Praise for *More than the Sum of Our*

"Ken Hubbell has crafted a remarkable exploration of our technological future that transcends the typical AI hype to deliver genuine insights into human-machine collaboration. "More than the Sum of Our Parts" presents a compelling vision of "Homo Gestalt" - not as science fiction, but as a practical roadmap for organizations navigating the integration of artificial intelligence into their core operations.

What sets this work apart is Hubbell's focus on synergy rather than replacement. His concept of Augmented General Intelligence (AuGI) emphasizes technology that amplifies human capabilities rather than competing with them. This perspective is particularly valuable for leaders grappling with the real challenges of AI implementation - from prompt engineering and bias mitigation to the evolving nature of teamwork itself.

The book's treatment of ethical AI deployment and the critical importance of human oversight resonates deeply with anyone building AI systems intended for collaborative use. Hubbell's insights into "Transhuman Resources" and the practical frameworks for managing human-AI teams offer actionable guidance for organizations serious about responsible AI adoption.

Perhaps most importantly, the author maintains that human agency, values, and judgment remain paramount in directing our technological future. This human-centered approach to AI development and deployment provides both reassurance and practical wisdom for navigating the complex landscape of artificial intelligence integration."

Nikolas Kairinos
Founder & CEO, Fountech AI

More than the Sum of Our Parts

The Age of Homo Gestalt and

Augmented General Intelligence

By Ken Hubbell

More than the Sum of Our Parts

*The Age of Homo Gestalt and
Augmented General Intelligence*

Paperback: ISBN 979-8-9885794-3-4

Library of Congress Control Number: 2025911240

First paperback edition June 2025.

Art by Ken Hubbell and ChatGPT.

Printed by Kindle Direct Publishing in the USA.

https://kdp.amazon.com/

Published in Raleigh, North Carolina

"He saw himself as an atom

and his Gestalt as a molecule.

He saw these others as a cell among cells,

and he saw in the whole the design of what, with joy,

humanity would become."

- Theodore Sturgeon, "More Than Human"

"To exist in the 21st Century,

we must rethink how we work, live, and grow

with our human, augmented human,

and non-human counterparts."

- Ken Hubbell, "There is AI in Team"

For Trudie, my best friend, mother of our three amazing children, and partner for life. Without your faith in me and a passion for the human side of technology, this book would never have been written. You are tireless and often relentless, but always there for me.

Everyone needs a Trudie in their life.

Preface: Read Me First

Some of my earliest memories are of a small cinder block house at the base of a triangle-shaped park in St. Petersburg, Florida. We had five television channels, a wall-mounted telephone, and a local pool we could ride our bikes to on hot summer days—no parents, no helmets. The highlight of the summer months was watching the spectacular heat lightning ripping across the 4 PM skies each evening as we sat on the front steps eating Charles' Chips from the huge tin delivered weekly to our home. It was a typical 1970s existence in the retirement capital of the USA.

While swimming and cycling were critical to my social life, I was also a bit of a geek back at a time when being a geek was neither cool nor popular. I truly enjoyed reading a good book or working in solitude. On humid days when the pool was closed, I discovered two air-conditioned places of refuge: the public library bookmobile and Radio Shack.

For those unfamiliar, the bookmobile was an Airstream camper filled with shelves of books. Once a month, it would arrive at the same strip mall a short bike ride from my home where I would pedal madly to get the best picks. After I read the best of the children's books, I learned I could request books from the main library through the librarian who stamped my selections each visit. With her guidance, I ventured beyond the kids' section. She became my first knowledge management system, and through her I became connected with what at that time seemed like everything.

My fascination with the intersection of technology and humanity grew with every book I read. From Isaac Asimov's "I, Robot" to Martin Caiden's "Cyborg" (the basis for "The Six-Million Dollar Man"), I was obsessed with artificial intelligence and human augmentation. This obsession wasn't just theoretical. I started programming simulations on a TRS-80. This led to me building electronics projects from Forrest M. Mims's books I thumbed through at the local Radio Shack. My first robot involved a trip with my uncle down Canal Street in New York City, hunting for cheap motors and ICs to build a mobile platform powered by a Timex Sinclair computer running on a staggering 4k of RAM.

Throughout high school, my interests were all over the map. I was an actor, musician, artist, and programmer. Thankfully, no one pigeon-holed us into a single career choice back then, because I would have been lost. I started college at West Point, planning to become a mechanical engineer in the Army, but soon realized my passion was for industrial design and that just didn't fit with a career in the military. I transferred to North Carolina State University's Design School, where I worked with the first video graphics cards, creating animations that led to corporate training programs. My programming skills roared back to life with the arrival of Macromedia Director, and my professional world shifted permanently into the realm of Human Resources.

I share this journey with you to illustrate the impact technological change has had on my life, and on the lives of so many I've worked with. At any point, I could have looked up and said, "The sky is falling," or felt that technology was replacing everything I knew. Instead, I was lucky to have people around me who helped me see that change is inevitable, and within it lies incredible opportunity. I hope this book will serve you in the same way.

Today, several decades later, I have that same childhood feeling of excitement for the future. What's amazing is I see that same emotion in the faces of millions around the globe. Where once only a handful of us were interested in these technologies, now it seems everyone is jumping on board. AI and robotics are rapidly touching every part of our lives. This evolution inspired me to completely reassess my own views on more radical topics like synthetic biology and human evolution. Ready or not, these issues are here.

My work focuses on helping people and businesses understand how technology's rapid growth offers immense advantages while navigating the human and ethical challenges it presents. I am still building products for EdTech, although I am now powering the engines of creation with generative AI. Bill Gates predicted that AI will soon take on tasks traditionally done by humans, enhancing our abilities and driving innovation. Based on what I see that future is arriving even faster than we think. Fortunately, I believe this is a story of augmentation and integration, not replacement.

To bring this future to life, I have scattered a set of fictional scenarios and real-world examples throughout this book. These stories explore how technologies like AI, neural interfaces, and robotics might impact our organizations and each of us personally. You may discover connections to yourself, your employees, your children, and perhaps even your Roomba™. The insights within these pages, enriched by real-world examples, will help you see how to embrace the changes ahead and prepare for humanity's next phase.

Since many of the terms associated with AI may be new to you, I've created a handy **Glossary** for quick reference, as well as a **Quick Start Guide** at the very end to help your organization get started.

So, sit back, dive in, and enjoy being part of the next generation of humanity.

Part 1: The Promise of Synergy

More Than the Sum of Our Parts

Chapter 1: Tomorrow, Today
The Emerging Gestalt

If you've felt the ground shifting beneath your feet recently, the sudden ubiquity of AI tools like ChatGPT writing emails or creating stunning images, headlines announcing robots working alongside warehouse staff, or perhaps even contemplating the implications of technology enhancing human senses or memory, you're not alone. Now is the time to embrace the opportunity to shape your future. This accelerating integration of humans and technology, this merging of endeavors, points towards a potential new stage, a synergistic system greater than the sum of its parts. The next generation of humanity, Homo Gestalt.

Helena's Heart

The third-floor office of Continuum Care smelled of old brick, strong coffee, and the sterile lemon scent of the overnight cleaning crew. Helena's corner was an oasis of controlled chaos, a testament to a mind that thrived in motion. A half-dead fern she'd named Phil drooped valiantly on her filing cabinet, and her coffee, as usual, was lukewarm. She was about to take a reluctant sip when the chime sounded.

It was a soft, melodic tone, nothing like the jarring urgency of a calendar alert. It was AURA, their AI agent, and its chime was less of an alarm and more of a quiet, digital tap on the shoulder. On her screen, a soft, yellow pulse appeared next to a name: Leo Martinez.

Helena's heart did a familiar little dip. Leo was one of their angels—a gerontology case worker whose clients adored him for his uncanny ability to listen not just to their words, but to the spaces between them. By every old-world metric, he was a superstar.

She clicked his name. The dashboard that appeared wasn't a spreadsheet of billable hours. It was a weather map of a human soul. AURA, with its access to anonymized metadata, showed her a pattern. Leo's visit notes, usually rich, anecdotal novellas, had become clipped and clinical. The sentiment analysis of his team-chat messages showed his usual upbeat tone had flattened. Most critically, he'd gone silent on the company's optional audio-journal, a tool most caregivers used as a pressure-release valve.

AURA had already connected the dots. It highlighted his schedule for the last three weeks: a brutal gauntlet of clients in late-stage hospice care. It was the emotional equivalent of running a marathon every day.

Proactive Measures Initiated, the screen read. AURA had deposited two "Respite Hours" into Leo's time-off bank and drafted a text message, awaiting her approval. "Hi Leo, just checking in. I see you've been on some of our most challenging cases. Just a reminder that your Respite Hours are there if you need a breather. We appreciate you. –Helena"

She hit send, a quiet marveling at the process. A few years ago, this would have started with an angry call from a client and ended in a disciplinary meeting. Now, it started with a whisper of data and ended with a gesture of support.

Leo's reply was almost instant. "Thanks, Helena. I really needed that today."

This small victory was the fuel for her afternoon. The "Innovation & Risk" quarterly review. The meeting was in the glass-walled conference room they all called "The Fishbowl," and today, Helena felt like the main exhibit. Mark from Legal was already there, his tablet perfectly squared with his notepad.

"Helena," he began before she'd even sat down. "I spent last night reading the latest CCPA interpretations. AURA is a lawsuit waiting to happen. And this new proposal..." He waved a hand at the agenda. "'Lift-Assist' exoskeletons? We're a care provider, not a DARPA project. The liability is astronomical."

Helena let him finish, taking a slow sip of water. "Mark, bless your risk-averse heart," she said, her voice even. "A few years ago, we lost Maria Flores, one of our best, to a career-ending back injury. She was 42. She was lifting a client, her foot slipped, and that was it. The Lift-Assist isn't a sci-fi fantasy; it's the best darn back brace ever invented. It's PPE for a caregiver's body. AURA is PPE for their soul. It helps us see the strain before the snap."

"The bias, Helena! The hiring tools scanning social data..."

"Professional data, Mark. Not their vacation photos," she corrected gently. "And it doesn't make decisions. It surfaces humanity. It found our new hire, Samir, because he runs a photo blog celebrating elderly shopkeepers. You think a keyword search for 'gerontology degree' would have found that kind of heart? We're not just filling roles anymore; we're casting for them. The AI helps me find people who fit the part."

The head of client services, a warm, pragmatic woman named Rosa, chimed in. "Our client churn is the lowest it's ever been. The new AI scheduler matches caregivers to clients based on communication styles. It gave a family grappling with a new Alzheimer's diagnosis to Leo, who is famously calm under pressure. The family felt supported from the first call. That's not a line item, Mark. That's our reputation."

Helena leaned forward, her gaze steady. "Your job is to protect us from the storm outside. My job is to make sure this house is strong enough to withstand it. That means building a place where our people can do this incredibly difficult, emotionally taxing work without breaking. These tools are the scaffolding that lets them do that."

She didn't get a full green light, but she got a pilot program. A win.

A month later, Helena walked through the new training wing. She saw Samir, his thin frame looking surprisingly sturdy inside the sleek Lift-Assist harness. He was practicing a transfer with a high-tech mannequin, but he wasn't focused on the mechanics. His hands were gentle, his voice was a low murmur, explaining every step. The harness bore the weight, leaving him free to do the real work: connecting.

That evening, the office was quiet, bathed in the orange glow of the setting sun. Helena stood by the window, looking down at the street. Her phone buzzed. It *was a notification from Continuum's public-facing customer support bot. A woman whose mother was a new client had spent twenty minutes asking the bot anxious questions about billing and medication schedules. The bot had handled it all, leaving a final note: "I've flagged your mother's file for a non-urgent, 15-minute wellness check-in call from her case manager tomorrow morning, just to make sure she's settling in well."*

The bot hadn't just answered questions. It had anticipated a need. It had shown foresight. It had, in its own way, shown care.

Helena walked back to her desk and gave Phil's drooping leaves a little water. Her coffee was stone cold, but she didn't mind. Her job wasn't about policies and paperwork anymore. It was about building a resilient, human-centered ecosystem. She was a strategist, an ethicist, an architect of a new kind of workplace. The machines handled the data, the heavy lifting, the noise. They left her, and her people, with the part that mattered most: the heart.

The Origins of Homo Gestalt: From Fiction to Foresight

Understand that the term Gestalt originates from psychology, signifying a configuration where the **whole is perceived as greater than the sum of its parts.** Applied to human evolution, the idea of a collective entity achieving synergy isn't entirely new. In 1953, science-fiction writer **Theodore Sturgeon** introduced the concept of **"Homo Gestalt"** in his novel *More Than Human*. In the story, six individuals with unique powers learn to "blesh" (blend + mesh) their abilities, acting as one organism and achieving a collective consciousness – a fictional representation which Sturgeon described as **"the next step in human evolution"** (Sturgeon, 1953).

> **Understanding the Gestalt Shift**
>
> **Key Concept:**
> The idea of "Homo Gestalt," drawn from speculative fiction, is now grounded in technological reality through cybernetics, AI, and man-computer symbiosis.
>
> **Why It Matters:**
> Recognizing the roots of this concept helps frame our current moment as one of intentional design, not accidental convergence. We can build it consciously.
>
> **Actionable Tip:**
> Use historical foresight like Licklider's man-computer symbiosis as a framework to guide today's AI-human partnerships toward ethical and high-impact outcomes.

What Sturgeon imagined metaphorically now resonates through technology. Decades ago, pioneers like psychologist **J.C.R. Licklider** foresaw an intimate **"man-computer symbiosis"** (Licklider, 1960). He envisioned a tight coupling where human brains and computers would cooperate, enabling them to **"think as no human brain has ever thought"** and solve problems far more effectively than either could alone. Licklider predicted humans would set goals and perform evaluations, while computers handled routine work, resulting in powerful intellectual partnerships (Licklider, 1960).

Later, cognitive scientist **Andy Clark** argued that humans are **"natural-born cyborgs,"** inherently adept at incorporating external tools into our thinking (Clark, 2003). He noted, *"We humans have always been adept at dovetailing our minds and skills to the shape of our tools and aids. But when those tools start dovetailing back... the line between tool and user becomes flimsy indeed."* (Clark, quoted in AZQuotes). For Clark, the boundary between human and machine blurs as technology integrates more deeply into our cognitive processes.

Fast forward to today, and this integration is moving from theory towards practice. Throughout this book we will examine the intersection of artificial intelligence, human enhancement, and human resources. Imagine each of these topics as the rings of a Venn diagram with the union of the three representing the new era of teams. I introduced the concept of the **new workforce** in my 2023 book, *There is AI in Team*. Now, in *More than the Sum of Our Parts*, I go one step further by defining **Homo Gestalt** not as Sturgeon's psychic collective, but as *"a future state characterized by deep, seamless human integration with a technological ecosystem... creating a new synergistic whole"*. This vision builds on the work of my first book and re-emphasizes **augmentation over replacement** – technology amplifying human intellect, perception, and collaboration. Importantly, it distinguishes itself from the pursuit of purely machine-based Artificial General Intelligence (AGI). Homo Gestalt is *human*-centered, focusing on **Augmented General Intelligence (AuGI)** – the enhanced collective intelligence of humans interwoven with AI. It suggests a new kind of societal "organism" that blends biological and artificial parts to work in concert.

Why This Matters *Now*

This isn't a theoretical discussion about a distant tomorrow. We are in an era where AI handles many tasks once exclusive to humans, making intelligence "free and commonplace." This accelerating integration makes understanding the Emerging Gestalt a critical imperative today.

Businesses are grappling with:

Competitive Pressure: Companies effectively leveraging AI and automation are achieving tangible gains. A recent PwC survey found 63% of CEOs believe AI will have a larger impact than the internet (PwC CEO Survey Data, 2023). Staying competitive increasingly means mastering this synergy, driven partly by the relentless pursuit of shareholder value and efficiency Neal Cross highlights (Cross, N./LinkedIn). As a recent Anthropic guide emphasizes, developing a clear AI strategy is moving from optional to essential (Anthropic Guide).

Talent Disruption: The skills landscape is shifting rapidly. While AI creates new roles, it transforms existing ones, impacting fields from design and law to customer service (China Daily; Stanford HAI AI Index Report 2023). A significant challenge that executives cite is the shortage of talent and skills needed to implement AI strategies. Effectively managing talent now requires understanding human-AI collaboration needs.

Ethical Minefields: The AIAAIC database tracking AI incidents shows a 26-fold increase since 2012. Issues like bias in AI hiring tools (Reuters, 2018), the spread of deepfakes, fabricated information or "hallucinations" (Mitchell, 2024; China Daily; Wagner, M.G./Substack), and the profound ethical that technologies like biological computers (Sparkes, 2022; Gizmodo) and neurotechnology (Farahany, 2023) raise are immediate operational and ethical challenges demanding robust governance.

Strategic Uncertainty: Leaders need frameworks to make informed decisions about AI adoption, team restructuring, ethical guardrails, and governance to navigate the hype cycle and make sound investments. The journey involves methodical steps: identifying use cases, building foundations, and scaling what works.

For individuals, the questions are just as urgent:

Career Relevance: How do my skills align with this future? What new skills do I need to learn *now* to remain valuable?

Navigating Tools: How can I use powerful AI tools effectively and ethically to enhance my own work and creativity, without falling prey to their limitations?

Information Trust: In a world awash with potentially AI-generated content, how do I discern truth from fiction?

Personal Impact: How will these changes affect my sense of purpose, my well-being, and my connection with others?

Ignoring these questions is like navigating a storm without a map or compass. Proactive understanding and strategic adaptation are essential for both organizational survival and individual thriving.

The Promise of this Book: Your Guide to the Gestalt

This book is designed to be that map and compass. It provides a clear framework, the **Synergy/Gestalt** model, to understand the complex interplay of forces shaping our future. We won't just admire the potential or dwell on the risks; we will equip you with the knowledge and perspectives needed to navigate this transformation effectively.

Inside these pages, you will:

Understand the 'Parts': Gain a clear, practical understanding of the core components: the enduring strengths of humans, the realities of AI, especially Generative AI, the capabilities of robotics and automation, and the potential of human augmentation.

Master the 'How': Learn the essential skills for enabling synergy, particularly the art and science of **Prompt Engineering**. Critically, you'll also grapple with the **ethical challenges** and understand the emerging landscape of **AI Governance**.

See the 'Whole' in Action: Explore real-world examples and practical implications for **team collaboration**, the necessary evolution of **Human Resources**, and the crucial strategies for **workforce adaptation and reskilling**.

Grasp the Broader Impact: Consider the effects on **mental health**, the **economic shifts** challenging zero-sum thinking, and the ultimate potential trajectory towards a more integrated **Homo Gestalt**.

Your Role as Architect

This book is not just an analysis; it's a call to engagement. We have not predetermined the shape of the Emerging Gestalt nor the future of human-machine collaboration. It will be built by the choices we make, the skills we cultivate, the ethical lines we draw, and the governance structures we implement.

Whether you are a CEO charting your company's strategic course, an HR professional redesigning talent management, a manager leading a newly blended team, an educator preparing the next generation, or an individual navigating your own career path, you are an architect of this future. This book provides the foundational knowledge, practical insights, and critical perspectives you need to build wisely.

It requires optimism about the possibilities, tempered with clear-eyed realism about the challenges highlighted by researchers like Melanie Mitchell regarding AI reasoning (Mitchell, 2024) and practitioners grappling with implementation. It demands we embrace learning and adaptation. Most importantly, it requires recognizing that even as technology becomes more integrated into our lives, human values, human judgment, and human connection remain the indispensable core. As Bill Gates noted, referencing Harlow's experiments, the personal relationship aspect is something AI may struggle to replicate (Gates, B. in Popular Mechanics, 2024).

> **Science Fiction to Strategic Foresight**
>
> **Key Concept:**
> The integration of AI, robotics, and human augmentation is moving us from isolated tools to an emergent system—an Emerging Gestalt—where the whole exceeds the sum of its parts.
>
> **Why It Matters:**
> This shift reframes how we define labor, value, inclusion, and human potential in a rapidly augmenting world. It calls for new models of collaboration and evaluation.
>
> **Actionable Tip:**
> Begin designing work environments and roles that account for hybrid capabilities—evaluate not just people or tech alone, but their synergy as a system.

Having established the concept of the Emerging Gestalt—this multiplicative integration of human and non-human capabilities—our exploration must begin with the most crucial and enduring component. Before delving into the powerful technologies reshaping collaboration, we must first ground ourselves in the unique strengths, adaptability, and inherent value of **The Essential Human Part**. Understanding what makes us uniquely human is the critical first step in effectively orchestrating our role within this rapidly evolving technological ecosystem, because ultimately, the purpose and direction of the Gestalt stem from human intention and values. The beauty of it all is it's still, fundamentally, all about us. Let's begin.

Chapter 2: The Essential Human Part

Adaptability, Creativity, and Connection

In the last chapter, we introduced the concept of the 'Emerging Gestalt'---a cooperative whole forming from the integration of humans, augmented humans, and non-human technologies like AI and robotics. We established that understanding this synergy requires examining its constituent parts. Logically, and perhaps essentially, we begin this examination by grounding ourselves in the most fundamental, adaptable, and arguably most vital part of this equation: **us**. What are the enduring human qualities that not only remain relevant but become *more* critical in an age of intelligent machines? Understanding the unique strengths of the "human part" is the first step towards effectively orchestrating the synergy of the Gestalt. This aligns with early visions like Licklider's, which emphasized that in effective man-computer symbiosis, humans would provide the crucial elements of goal-setting, insight, and evaluation (Licklider, 1960). Act now to understand your indispensable role in the Emerging Gestalt. Examine the human part first and lead the synergy that will define our future.

Maya's Muse

Maya stared at the blank canvas—not a physical one, but the intimidatingly empty project file for the new indie game her tiny studio, PixelBloom, was developing. For weeks, the concept art phase had stalled. Their lead artist, Ben, was brilliant but swamped, and their budget couldn't stretch to hiring freelance help for every iteration. Doubt gnawed at her; maybe the ambitious fantasy world they envisioned was simply too much for their small team.

Remembering a workshop she'd attended, Maya hesitantly opened "ChromaCanvas," one of the new diffusion model AI tools. She typed a tentative prompt: "Concept art for a bioluminescent forest at twilight, glowing mushrooms, ethereal style." The results were... interesting, but generic. Disappointed but not defeated, she recalled the workshop's emphasis on detail and context.

Taking a deep breath, she tried again, pouring her team's vision into the prompt field: "Act as a senior concept artist for an indie fantasy RPG. Generate concept art for the 'Whisperwood Glade' location. Setting: a dense, ancient forest at deep twilight. Key features: Giant, bioluminescent mushrooms casting a soft blue and purple glow; shimmering, almost invisible sprites flitting between trees; ancient, moss-covered stones carved with faint, glowing runes. Style: painterly, reminiscent of Studio Ghibli but with slightly darker, more mystical undertones. Mood: Enchanting, mysterious, slightly melancholic. Aspect ratio: 16:9."

She hit 'generate'. Pixels blurred, coalesced. And then... they emerged. Four distinct images, each capturing the essence of the Whisperwood Glade far better than she'd dared hope. One image in particular nailed the melancholic enchantment perfectly, the light from the mushrooms reflecting on dew-kissed ferns, a barely visible sprite caught mid-flight.

It wasn't finished art, not by a long shot. There were oddities including a mushroom that looked slightly distorted, a rune that didn't quite make sense. But it was a powerful start. Maya quickly shared the image with Ben via their team chat.

"Whoa," Ben replied almost instantly. "Where did this come from? This feels right. That lighting gives me an idea for the particle effects..."

Over the next hour, Maya didn't replace Ben; she augmented him. She used ChromaCanvas to generate variations based on his feedback, "Okay, same scene, but make the runes glow brighter," or "Let's see it from a lower angle, focusing on the mossy stones." She even used a separate LLM tool, feeding it descriptions of their game's lore, to generate placeholder names for the sprites and runes depicted in the AI's art.

By lunchtime, they hadn't just broken through the creative block; they had a rich, visually grounded direction for a key game location, complete with initial lore integration. The AI hadn't done the real creative work. That spark came from Maya's vision and Ben's artistic judgment. But the generative tools acted as an incredibly fast, responsive, and tireless brainstorming partner and initial sketch artist. It allowed their small team to punch far above their weight, exploring visual ideas at a speed previously impossible.

Maya smiled while saving the generated images and the AI-suggested names. The revolution wasn't about machines taking over; it was about humans learning to collaborate with a new kind of intelligence, using these synthetic capabilities to bring their own uniquely human visions to life, faster and more vividly than ever before. Her canvas was no longer blank.

The Collaborative Instinct: Our Deepest Design

Recognize that human history is, at its core, the story of collaboration. Use this insight to strengthen your own teams and relationships. From the earliest hunter-gatherer bands sharing resources for survival to the monumental efforts required to build the Great Pyramids of Egypt around 2560 BCE, our progress has always been driven by the ability to work together. Individuals alone did not achieve that colossal feat; rather, tens of thousands of laborers, architects, artisans united by a shared vision and complex communication accomplished it. This innate drive to team up, to pool resources, skills, and knowledge, is arguably our species' defining advantage It forms the bedrock of civilizations and provides the foundation for the human-machine collaborations that shape the Emerging Gestalt. While technology offers powerful new ways to connect and coordinate, the fundamental *will* to collaborate remains deeply human. Modern research on collective intelligence further examines how groups, now including AIs, can achieve intelligence beyond individual members (Malone & Bernstein, 2015).

> **The Collaborative Instinct is Our Deepest Design**
>
> **Key Concept:**
> Human beings are evolutionarily wired for teamwork. From pyramid-building to modern project teams, collaboration is what built civilization.
>
> **Why It Matters:**
> As AI systems enter teams, it's essential to recognize that their success depends on the deeply human will and skill to collaborate.
>
> **Actionable Tip:**
> In tech-integrated projects, prioritize shared goals, social cohesion, and communication frameworks that honor the human drive to team up.

The Power of Connection: Empathy as the Glue

Beyond mere coordination, what truly elevates human collaboration is our capacity for communication and, crucially, **empathy**. Consider the poignant Christmas Truce of 1914 during World War I. Amidst brutal conflict, soldiers spontaneously laid down their arms, shared gifts, and recognized their shared humanity across enemy lines. It was a powerful, albeit temporary, demonstration of empathy overriding programmed hostility.

Apply this capacity for genuine understanding and connection in every sphere, especially where technology intersects with human needs. Think of Dr. Paul Farmer, co-founder of Partners In Health. His organization revolutionized global health not just through medical expertise, but by deeply listening to and empathizing with the needs of marginalized communities, fostering collaboration between doctors, patients, and governments based on compassion. (Kidder, 2003). Can an AI, trained on text data, truly replicate this depth of understanding? While AI can simulate empathetic language, it lacks genuine subjective experience. As Bill Gates alluded to when discussing AI tutors and doctors, referencing Harry Harlow's experiments with monkeys, the lack of a personal, relational connection is a significant gap AI may always struggle to fill (Gates, B. in Popular Mechanics, 2024). This capacity to connect, build trust, and understand unspoken needs remains a cornerstone of effective leadership, customer service, patient care, negotiation, and team cohesion—the essential glue holding the human elements of the Gestalt together. Ethical frameworks for AI consistently emphasize keeping human values central, and empathy is a core human value.

> **Empathy is a Strategic Advantage**
>
> **Key Concept:**
> Unlike AI, humans feel with and for others. Empathy creates trust, loyalty, and connection that technology can't replicate.
>
> **Why It Matters:**
> Empathetic leadership and service directly affect client retention, team morale, and conflict resolution outcomes.
>
> **Actionable Tip:**
> Train teams not just in tech, but in emotional intelligence. Use empathy check-ins during AI-mediated communications to maintain human connection.

Recognize and cultivate these 'soft' skills, particularly empathy, because they remain essential to success in technology-integrated environments. Consider the modern customer service center, where agents utilize sophisticated Customer Relationship Management (CRM) systems, knowledge bases, and potentially AI-powered assistance tools to manage interactions. Despite the technological efficiency, research consistently demonstrates a direct link between agent empathy and key business metrics. Studies synthesized by firms like Deloitte show that customers who perceive genuine empathy during service interactions, even brief ones mediated by technology, report significantly higher satisfaction levels (CSAT) and Net Promoter Scores (NPS). More critically, this empathetic connection translates into measurable loyalty; these customers are demonstrably less likely to switch to competitors and often express a willingness to pay a premium for services from companies they feel understand and value them. (Deloitte Digital, "The Human Experience Edge" series or similar CX reports). This isn't just about feeling good; it's about measurable economic impact driven by a core human skill operating symbiotically within a technological framework. Technology might handle the transactional elements, but the human touch, specifically empathy, builds the relationship and secures the value.

Empathy's Tangible Value:

- **Customer Loyalty:** Studies show customers perceiving genuine empathy during service interactions report higher satisfaction (CSAT/NPS).

- **Business Impact:** Empathetic connection demonstrably reduces customer churn and can support premium pricing. (Source: Deloitte Digital CX reports)

- **Technology Limitation:** While AI can mimic, it cannot replicate genuine human feeling and connection.

Our Superpowers in the Age of AI: Humans Still Reign

As AI takes over routine analytical and generative tasks, the value proposition shifts. Certain human capabilities don't just remain relevant; they become premium skills, essential for directing, interpreting, and ethically guiding the powerful technological parts of the Gestalt:

1. **Creativity and Innovation:** While Generative AI can produce novel combinations based on its training data, true human creativity involves more. It's about asking entirely new questions, making intuitive leaps, connecting seemingly unrelated domains (like applying biological principles to architectural design), and generating truly original concepts born from experience, emotion, and imagination. AI is a powerful brainstorming partner, but the spark of paradigm-shifting innovation often comes from the human mind thinking *beyond* existing patterns (China Daily). Research suggests human intuition and diverse experiences are key contributions alongside AI's processing power (ScienceDirect article on AI-enhanced collective intelligence).

2. **Critical Thinking and Complex Judgment:** AI finds patterns, humans evaluate context and ambiguity. As AI generates plausible outputs, critically assessing accuracy (spotting hallucinations – Mitchell, 2024; China Daily; Wagner, M.G./Substack), identifying bias, and judging applicability is paramount. This human oversight is indispensable, especially as we often

don't fully understand the complexities of our *own* cognition, let alone AI's potentially different processes (Wagner, M.G./Substack). We must be wary of anthropomorphizing AI or assuming its "reasoning" mirrors ours; it may often be sophisticated mimicry or post-hoc justification (Mitchell, 2024; Wagner, M.G./Substack).

3. **Strategic Thinking and Vision:** AI can analyze trends and project futures based on past data, but strategic leadership requires more. It involves setting a long-term vision, understanding the complex interplay of market forces, human behavior, and competitive dynamics, adapting plans based on intuition and experience, and aligning diverse efforts towards a shared goal. Humans provide the "why" behind the "what," setting the direction for the entire Gestalt system, echoing Licklider's vision of humans setting goals (Licklider, 1960).

4. **Empathy and Emotional Intelligence:** As mentioned, genuine empathy remains uniquely human. This translates into crucial abilities: building strong client relationships, motivating diverse teams, providing compassionate care, navigating sensitive negotiations, and understanding the subtle emotional currents that drive human decision-making. These skills are vital for effective leadership and any role requiring deep interpersonal connection.

5. **Ethical Reasoning and Values:** While AI can be programmed with ethical rules, navigating truly complex moral dilemmas requires human judgment informed by values, cultural context, and a deep understanding of potential consequences. Deciding the *right* course of action, especially when principles conflict, is a profound human responsibility, essential for steering the Gestalt ethically.

Adaptability: Our Evolutionary Edge, Accelerated

If collaboration is our foundational strength, adaptability is our mechanism for survival and progress. Throughout history, humans have faced disruptive change: the agricultural revolution, the Industrial Revolution, the digital age. Each required significant adaptation in skills, social structures, and ways of thinking. The Industrial Revolution, for instance, displaced agrarian workers but simultaneously created new factory roles and spurred urbanization, forcing massive societal adaptation. Cognitive scientist Andy Clark suggests this integration with tools is part of our nature as "natural-born cyborgs" (Clark, 2003). Furthermore, the Extended Mind thesis posits that our cognitive processes readily incorporate external tools (Clark & Chalmers, 1998).

Today, the pace of change driven by AI and related technologies is dramatically faster. What distinguishes us is our inherent neuroplasticity or ability to learn, unlearn, and relearn throughout our lives. While the challenge is greater, our capacity to adapt remains our key advantage. Thriving in the Emerging Gestalt demands embracing **lifelong learning** and cultivating **cognitive flexibility,** the willingness to constantly update our mental models and acquire new skills, including how to effectively partner with our technological counterparts, recognizing that even our understanding of *how* we think and learn is still evolving (Wagner, M.G./Substack). Those who cultivate adaptability will find opportunity; those who resist may struggle.

> **Adaptability is the Superpower AI Doesn't Have**
>
> **Key Concept:**
> Humans excel at pivoting in ambiguity, learning from one context and applying insight to another. It's what makes us resilient.
>
> **Why It Matters:**
> While AI scales tasks, it doesn't reimagine them. Human flexibility fills the critical gaps in creativity, improvisation, and cross-domain insight.
>
> **Actionable Tip:**
> Design AI-integrated workflows that leave space for human reinterpretation, and reward flexible thinking in performance evaluations.

The Irreplaceable Human Touch

Despite the power of automation and AI, there remain domains where the direct "human touch" provides value that technology struggles to replicate. Think of the nuance a skilled therapist brings to understanding a patient's unspoken pain, the inspiration a passionate teacher ignites in a student beyond mere information transfer, the creative judgment an artist applies to finalize a masterpiece started with AI assistance, or the trust built through face-to-face negotiation. These interactions involve intuition, shared experience, non-verbal cues, and emotional resonance. Michael G. Wagner compellingly argues that even our own conscious awareness might function less like a driver and more like an interpreter, constructing narratives *after* deeper neural processes initiate action (the "readiness potential") (Wagner, M.G./Substack). Recognizing and valuing these contributions is essential as we design integrated systems, ensuring technology augments rather than entirely replaces these vital human roles.

As we continue our exploration of the technological marvels contributing to the Emerging Gestalt, let's hold this firmly in mind: the human element is not a legacy component waiting to be phased out. It is the **foundational, directing, and sense-making part** of the system. Our innate collaborative drive, our capacity for empathy and connection, our unique cognitive strengths in creativity, critical judgment, and ethical reasoning, and our profound adaptability are the very qualities that enable us to harness the power of AI and robotics responsibly and effectively. The challenge isn't to compete with machines on their terms (speed, data processing), but to cultivate and leverage our distinct human advantages.

We can now turn our attention to the first major technological component reshaping teamwork: **The Cognitive Catalyst**. Understanding Artificial Intelligence, particularly its generative power, is key to unlocking its enhancing potential within the Gestalt.

Reflection:

As AI augments business processes, leaders must double down on empathy and human judgment. You must focus on building trust, investing in emotional intelligence training, and designing roles that maximize human creativity.

How are you ensuring your teams remain adaptive and human-centered in the face of automation?

Chapter 3: The Cognitive Catalyst

Understanding AI and Generative Power

Having explored the foundational human element in Chapter 2, our unique adaptability, creativity, and inherent drive for connection, we now turn our focus to a powerful technological 'part' that is dramatically reshaping the landscape of collaboration: **Artificial Intelligence (AI)**. It's tempting to think of AI simply as software, perhaps a more advanced version of the programs we've used for decades. But that view misses the profound shift underway. AI, particularly in its modern forms, acts more like a **cognitive catalyst** within the Emerging Gestalt we introduced. It's an engine capable of processing information, identifying patterns, and increasingly, *generating* novel content at speeds and scales that augment and amplify human thought and creativity in unprecedented ways. This aligns with early visions of technology augmenting human intellect (Engelbart, 1962) and enabling human-computer symbiosis (Licklider, 1960). To effectively integrate this potent component and harness the synergy it enables, resulting in the whole truly being greater than the sum of its parts, we must first gain a clear understanding of this catalyst: its remarkable capabilities, its underlying principles, and, just as importantly, its critical limitations. Embrace this shift now. Understand AI's transformative role and apply its generative power to elevate your collaborative efforts.

David and the Data Deluge

David sighed, rubbing his temples as he stared at the mountain of research papers cluttering his virtual desktop. The deadline for the policy brief on renewable energy adoption trends was looming, and synthesizing the key findings felt like trying to drink from a firehose. He'd hoped his new AI assistant, "SyntheSys," would be the answer, a digital teammate to help him navigate the data deluge.

His initial attempts were frustrating. "SyntheSys, summarize these articles on solar panel efficiency," he'd prompted, uploading a dozen dense PDFs. The result was a sprawling, multi-page document that seemed to just rehash sections of the papers without clear focus. It was "more" text, not less. He tried again: "Give me the main points about wind energy growth." SyntheSys produced a generic listicle that could have come from a basic web search, missing the nuances of the specific research he needed. "Useless," David muttered, feeling the pressure mount.

Then, he remembered a key takeaway from a recent internal training session, something about not just "asking" the AI, but "directing" it, like explaining a task clearly to a new human assistant. He recalled the term: prompt engineering. It wasn't magic; it was communication.

He decided to try a different approach, focusing on just one critical paper first. He took a breath and typed carefully:

"Act as a research analyst summarizing technical papers for a non-expert audience. Analyze the attached paper titled 'Grid Integration Challenges for Variable Renewables'. Identify ONLY the top 3 practical challenges discussed regarding grid stability. Present these challenges as a bulleted list, with a single concise sentence explaining each challenge in simple terms. Ignore theoretical discussions and focus solely on actionable problems identified."

He attached the paper and waited. SyntheSys responded almost instantly. This time, the output was different:

- *Intermittency Management: Difficulty ensuring a consistent power supply when wind and solar generation naturally fluctuates.*

- *Transmission Capacity: Existing power lines may lack the capacity to transport large amounts of renewable energy from generation sites (often remote) to population centers.*

- *Inertia and Frequency Control: Replacing traditional power plants reduces grid inertia, making it harder to maintain stable frequency and recover from disturbances.*

David blinked. It was exactly what he needed: clear, concise, relevant, and directly addressing the prompt's constraints. He hadn't just asked for a summary; he had specified the "role", the "source", the "focus" (practical challenges), the "format" (bulleted list), the "audience" (non-expert), and even what to "ignore".

He realized his mistake hadn't been using the AI, but using it lazily. He started applying the same principles to the other papers, iterating slightly as needed. "Okay, SyntheSys, using the same format, now analyze this paper on battery storage costs, focusing on projected cost reductions by 2030." The AI obliged, sticking to the structure he'd established.

Hours later, David wasn't just wading through summaries; he was actively synthesizing insights drawn from precisely targeted AI outputs. He felt less like a frustrated manager and more like a conductor, guiding a powerful instrument to play the specific notes he needed. Prompt engineering wasn't just a buzzword; it was the skill that transformed SyntheSys from a source of overwhelming noise into a genuinely valuable, efficient member of his research team. He was still doing the critical thinking, but the AI, properly directed, was handling the heavy lifting of information extraction at lightning speed. The deadline suddenly felt manageable again.

From Analyzing the Past to Generating the Future: The AI Evolution

AI researchers initially focused on building systems to analyze existing information. Recognize this shift and explore how generative AI now creates new possibilities for innovation in your work. These analytical AI systems mastered tasks such as recognizing faces, classifying spam emails, predicting stock market trends based on historical data, or identifying cancerous cells in medical images (Reviews of AI in radiology/finance; Bhandari, 2024). Researchers showed them many examples, enabling them to learn patterns and make predictions, proving immensely valuable to the researchers in optimizing processes and uncovering insights hidden within vast datasets.

This analytical prowess relies heavily on foundational **Machine Learning (ML)** techniques. Instead of programmers writing explicit step-by-step instructions for every possible scenario, ML algorithms allow systems to *learn* from data. Think of teaching a child to recognize cats: you don't list every defining feature; you show them many examples, and they gradually learn the underlying patterns. ML works similarly, adjusting its internal parameters based on data exposure to improve performance on a specific task. **Deep Learning (DL)**, a powerful subset of ML, takes this further by using complex, multi-layered **artificial neural networks**. Inspired by the interconnected structure of the human brain, these deep networks can automatically learn intricate hierarchies of features directly from raw data, identifying edges, then shapes, then objects in an image, for example, enabling breakthroughs in areas like computer vision and speech recognition.

However, the current wave washing over us, the one causing such excitement and disruption, is fueled by a different flavor of AI: **Generative AI**. While built upon ML and DL foundations, its goal isn't just to analyze or classify, but to *create* something novel that mimics the patterns and structures learned from its training data. This leap from analysis to creation—from interpreting the world to adding original (or seemingly original) content *to* it—is what positions Generative AI as a uniquely powerful cognitive catalyst, capable of participating in creative and knowledge-based tasks alongside humans, acting as a "cognitive collaborator" or even an "extended phenotype" externalizing the user's reasoning and intent.

The Engines of Generation: LLMs and Diffusion Models Explained

Let's first turn our attention to the **Large Language Models (LLMs)**, the powerhouses behind the surprisingly coherent conversations and versatile text creation you've likely experienced with popular tools such as OpenAI's ChatGPT, Google's Gemini, or Anthropic's Claude. These systems, capable of holding extended dialogues, drafting diverse creative formats, and answering a wide array of questions, are truly redefining what we expect from a cognitive partner. The term 'large' is no mere flourish; it speaks to the monumental scale of their training. These engines propel much of today's AI revolution, enabling a new form of cognitive collaboration.

> **Generative AI as a Cognitive Catalyst**
>
> **Key Concept:**
> Generative AI marks a leap from analyzing the past to generating new content—text, images, or code—based on learned patterns, transforming it into a true collaborator.
>
> **Why It Matters:**
> This shift positions AI not just as a tool, but as an assistant capable of participating in ideation, content development, and strategy.
>
> **Actionable Tip:**
> Treat LLMs and generative tools as creative co-pilots—break tasks into stages, compare drafts, and iterate collaboratively using feedback loops.

Machine learning engineers immerse these models in truly colossal oceans of text and code—potentially trillions of words harvested from the vast expanse of the internet, digitized books, scientific papers, and sprawling software repositories. This 'largeness' also shows their profound internal complexity: they contain billions, or even trillions, of parameters. It's helpful to think of these parameters as an intricate network of adjustable knobs or perhaps synaptic connections; the greater their number, the more nuance and sophistication the model can potentially learn and represent about the vast and subtle landscape of human language.

Immersed in this digital ocean of words, LLMs embark on a unique learning journey. They don't 'understand' in the human sense, but rather discern and internalize the statistical relationships between words, phrases, and concepts. Through this intensive processing, they absorb the rules of grammar, the nuances of syntax, a wealth of factual information, and even the implicit cultural contexts and varied writing styles embedded within their training data. Their core objective during this deep learning phase is often deceptively simple: to predict the next word (or 'token') in a sequence, given the words that came before. If presented with the phrase "The cat sat on the...", the model learns through countless examples that 'mat' is a highly probable and contextually fitting continuation.

To truly appreciate their role within the Gestalt, it's vital to peek 'under the hood,' as their operational mechanism is quite different from human cognition. LLMs operate by converting text into numerical representations (transforming tokens into numbers) and then processing these numbers within an incredibly complex, high-dimensional 'shape' space. Their impressive ability to generate coherent and contextually relevant text stems not from a deep grasp of semantic meaning, but from learning the statistical likelihood of various word sequences appearing within this intricate geometric space. As D. Shannon might observe, they become masters of linguistic patterns and structure. The sophisticated Transformer architecture, often the backbone of these models, employs an ingenious 'attention mechanism' that allows them to weigh the importance of different words in an input sequence, further refining their ability to produce outputs that feel remarkably relevant and appropriate.

But the story of LLMs doesn't end with sophisticated mimicry. Researchers are relentlessly pushing these models towards something more akin to reasoning, giving rise to what are sometimes called Large Reasoning Models (LRMs). Innovators like OpenAI with their o1 model, or DeepSeek with R1, are specifically training these advanced systems. They often employ techniques like reinforcement learning on vast datasets of human-generated 'chain-of-thought' examples to tackle problems that demand step-by-step logical deduction, a development highlighted by Melanie Mitchell in 2024. This involves the AI generating not just a final answer, but a plausible sequence of reasoning steps, thereby mimicking, and potentially augmenting, human problem-solving processes.

The sheer scale of these models, even when operating on predictive principles, unlocks a breathtaking suite of emergent abilities that directly enhance human productivity and creativity. Imagine drafting emails, complex reports, or engaging marketing copy with their assistance; or having vast research papers and lengthy meeting transcripts condensed into concise, digestible summaries. They can provide informative answers based on their extensive training (though, as we'll explore in Chapter 7, human verification remains absolutely crucial), translate text between numerous languages with increasing fluency, and even generate functional code snippets or entire programs in various programming languages, exemplified by tools like GitHub Copilot. Furthermore, their capacity for extended, context-aware dialogue and their utility in brainstorming sessions where they generate lists of ideas, suggest alternative phrasings, or propose different approaches to a problem positions them as invaluable cognitive collaborators.

If LLMs are the eloquent wordsmiths of this new AI era, then **Diffusion Models** are their visual counterparts, the digital artists conjuring images from the ether of pure data. These are the models driving the current explosion in AI image generation, familiar to users of tools like Midjourney, DALL-E 3, and Stable Diffusion, and central to scenarios like Maya's Muse. Their method of learning is a fascinating conceptual ballet of destruction and reconstruction. Trainers expose them to countless real images, then algorithms add noise. Layer-by-layer, random visual 'noise' like the static on an old television screen is systematically added until only a field of pure noise remains. The crucial, almost magical step is that, simultaneously, the model learns the intricate statistical process required to reverse this degradation. It learns to predict and meticulously remove the noise, step-by-step, to recover the original image's underlying structure and patterns.

> **Understanding the Engines of Generation**
>
> **Key Concept:**
> LLMs and diffusion models are foundational technologies powering today's generative capabilities, each with distinct strengths and risks.
>
> **Why It Matters:**
> Knowing how these models work improves your ability to use them responsibly, avoiding blind trust and misuse.
>
> **Actionable Tip:**
> When choosing a tool, assess what type of model powers it, what data it was trained on, and its alignment and safety mechanisms.

After training rigorously, the creative process begins with a human touch—a text prompt describing the desired image, perhaps "a cinematic photo of a bioluminescent jellyfish floating through a nebula, vibrant colours." The model then starts with a canvas of pure random noise and, guided by the instructional prompt and the vast library of visual patterns it has internalized, meticulously 'denoises' this canvas over many iterations. Gradually, elegantly, it shapes the chaos into the requested image, translating textual concepts into visual reality.

The visual tapestries they can weave from these prompts are astonishingly diverse. They can conjure believable images of objects or scenes that have never existed with startling photorealism; they can mimic the distinct styles of famous artists or entire art movements like Impressionism or Surrealism, or capture specific aesthetics such as cyberpunk or high fantasy. This makes them incredibly powerful tools for concept visualization, rapidly generating visuals for product designs, architectural mock-ups, character ideas for games or films (as Maya discovered), or even entire storyboards. Beyond grand concepts, they are also adept at creating practical graphic assets—logos, icons, textures, and backgrounds—for a myriad of uses, further empowering human creators.

A Synergistic Cognitive Partner: Amplifying the Whole

When teams effectively integrate these powerful generative AI 'parts' into human workflows, they act as potent catalysts, enabling synergy and making the collective 'whole' far more capable. Harness this synergy and seek opportunities where AI can amplify your human strengths and drive extraordinary results:

Amplified Creativity: Generative AI becomes an inexhaustible brainstorming partner and initial drafter. It can instantly generate dozens of variations on an idea, visualize concepts described in words, or help overcome the "blank page" problem by providing starting points. This allows human creativity to focus on higher-level ideation, refinement, strategic intent, and adding the unique spark of originality, rather than getting bogged down in initial execution. AI functions as a collaborative assistant, offering suggestions and inspiration, while human oversight remains crucial (China Daily; Eapen et al., 2023). Studies have found that writers given AI suggestions produced stories rated more creative, especially for less experienced writers (Yang et al., 2023), and AI assistance improved creative marketing slogan generation (Hong & Zhou, 2022).

Enhanced Productivity & Efficiency: Routine cognitive tasks that consume significant human time can be dramatically accelerated. Drafting standard reports, summarizing meeting notes (e.g., tools like Otter.ai, Fathom), writing initial code blocks, answering frequently asked questions, or creating basic presentation slides can often be handled rapidly by AI, freeing human workers for tasks requiring deeper analysis, critical judgment, complex problem-solving, or interpersonal engagement. (Recall the Stanford/MIT study showing significant agent productivity boosts - Brynjolfsson, Li, and Raymond, 2023). This is a primary driver for enterprise adoption, with significant measured gains across various roles (Anthropic Guide).

Democratized Skill Access & Capability: Generative AI acts as a powerful skill equalizer. Someone lacking strong writing skills can produce professional communications; a manager needing a quick data visualization might generate a chart without needing specialized software skills; an entrepreneur can create marketing materials without hiring a dedicated designer immediately. This lowers the barrier to entry for many tasks, empowering individuals and smaller teams to achieve more.

Accelerated Learning & Knowledge Synthesis: AI tools can explain complex subjects in personalized ways, summarize dense academic papers into key takeaways (e.g., tools like Elicit, Scite), translate research across language barriers, and even help generate quizzes or study aids tailored to an individual's learning needs. This ability to quickly access, synthesize, and learn from vast amounts of information is crucial for navigating the rapid knowledge expansion of our time.

Evolving Partnership - Towards Agents: The relationship is evolving beyond simple tool use. AI systems are becoming more proactive "cognitive collaborators" capable of analyzing their own outputs, anticipating objections, and exploring alternatives. This leads towards the concept of **AI Agents** – systems designed to reason through complex problems, create actionable plans, and execute those plans using a suite of tools (like web searches, APIs, or other software) (Ruiz, A.; Anthropic Guide). These agents typically include core reasoning (often an LLM), memory, planning capabilities, and access to tools, enabling them to autonomously pursue goals set by humans. This represents a more sophisticated level of integration within the Gestalt.

Empirical Evidence of Synergy (and its Challenges): While the potential is clear, achieving consistent synergy isn't automatic. A comprehensive meta-analysis of 106 studies by Vaccaro et al. (2024) in *Nature Human Behaviour* found nuanced results. On average, human-AI teams did *not* always outperform the best individual (human or AI) alone, often due to coordination challenges or suboptimal integration. However, the study found significant performance *gains* from human-AI collaboration specifically in tasks involving **creative generation**. Conversely, for purely analytical decision tasks, teams sometimes underperformed an optimal AI. Synergy emerged most strongly when humans contributed complementary strengths (like domain expertise or creativity) or when AI augmented areas where humans were weaker. This highlights that effective integration requires careful design to leverage differences and align strengths (Vaccaro et al., 2024). Trust and interaction dynamics are also crucial for success (Frontiers article on Intentional Behavioral Synchrony).

Critical Understanding: Recognizing the Catalyst's Flaws

However, embracing AI as a cognitive catalyst requires a clear-eyed understanding of its significant limitations. Treating these tools as infallible black boxes is not just inefficient; it's potentially harmful. Effective synergy depends on recognizing and managing these inherent flaws. Acknowledge these limitations to use AI responsibly and effectively; and, train yourself and your team to question outputs and refine your critical thinking:

The Hallucination Hazard: Key Limitation. LLMs prioritize fluency and statistical likelihood over factual accuracy. They can, and frequently do, invent facts, sources, citations, or entire narratives that sound plausible but are completely wrong. **Never trust AI-generated factual claims without independent verification from reliable sources.** This requires cultivating critical evaluation skills.

Embedded Bias: Key Limitation. Because training data originates from humans, AI models inherit its biases. They can perpetuate stereotypes related to gender, race, profession, or culture in their text or image outputs. **Outputs must be carefully reviewed for potential bias, and steps taken (prompting techniques, diverse data, auditing) to mitigate unfair or discriminatory outcomes.** Ethical deployment demands awareness of this deep-seated issue.

> **Respecting the Limits of Intelligence Without Understanding**
>
> **Key Concept:**
> Despite their impressive outputs, generative AIs lack true comprehension. Even the newer "reasoning models" with their fluency and analysis can mask a fundamental absence of true reasoning.
>
> **Why It Matters:**
> Overtrusting AI without understanding its limitations can lead to flawed decisions, ethical lapses, or safety failures.
>
> **Actionable Tip:**
> Use prompts that demand justification ("Explain your reasoning"), always review for hallucination, and never deploy unverified outputs in critical contexts.

Lack of True Understanding & Common Sense: Key Limitation. Current AI doesn't *understand* like humans. It operates on statistical patterns and geometric relationships between concepts, not deep meaning or causality (Shannon, D.). Its reasoning, even in advanced LRMs, might be sophisticated mimicry rather than genuine, robust intelligence (Mitchell, 2024). It lacks consciousness and true common sense. As Michael G. Wagner points out, AI's generated "chain-of-thought" explanations might be akin to human *post-hoc* storytelling – rationalizing a result reached through opaque processes, rather than reflecting the actual 'thought' process itself (Wagner, M.G./Substack). **Do not rely on AI for nuanced ethical judgments or tasks requiring deep world knowledge.** Human judgment remains irreplaceable here.

Data Limitations (Staleness & Relevance): AI models generally don't access real-time information beyond their last training date. Their knowledge is static and can become outdated quickly. Furthermore, their effectiveness depends heavily on the relevance and quality of their training data for the specific task at hand.

Potential for Malicious Use: The very power that makes Generative AI useful also makes it dangerous in the wrong hands. It can be easily weaponized to create highly convincing deepfakes, spread misinformation at scale, automate scam operations, or generate harmful content. **Societal awareness and robust governance are essential to mitigate these risks**.

Computational & Environmental Costs: Training large-scale models requires immense computational power and energy, contributing to environmental concerns. The accessibility and sustainability of these powerful tools are ongoing considerations (Strubell et al., 2019).

Interpretability Challenges (The Black Box): While techniques like chain-of-thought aim to make reasoning more transparent (Mitchell, 2024), the internal workings of large models often stay opaque ("black box"), making it hard to fully debug or guarantee safety (Shannon, D.). Anthropomorphic language used by models ("I think...", "Hmmm...") can mislead users into over-trusting systems whose underlying mechanisms are not truly understood (Mitchell, 2024).

Understanding these limitations isn't about fostering fear; it's about fostering **responsible and effective use**. It's about knowing when to trust the AI's output, when to question it rigorously, and when to rely solely on human judgment. It's the difference between using a powerful catalyst effectively and causing an uncontrolled, potentially damaging reaction.

Effective synergy, therefore, demands not just using AI, but skillfully directing it through techniques like prompt engineering, maintaining rigorous critical oversight, understanding its fundamental limitations, and preparing for the rise of more autonomous AI agents. Having explored this cognitive catalyst, let's now turn to the 'part' that gives the Gestalt physical agency: **Embodied Action & Automation**.

Reflection:

Generative AI transforms how we think and work. Leaders must champion experimentation with AI while establishing guardrails around accuracy and ethical use. Prioritize prompt engineering training and establish governance frameworks that align AI outputs with organizational values.

How are you ensuring your teams understand and effectively apply prompt engineering to maximize AI's value?

Chapter 4: Embodied Action & Automation
The Robotic Part

In the preceding chapters, we established the indispensable human 'part' with its unique creativity and adaptability and explored the transformative power of Artificial Intelligence as the cognitive catalyst. We saw how AI can process information and generate insights at superhuman speeds. But ideas and analysis alone don't change the physical world. For the Emerging Gestalt this synergistic whole promises capabilities greater than the sum of its parts to truly interact with, manipulate, and shape our environment, it needs hands, legs, sensors, and effectors. It requires the ability to translate digital intelligence and human intent into tangible action. The **Robotic Part** fulfills this crucial function through the diverse and rapidly evolving ecosystem of automated systems, collaborative robots (cobots), and autonomous machines that serve as the **embodied action** component of the Gestalt, extending its reach, precision, and endurance far into the physical realm. This is a pivotal point for all industries. You must take steps now to apply the power of robotics to transform ideas into tangible action in your organization.

From Clockwork Dreams to Collaborative Partners: The Evolution of Embodied AI

The human desire to imbue inanimate objects with movement and purpose is ancient. Consider how this ancient drive now empowers you to integrate robotics as collaborative partners rather than just tools. Myths across cultures tell of artificial beings, like the bronze giant Talos defending Crete or the Golem of Prague crafted from clay (Classical Mythology; Jewish Folklore). The meticulous clockwork automata of the 18th century, such as Vaucanson's Digesting Duck or the elegant musicians and writers created by Pierre Jaquet-Droz, were marvels of mechanical engineering that simulated life with astonishing detail (Riskin, 2003). These early creations, while not intelligent, reflected a deep-seated aspiration to replicate biological function through mechanical means.

The transition to truly functional robotics began in the mid-20th century, enabled by advances in electronics, control theory, and computation. The pioneering work of George Devol and Joseph Engelberger enabled General Motors to deploy the first industrial robot, the Unimate, on its assembly line in 1961 (Robotics Industries Association History; Engelberger, 1980). These early robots were powerful but largely "unaware" of their surroundings, programmed for repetitive tasks like lifting heavy objects or spot welding, and typically isolated within safety cages to prevent accidental contact with human workers. They were highly effective automation tools, distinct 'parts' operating separately from the human workforce. The journey towards genuine synergy, towards robots becoming integrated partners within the Gestalt, required significant advancements in sensing, intelligence, and safety.

The Modern Robotic Ecosystem: A Spectrum of Embodied Capabilities

Today, the "robotic part" is far from monolithic. It encompasses a vast spectrum of technologies, each optimized for different tasks and environments, increasingly incorporating AI for adaptability and intelligence. Explore how today's robots build real synergy with human teams:

Industrial Robots: Still the backbone of automated manufacturing, these systems handle high-volume, high-precision tasks.

- *Applications:* Welding, painting, assembly, pick-and-place operations, quality inspection using machine vision.

- *Evolution:* While large, powerful arms (from companies like FANUC, KUKA, ABB, Yaskawa) remain common, there's a trend towards smaller, more modular robots, increased use of AI for tasks like bin-picking (identifying and grasping objects from random assortments), and integration with sophisticated simulation software (digital twins) for process optimization. (Manufacturer product lines; reports on smart factories/Industry 4.0).

Logistics & Warehouse Robots: Transform how goods are stored, moved, and sorted.

- *Key Technology:* Autonomous Mobile Robots (AMRs) navigate facilities dynamically, unlike older Automated Guided Vehicles (AGVs) that followed fixed paths. Examples include Amazon Robotics (formerly Kiva Systems), Fetch Robotics (now part of Zebra Technologies), Locus Robotics, and Geek+.

- *Impact:* Studies consistently show significant improvements in warehouse efficiency, order fulfillment speed, and reduced labor costs in facilities deploying AMRs. (MHI Annual Industry Report; Academic studies on warehouse automation ROI). Sophisticated AI often manages fleet coordination, enabling these systems to work collaboratively.

- *Example:* A prime example of this transformation is **Amazon Robotics** (formerly Kiva Systems). Their deployment of hundreds of thousands of AMRs in fulfillment centers allows the system to bring goods directly to human pickers, drastically reducing walking time and increasing order processing speed. While Amazon doesn't release precise, universal metrics, industry analyses consistently point to significant efficiency gains in facilities using these systems, enabling faster delivery times and higher throughput crucial for e-commerce logistics (Public information from Amazon Robotics; various industry analyses, e.g., by logistics consulting firms or publications like DC Velocity). The sophisticated AI managing the fleet coordination ensures optimized paths and minimizes congestion, showcasing the synergy between physical automation and intelligent control.

Service Robots (Human-Interacting): Operate in public spaces or service industries.

- *Healthcare:* Surgical assistants like the da Vinci system (Intuitive Surgical) provide surgeons with enhanced dexterity and visualization. Robots deliver medication and supplies within hospitals (e.g., Aethon TUG), disinfect rooms with UV light, and assist with patient mobility or rehabilitation (e.g., Ekso Bionics exoskeletons), and AI-powered monitoring systems enhance patient care and operational efficiency (ValueCoders; JR Marketing on senior care).

- *Hospitality/Retail:* Robots deliver room service (e.g., Savioke Relay), guide customers in stores, perform inventory checks, and provide automated cleaning services (e.g., Brain Corp AI platform for commercial cleaners).

- *Delivery:* Autonomous ground vehicles and aerial drones promise last-mile delivery solutions (e.g., Starship Technologies ground robots; Wing and Zipline aerial drones), though regulatory hurdles and operational complexities remain.

Agricultural Robots: Address labor shortages and enabling precision farming.

- *Applications:* Autonomous tractors plant and till (e.g., John Deere autonomous tractors), robotic systems perform precise spraying of pesticides/herbicides (reducing chemical use), robots automate harvesting of fruits and vegetables (e.g., Abundant Robotics for apples - operations ceased, but demonstrated potential), and drones use AI image analysis to monitor crops. Robots are also addressing labor shortages and enabling precision farming (like the potential demonstrated by UKKÖ Robotics for strawberries - Horecha, 2023) and data analysis.

- *Benefits:* Potential for increased yields, reduced resource consumption (water, fertilizer, chemicals), and operation around the clock. (Research on Precision Agriculture and AgTech).

Construction Robots: Improve safety and efficiency on building sites.

- *Examples:* Robots automate bricklaying (Hadrian X), finish drywall (Canvas), tie rebar, survey sites using drones and AI analysis, and print 3D concrete structures (e.g., ICON, Apis Cor). While these technologies are still emerging, they promise to alleviate labor shortages and speed up construction timelines.

Exploration, Inspection, and Maintenance Robots: Operate in hazardous or remote environments.

- *Applications:* Remotely Operated Vehicles (ROVs) conduct deep-sea exploration and infrastructure inspection, drones inspect wind turbines, bridges, or power lines, mobile robots like Boston Dynamics' Spot navigate challenging industrial sites or disaster zones, and robotic systems aid nuclear decommissioning and space exploration (NASA's Perseverance Rover).

Emerging Humanoid Robots: A significant development is the push towards general-purpose humanoid robots, powered by advanced AI.

- *Applications:* Projects like **NVIDIA's GR00T N1** aim to create foundation models for humanoid robots, enabling them to understand natural language instructions and learn complex tasks from simulation, human demonstration (teleoperation), and even video. These models often integrate Vision-Language Models (VLMs) for perception/ reasoning and Diffusion Transformers for generating precise motor actions.

- *Goal:* Create robots capable of diverse manipulation tasks in unstructured environments, potentially working alongside humans in homes, warehouses, or factories. While still early, this represents a convergence of advanced AI and robotics aiming for adaptable physical agency.

This diverse landscape demonstrates that robotics provides specialized physical capabilities across virtually every sector, acting as the hands, legs, and eyes of the broader intelligent system.

Cobots: The Bridge to Human-Robot Synergy

As we continue to map the landscape of the Emerging Gestalt, seeking ways for its diverse 'parts' to achieve true synergy, one development stands out as particularly transformative for enabling genuine human-robot teaming: the rise of the Collaborative Robot, or **Cobot**. These remarkable machines represent a fundamental paradigm shift. For decades, industrial robots operated largely in isolation, powerful but cordoned off from their human counterparts. Cobots, however, are engineered from the ground up not to operate *instead* of humans, but to work *with* them, sharing the same workspace and often the same tasks in close, dynamic proximity. Use cobots strategically to amplify your team's strengths; identify where synergy is most needed.

This new era of collaboration is built, first and foremost, on an unwavering commitment to **safety by design**. Manufacturers have meticulously engineered cobots with a suite of inherent safety features, effectively dismantling the need for the traditional, cumbersome safety cages that once defined robotic work cells. Imagine a system acutely aware of its surroundings; built-in sensors allow cobots to detect unexpected forces, such as inadvertent contact with a human, triggering an immediate stop or a gentle safety maneuver. Operators can precisely tune their operational parameters to ensure movements are slow and gentle enough to preclude injury. Even their physical form is considered, with rounded geometry and padded surfaces designed to minimize potential harm. Some advanced cobots even employ sophisticated vision systems, using cameras to actively monitor their workspace and intelligently adjust their paths to avoid collisions, all in adherence with stringent international standards like ISO 10218 and the technical specification ISO/TS 15066.

Beyond their safety-centric design, cobots are distinguished by their remarkable **ease of use and flexibility**. Designers have intentionally made them far simpler to program and deploy when compared to their traditional industrial predecessors. Many utilize intuitive teach pendants, handheld controllers that allow users, even those without deep robotics expertise, to program movements step-by-step. Perhaps even more impressively, many support lead-through programming: an operator can simply grab the robot's arm and physically guide it through the desired sequence of motions, which the cobot then diligently records and can repeat with precision. This significantly lowers the technical barrier to entry for automating tasks. This inherent flexibility, combined with their relative ease of setup and reprogramming, makes cobots exceptionally well-suited for high-mix, low-volume production runs or for tasks that change frequently—scenarios where traditional, more rigid automation might prove too costly or inflexible to implement effectively.

It is in **synergy in practice** that cobots truly shine, excelling at augmenting human capabilities by seamlessly taking over specific sub-tasks within a larger, shared process. Consider the realm of ergonomic assistance: cobots can tirelessly handle repetitive lifting, awkward twisting, or precision placement tasks that might otherwise cause strain or injury to human workers. BMW, for instance, has successfully integrated cobots for tasks like applying sealant, significantly reducing ergonomic stress on their human workforce. In many manufacturing sectors, cobots have become common sights in machine tending, diligently loading and unloading parts from CNC machines or injection molding presses, thereby freeing human operators to focus on more complex setup procedures, crucial quality control checks, or managing multiple machines simultaneously. They can also perform meticulous quality inspections, often using integrated cameras and AI, or handle delicate parts with unwavering consistency for precise measurement. And in assembly and finishing operations, cobots can execute precise screwing, gluing, polishing, or intricate assembly steps in direct collaboration with a human worker who might be handling the more complex, dexterous, or judgment-dependent parts of the task. We see this in small and medium-sized enterprises using cobots for assembling intricate electronics or carefully packaging goods.

The real-world impact of this human-robot synergy is not just conceptual; it is significant and demonstrably measurable. Take DCL Logistics, a third-party logistics provider, which implemented Universal Robots' UR10e cobots for the often mundane tasks of repetitive packaging and kitting. By automating these crucial steps, DCL reported a staggering 500% increase in productivity for those specific tasks and, remarkably, realized a full return on their investment in just six months. Crucially, their human workers were not displaced but freed up for more complex logistics operations that genuinely required their judgment and problem-solving skills. Similarly, SHAD, a manufacturer of motorcycle accessories in Spain, integrated an Omron TM cobot into its assembly line specifically for inserting and tightening screws on motorcycle cases. This collaborative approach allowed SHAD to increase its production by a notable 10% while simultaneously improving the ergonomics for the human worker, who previously shouldered the strenuous manual screw-driving task and now focuses on component preparation and final quality checks alongside their tireless robotic partner. Further, a major automotive supplier like Continental Automotive utilizes cobots for tasks demanding consistent force and unwavering precision, such as the assembly of delicate circuit boards. Here, the cobot handles the precise insertion or screwing operations, while human workers stationed nearby perform vital inspections and manage more complex component placements, effectively leveraging the cobot's steadfastness and the human's superior dexterity and visual acuity.

These examples vividly demonstrate how cobots act as a crucial interface layer. They allow the inherent physical power, endurance, and precision of robotics to be safely and effectively integrated directly into human workflows. In doing so, they create a truly collaborative physical 'part' within the team, a tangible manifestation of synergy where shared purpose and mutual support blurred the lines between human and machine contributors.

The Interconnected System: Automation, Autonomy, and the IoT

Its connection to the broader technological ecosystem significantly amplifies the effectiveness of each robotic 'part':

Automation vs. Autonomy: It's useful to distinguish here. *Automation* involves machines performing pre-programmed tasks repetitively. *Autonomy* implies the ability to make decisions and adapt actions based on sensor input and changing environmental conditions, often powered by AI. Modern robotics increasingly blends both, with systems capable of automated routines but also autonomous adjustments.

The IoT Sensory Network: The Internet of Things provides the essential data streams that enable robotic intelligence and coordinated action. Sensors on machines, in the environment, and tracking materials provide real-time status updates. This data feeds AI algorithms that optimize robotic tasks, predict maintenance needs (preventing downtime), and coordinate the actions of multiple robots or autonomous systems. IoT acts as the distributed nervous system, providing the awareness needed for intelligent embodied action. (Concepts of Cyber-Physical Systems and the Industrial Internet of Things - IIoT).

Bridging Worlds: Robotics as the Phygital Link

Robotics and automation form the indispensable bridge connecting the digital realm of information and AI-driven insight to the physical realm of action and consequence. This **"Phygital"** link is where computation translates into tangible work. Bridge the digital and physical worlds and use robotics to create seamless integration and unlock new possibilities:

- An AI optimizes a delivery route (digital), an autonomous truck drives it (physical).

- AI analyzes a medical scan (digital), a robotic surgical arm assists the surgeon (physical).

- A simulation optimizes a factory layout (digital), AMRs physically transport materials according to the new plan (physical).

- AI designs a custom protein (digital), robotic lab automation synthesizes and tests it (physical - bridging to **Appendix A** on SynBio).

The Rise of Phygital Intelligence

Key Concept:
Robotics bridges the digital and physical worlds. With AI, they now perceive environments, make decisions, and adapt in real-time.

Why It Matters:
These capabilities enable unprecedented flexibility—from last-mile delivery to search-and-rescue—amplifying human effort.

Actionable Tip:
Evaluate tasks for real-time responsiveness or sensory complexity—these are ideal candidates for AI-robotic integration.

Without this capacity for embodied action, the cognitive power of AI stays confined within the virtual realm. Robotics gives the Emerging Gestalt its ability to physically interact with and modify the world around us. This aligns with the view that augmentation, including robotics, serves as a "critical binding agent" marrying machine capabilities with human adaptability (Ministry of Defense, 2021).

38

Capabilities & Benefits: The Value Proposition of Embodied Action

The integration of this increasingly sophisticated robotic 'part' into the fabric of our collaborative endeavors, this tangible manifestation of embodied action, is not merely a technological novelty; it brings a cascade of substantial and transformative value to the synergistic 'whole' we are actively building. As these tireless mechanical partners join forces with human ingenuity and AI's cognitive prowess, the benefits ripple outward, reshaping our capacity for production, quality, safety, and operational adaptability. Maximize your team's potential by integrating robotics to add flexibility, precision, and endurance to your operations.

Perhaps most immediately apparent is the profound impact on **unlocking productivity**. Robots, unburdened by fatigue or the need for rest, can work tirelessly and consistently, often executing specific tasks at speeds far exceeding human capability. This relentless dedication naturally translates into a significant boost in overall output, allowing organizations to meet demands and achieve production targets that were previously unattainable.

> **Automation is a System, Not a Gadget**
>
> **Key Concept:**
> Robotic performance is amplified when linked with IoT sensors, AI prediction engines, and human workflows as part of a larger system.
>
> **Why It Matters:**
> Treating automation as plug-and-play underestimates the orchestration needed for meaningful gains.
>
> **Actionable Tip:**
> Think ecosystem-first: Map out how robotic parts interface with data flows, human teams, and decision-making loops.

Closely allied with this enhanced productivity is the assurance of **unwavering quality and precision**. In tasks characterized by repetition, the very nature of automation serves to minimize, if not entirely eliminate, the potential for human error. This leads to a higher degree of consistency in finished products or processes, bolstering quality standards and reducing costly rework or defects.

Beyond the metrics of speed and accuracy, the introduction of robotics profoundly **enhances human safety and well-being**. By thoughtfully delegating tasks that are dangerous, hazardous, or ergonomically challenging to their robotic counterparts, we significantly reduce the risk of workplace injuries and protect the physical health of human team members. This allows us to reassign human talent to roles that are not only safer but often more engaging and cognitively demanding.

The reach of this embodied action extends even into environments where human presence is difficult, if not impossible. Robots can **operate effectively in extreme conditions** that are wholly unsuitable for human physiology: the vacuum of space, areas with high radiation levels, the crushing pressures of the deep sea, or environments characterized by extreme temperatures. This capability opens up new frontiers for exploration, maintenance, and operational capacity.

Furthermore, the integration of robotics **enables unprecedented scale and flexibility**. Automation, by its very nature, allows for the rapid scaling of production or operational throughput to meet fluctuating market demands. And as modern robotics, particularly in the form of collaborative cobots and agile Autonomous Mobile Robots (AMRs), become increasingly sophisticated, they offer a remarkable degree of flexibility, allowing workflows and processes to adapt quickly to changing requirements or product variations.

Finally, these instrumented robotic systems are not just silent workers; they are also invaluable sources of information, **generating a continuous stream of actionable data**. Sensors embedded within them constantly monitor operational performance, providing rich datasets for AI algorithms to analyze. This data, in turn, fuels AI-driven optimization, allowing for the fine-tuning of processes, the prediction of maintenance needs (thereby preventing costly downtime), and the overall enhancement of system efficiency.

In essence, the robotic component, increasingly powered by sophisticated AI foundation models for advanced humanoids as envisioned by projects like NVIDIA's GR00T, and specialized systems already transforming industries like agriculture and healthcare, provides the essential physical agency for the Emerging Gestalt. From powerful industrial arms to nimble collaborative cobots and intelligent autonomous systems networked via the Internet of Things, robots translate cognitive insights and human intentions into tangible, world-altering action. The effective integration of this physical 'part' is therefore a cornerstone of our synergistic future, though it demands careful planning, robust safety protocols, thoughtful consideration of workforce impacts (as we will explore in Chapters 10 and 11), and skillful orchestration with its human and AI counterparts. Having now explored the cognitive catalyst of AI and the embodied action of robotics, our journey next takes us to examine the potential evolution of the human 'part' itself through the lens of Human Augmentation.

The robotic component, increasingly powered by sophisticated AI like foundation models for humanoids and specialized systems for industries like agriculture (Horecha, 2023) and healthcare (ValueCoders; Bhandari, 2024), provides the essential physical agency for the Emerging Gestalt. From industrial arms to collaborative cobots and intelligent autonomous systems networked via the IoT, robots translate cognitive insights into tangible action. Effectively integrating this physical 'part' requires careful planning, robust safety protocols, addressing workforce impacts, and skillful orchestration with human and AI components. Having explored the cognitive catalyst (AI) and embodied action (Robotics), we now examine the potential evolution of the human 'part' itself through **Human Augmentation.**

Reflection:

Automation is reshaping operations and logistics. Leaders should map which processes can benefit from automation and which require human oversight. Create a roadmap for integrating AI and robotics that includes clear communication, cross-functional teams, and ongoing skills development.

Have you identified which processes in your organization can be enhanced by automation while preserving human oversight?

Chapter 5: Evolving Ourselves

The Augmented Human Part

We have now explored several foundational 'parts' of the Emerging Gestalt: the uniquely adaptable human core, the transformative cognitive catalyst of AI, and the embodied action enabled by robotics and automation. These components are increasingly working together, adding skills and multiplying their capabilities. But the equation of this emerging whole isn't static. Perhaps the most profound and intimate aspect of this transformation involves the potential evolution of the *human part* itself. This is the domain of **Human Augmentation**, a rapidly advancing frontier where science and technology are beginning to modify, enhance, and even transcend our inherent biological limitations. Understanding augmentation is crucial because it signifies a potential shift from humans *using* technology as external tools to technology becoming *part of us*, fundamentally reshaping our capabilities, our integration into the Gestalt, and perhaps even our definition of what it means to be human. As the UK Ministry of Defense noted, augmentation could be a "critical binding agent that marries the capabilities of machines with the creativity and adaptability of people," becoming a key factor in future societal and competitive landscapes (Ministry of Defense, 2021).

Alex and the Augmented Assembly Line

The hum of the automated sorting machinery at the Apex Logistics Hub was a low, constant thrum, a counterpoint to the rapid-fire click of scanners and the occasional whirr of a lifting robot. Alex took a deep breath, the air conditioning cool against their face. Today was their first day on the floor, a position they'd frankly worried might be out of reach after the accident.

Alex looked down at their left arm – not flesh and bone, but gleaming carbon fiber and brushed polymer, subtly articulated, an extension of their will mediated by nerve signals and miniature motors. This wasn't just a replacement; it was a 'part' designed for this new era of work. Developed by a company specializing in neuro-integrated prosthetics, this arm wasn't just strong; it was sensitive. Tiny haptic feedback motors in the socket and a sophisticated sensor array in the hand translated pressure, texture, and even temperature into subtle signals Alex's brain had learned to interpret almost instinctively, a form of human augmentation blurring the line between biology and machine.

They inspected and sorted high-value, irregularly shaped items coming down a specialized conveyor belt—a task too delicate and variable for the standard pick-and-place robots further down the line but requiring speed and precision beyond what a single human could manage. It was a perfect example of the synergistic team – humans and technology collaborating.

Alex stepped up to their station. A small screen displayed instructions and metrics. A green light pulsed, indicating the next item was ready. Alex extended their prosthetic arm. It felt less like operating a tool and more like an integrated extension of their body, already anticipating the necessary grip based on the visual feed from the station's camera and the arm's own sensors, processed by its onboard AI.

The first item, a fragile ceramic vase, moved into position. Alex's prosthetic hand closed gently, the sensor data instantly confirming the weight and shape. On the screen, the station's AI interface (Cognitive Catalyst) cross-referenced the visual data with the manifest and Alex's grip parameters. "Item 734, Variant C. Confirmed. Sort Bay 9," a calm voice synthesized from the station's system announced. Alex smoothly pivoted and placed the vase in the designated bay, the arm's force feedback confirming secure placement.

Then came a box of heavy, dense electronics, followed by a package with an unusual, slick texture. The arm instantly adjusted its grip strength and angle. Alex's performance metrics on the screen, usually tracking human speed and accuracy, were augmented to include data from the prosthetic – grip force logs, object identification confidence scores, placement precision. The team evaluated their capability not just as "Alex," but as "Alex-with-Augmented-Arm-and-Integrated-Station AI."

Across the aisle, Alex noticed another worker, Sarah, strapping into an industrial exoskeleton – a powered suit providing lumbar and arm support, designed to help her safely lift and move larger, heavier packages without strain. Sarah's exoskeleton was another form of physical augmentation, turning a demanding physical task into something manageable, extending human endurance. She wasn't replaced by a forklift; she was enhanced to perform a different type of heavy lifting, working alongside forklifts, AMRs, and other automated systems.

Beyond Biological Baselines: Defining Human Augmentation and its Philosophical Roots

Human augmentation, when we broadly define it, is the application of science and technology to enhance human physical, cognitive, sensory, or even emotional capabilities beyond the typical biological baseline. Consider how augmentation can expand your capabilities and redefine your potential. While simple forms like eyeglasses or hearing aids have existed for centuries, the current wave involves interventions with far deeper implications. This field intersects significantly with philosophical movements like **Transhumanism**, which actively advocates for using technology to overcome fundamental human limitations like disease, aging, and cognitive constraints, and **Posthumanism**, which critically examines and questions the traditional boundaries of human identity in light of technological possibilities. (Bostrom, 2005; Hayles, 1999). The core idea isn't just fixing what's broken; it's about potentially *improving* upon the original design, making the human part a more dynamic and adaptable component within the larger system.

> **Human Augmentation Redefines What It Means to Be Human**
>
> **Key Concept:**
> From prosthetics to neurotech and gene editing, augmentation expands the human baseline, pushing the boundary of what "human ability" means.
>
> **Why It Matters:**
> These tools change not only capability but identity, forcing societies to confront ethical, legal, and philosophical questions.
>
> **Actionable Tip:**
> Build inclusive policies and dialogues now—engage voices from ethics, disability advocacy, and science fiction to shape norms before mass adoption.

As David W Sime of Riiot Digital observed about the learning process between a user and an intelligent prosthetic, "...they become a partnership... it's an 'us together' one." (2022 interview, Riiot Digital). This highlights a key aspect: augmentation often involves creating a new, integrated system where biology and technology learn and adapt together, blurring the lines between user and tool, echoing Andy Clark's ideas about the flimsy boundary between tool and user (Clark, 2003).

Physical Augmentation: Reshaping Our Bodies, Redefining Action

This is often the most tangible form of augmentation, directly altering our physical interaction with the world. Adopt new technologies that integrate seamlessly into your daily life. Use them to enhance your mobility, strength, and safety:

Advanced Prosthetics: From Restoration to Potential Enhancement: Modern prosthetics are rapidly evolving from passive replacements to active, integrated extensions of the body.

- *Restoring Function:* Technologies aim to replicate natural movement with increasing fidelity. **Myoelectric prosthetics**, for instance, use sensors to detect electrical signals from remaining muscles in a residual limb, allowing intuitive control over the artificial hand or arm (Engineering literature on prosthetic control systems). **Osseointegration**, a surgical technique pioneered by Dr. Per-Ingvar Brånemark, involves implanting a titanium fixture directly into the bone, creating a stable anchor point for attaching a prosthesis, improving control and sensory feedback compared to traditional socket-based systems (Brånemark R, et al. publications). These allow individuals like **Enzo Romero**, the Peruvian engineer who designed his own functional bionic hand, to regain significant dexterity (News reports). Some advanced prosthetics even incorporate sensory feedback, allowing users to "feel" texture or pressure.

- *Beyond Restoration?:* The line blurs with devices designed for specific high performance. Athlete **Hunter Woodhall**'s carbon-fiber running blades enable him to compete at an elite level, raising questions about whether such technology offers advantages beyond merely compensating for his biological difference (Discussions in sports ethics and Paralympic classifications). Experimental devices might offer capabilities like 360-degree wrist rotation or enhanced grip strength.

- *Expanding Scope:* Prosthetics aren't limited to limbs. Research into **artificial retinas** aims to restore partial sight for certain types of blindness (Example: Argus II Retinal Prosthesis System), and work continues on developing functional **artificial hearts** and other internal organs, though challenges remain immense (Medical device research publications).

Exoskeletons: Wearable Strength and Support: These external robotic frameworks amplify human physical capabilities.

- **Industrial Impact:** Reducing workplace injuries and boosting endurance is a key driver. **Ford Motor Company**, for instance, has deployed the EksoVest, developed by Ekso Bionics, in several plants. This upper-body exoskeleton provides lift assistance for workers performing repetitive overhead tasks, significantly reducing shoulder strain and fatigue, aiming to decrease injury rates and improve worker well-being (Ford News Releases; Ekso Bionics Case Studies, e.g., "Ford Rolls Out Exoskeleton Vests Worldwide..."). Similarly, **Delta Air Lines** conducted pilot programs with a Sarcos Robotics powered exoskeleton (Guardian XO) designed to help baggage handlers lift heavy luggage, exploring the potential to enhance safety and efficiency in physically demanding airport operations (Sarcos Robotics Press Releases/News Reports on Delta trial, e.g., from 2020). Militaries also invest heavily in exoskeletons to augment soldier load-carrying and endurance (Ministry of Defence, 2021). These systems exemplify how augmentation allows the human part to exert greater force or sustain effort longer, directly impacting physical task performance within the Gestalt.

- *Medical and Personal Applications:* Rehabilitation exoskeletons from companies like **Ekso Bionics** or **ReWalk Robotics** help patients with spinal cord injuries or stroke regain mobility. Lighter-weight designs aim to provide daily mobility assistance for individuals with muscle weakness or other impairments. **Open Bionics** continues to innovate with affordable, aesthetically engaging bionic hands, emphasizing personalization (Company websites, medical technology reviews).

Cognitive & Sensory Augmentation: Upgrading Perception and Thought

Augmenting the mind and senses offers perhaps even more profound integration possibilities within the data-rich environment of the Emerging Gestalt. Leverage these tools to upgrade your perception and decision-making. Train yourself to think with, rather than against, these technologies:

Brain-Computer Interfaces (BCIs): The Direct Neural Link: BCIs create a direct communication channel between brain activity and external devices, bypassing traditional motor pathways.

- *Mechanism:* BCIs range from non-invasive methods using **EEG (electroencephalography)** caps to read electrical signals from the scalp (Example: Used in some neurofeedback therapies or experimental device control), to highly invasive methods that require surgical implantation of electrode arrays to read signals directly from neurons (Example: Neuralink's approach; Utah Array used in much academic research). The global BCI market is projected to grow significantly, indicating increasing research and potential application (Market research reports like Global News Wire BCI Market Analysis 2023 estimate $5.34B by 2030).

- *Restorative Uses:* Established applications include **cochlear implants** for deafness. Research focuses on restoring movement control for paralyzed individuals by translating thought into commands for robotic limbs or computer cursors (Academic publications from labs like BrainGate). Recent breakthroughs let individuals with paralysis type via 'mental handwriting' at speeds approaching 90 characters per minute (NIH News Releases, 2021; Brown University News, 2021).

- *Enhancement & Control:* Beyond restoration, BCIs offer potential for direct control of complex systems, as seen in the **Australian Army's robot control experiments** (Defence Science and Technology Group reports). Research explores using BCIs for enhanced focus, accelerated learning, or even "silent communication" (Meta Reality Labs BCI research). This represents the potential for the human mind to become a direct, high-bandwidth controller and processor within the Gestalt. However, this potential raises profound ethical questions about **cognitive liberty** (Farahany, 2023).

External Cognitive Aids: The Extended Mind: Much of our current cognitive augmentation happens *outside* the body. Smartphones act as ubiquitous memory banks, navigation aids, and communication hubs. AI assistants like Siri, Alexa, or ChatGPT can retrieve information, summarize text, and perform cognitive tasks on command. This aligns with the Extended Mind thesis (Clark & Chalmers, 1998). Furthermore, **Augmented Reality (AR)** systems (glasses or heads-up displays) can overlay relevant data onto our field of vision. For example, **GE Vernova's Gas Power division** uses AR headsets (like the RealWear Navigator 500) to provide field service engineers with hands-free access to documentation, schematics, and real-time remote expert support during complex maintenance and repair operations on power generation equipment. This reduces downtime, improves first-time fix rates, and enhances safety by keeping the engineer's hands free and attention focused (Source: GE Vernova and RealWear partnership announcements and case studies). These tools function as components of our "extended mind," integrating external processing power and information directly into our cognitive workflow. (Example: Microsoft HoloLens applications in industry; Google Glass enterprise editions).

Sensory Augmentation/ Substitution: Technology can enhance existing senses or even create new ones. Advanced hearing aids use AI to filter noise and clarify speech.

Research explores devices that translate data streams (like stock market fluctuations or Wi-Fi signals) into tactile sensations (haptic feedback) or allow individuals to "feel" magnetic north, effectively adding new sensory inputs to human perception (Research by David Eagleman on sensory substitution; Cyborg Foundation projects). The work towards simulating mammalian brains (Markram, H./LinkedIn) might eventually inform the development of more sophisticated BCIs or cognitive aids by providing deeper insights into neural function. Ethnographic studies examine individuals self-identifying as "cyborgs" due to implants (Gray, 2017).

The Genetic Frontier: Potential to Edit the Blueprint

Perhaps the most fundamental level of augmentation involves altering our genetic code. Explore these genetic frontiers thoughtfully and understand the profound ethical and personal choices they entail:

CRISPR and Precision Gene Editing: Technologies like CRISPR-Cas9 act like programmable molecular 'scissors,' allowing scientists to make precise changes to DNA sequences with relative ease (Doudna & Charpentier Nobel Prize literature).

- *Therapeutic Promise:* The primary focus is treating genetic diseases by correcting the underlying mutation. Clinical trials are underway for conditions like sickle cell anemia and inherited blindness (ClinicalTrials.gov database). The UK's pioneering use of **mitochondrial donation** prevents specific inherited diseases by using genetic material from three individuals (HFEA reports, May 2023). Importantly, most current therapeutic efforts focus on somatic gene editing, affecting only the individual patient without passing changes to offspring.

- *The Enhancement Debate:* The potential exists to use these tools for *germline* editing (modifying sperm, eggs, or embryos), which would create heritable changes, or for enhancing non-disease traits (intelligence, athleticism). This prospect raises profound ethical alarms about unforeseen ecological consequences, exacerbating social inequalities ("genetic haves and have-nots"), and the potential for a new eugenics. There is currently broad international scientific and ethical consensus against non-therapeutic germline enhancement (Statements from international scientific bodies like the Hinxton Group; National Academies reports on human genome editing).

The Radical Frontier: Biological Computing? A striking, albeit highly experimental, example pushing the boundaries of augmentation and computation is the work of companies like **Cortical Labs** (Sparkes, 2022; Gizmodo). They are developing what they term "biological computers" (like the CL1) powered by lab-grown human brain cells integrated with silicon chips. While primarily aimed at research (e.g., drug discovery, understanding learning), their "Wetware-as-a-Service" concept and the ability to teach these biological systems tasks (like playing Pong) represent a profound blurring of lines between biology and computation. Though nascent and fraught with ethical questions (the marketing described as "morbid"), this research points towards potential futures where computation isn't just silicon-based but incorporates living neural tissue, raising fundamental questions about identity, consciousness, and the very definition of "augmentation."

Navigating the Augmented Reality: Opportunities and Deepening Challenges

As we contemplate the integration of this potentially enhanced human 'part' into the dynamic fabric of the Emerging Gestalt, a vista of transformative possibilities unfolds before us. Yet, this same horizon is shadowed by the amplification of existing ethical and societal challenges, demanding our most careful consideration and proactive stewardship. The journey into an augmented reality is one of immense promise but you must navigate a landscape where these values and structures will face profound tests.

The **key opportunities** presented by human augmentation are compelling and speak to some of our most fundamental aspirations. Imagine **revolutionizing accessibility and inclusion** on an unprecedented scale; restorative augmentations hold the potential to dramatically improve the quality of life for individuals with disabilities, breaking down barriers and enabling their fuller, more active participation in all aspects of society. Consider, too, the potential for **boosting safety and performance** in demanding environments. Augmentations like exoskeletons can shield workers from injury in physically strenuous jobs, while sophisticated cognitive aids could significantly reduce errors in complex, high-stakes tasks. Furthermore, the prospect of **enabling even deeper human-machine synergy** is tantalizing. Advanced interfaces, such as the Brain-Computer Interfaces we've touched upon, could theoretically allow for more seamless, intuitive, and high-bandwidth control and collaboration with the complex AI and robotic systems that form other crucial 'parts' of the Gestalt.

However, these bright opportunities are inextricably linked with **significant challenges and profound ethical considerations** that we must confront with open eyes and unwavering resolve. Perhaps the most pressing is the specter of **equity and access, giving rise to the critical challenge of an "augmented divide."** The high costs often associated with advanced prosthetics, sophisticated implants, or potential future genetic enhancements risk creating a stark and potentially insurmountable chasm between those who can afford such enhancements and those who cannot. How, as a society, do we ensure that these transformative benefits don't merely accrue to the wealthy, further entrenching existing inequalities? Crafting thoughtful policies that address insurance coverage, explore potential subsidies, and actively encourage the development of lower-cost, open-source alternatives, much like Enzo Romero's inspiring work with his 3D-printed hand, becomes absolutely vital.

51

The very intimacy of these technologies also brings to the forefront concerns regarding **safety, security, and inherent biological risks.** The long-term health impacts of implanted devices, the potential for immune rejection or device malfunction, and the glaring security vulnerabilities of connected augmentations are major areas of concern. BCIs in particular raise the chilling question of whether they could be hacked. Nothing less than rigorous pre-market testing, secure-by-design engineering principles, and diligent long-term monitoring will suffice to mitigate these risks.

Then there is the deeply personal frontier of **privacy and the emerging imperative of cognitive liberty.** Augmentations, especially those generating biological or neural data, create unprecedented privacy risks. Who truly owns this incredibly intimate data? How will it be used, and by whom? The very concept of "cognitive liberty" or the fundamental right to mental self-determination, free from unwanted technological manipulation or surveillance is rapidly emerging as a critical area for legal and ethical development, a theme we will revisit when discussing mental well-being in Chapter 12. As pioneers like Nita Farahany have meticulously detailed, and as early work by scholars such as Bublitz, Ienca, and Andorno has highlighted, even currently available brain wearables present these thorny issues, demanding our immediate attention.

Beyond the practical, augmentation forces us to grapple with fundamental questions of **identity, authenticity, and what it truly means to be "human."** Where does the biological human end and the integrated technology begin? How much alteration can our physical or cognitive selves undergo before we perceive a shift in our fundamental identity? Does an increasing reliance on cognitive enhancement inadvertently diminish the value we place on natural learning, inherent effort, or even the beautiful imperfections of the human mind? These are not mere philosophical musings; they challenge our core concepts of selfhood and the very essence of our lived experience.

The integration of augmentation into the workplace also raises significant concerns about **coercion and informed consent.** Could employers, in a relentless pursuit of productivity, subtly or overtly pressure employees to adopt performance-enhancing augmentations? How do we ensure truly informed consent for invasive procedures or for technologies whose long-term effects may still be largely unknown?

And finally, the challenge of **fairness and the prevention of discrimination** looms large. We must proactively develop policies that prevent discrimination *against* augmented individuals, who might encounter fear or prejudice due to their enhancements. Simultaneously, we must address the potential for augmentation to create unfair advantages *over* non-augmented individuals in competitive settings like hiring, promotions, or compensation.

These ethical dilemmas surrounding equity, safety, privacy (especially the critical frontier of **neuro-privacy**, as detailed by Farahany (2023)), identity, coercion, and fairness are not merely abstract philosophical concerns. These ethical dilemmas directly precede the **complex, practical challenges that Transhuman Resources (THR) must navigate**, as we will explore in detail in Chapter 10. The ethical questions raised here:

Who gets access?

How do we ensure safety and privacy?

How do we define fair performance when capabilities differ so vastly?

become the specific policy gaps, recruitment dilemmas, performance management conundrums, and DEI imperatives that THR leaders must address proactively.

Consider a relevant real-world analogy that, while often biochemical rather than technological, mirrors the emerging challenges: the documented off-label use of prescription stimulants (like Adderall or Modafinil) by healthy individuals seeking cognitive enhancement for improved focus and productivity in highly competitive academic and professional environments. (Greely et al., 2008; Sahakian & Morein-Zamir, 2007). This phenomenon already forces organizations (and society) to grapple with issues directly parallel to technological augmentation:

- **Equity & Fairness:** Does this create an unfair playing field where those with access (via prescription or illicit means) gain an advantage? How does this impact performance evaluation?

- **Coercion:** Does intense pressure to perform implicitly coerce individuals into seeking such enhancements?

- **Safety & Well-being:** What are the health risks and how should organizations respond if use impacts workplace safety or employee health?

- **Policy Gaps:** Most workplace policies focus on illicit drug *abuse*, not necessarily the nuanced ethics of enhancement use by otherwise healthy individuals.

This existing struggle with cognitive enhancement via pharmaceuticals provides a concrete preview of the types of issues THR must develop robust frameworks for as *technological* augmentations become more sophisticated and prevalent. THR cannot wait for widespread adoption; the ethical groundwork laid (or ignored) now will shape the fairness and effectiveness of managing the augmented workforce of tomorrow.

Human augmentation represents a potentially radical evolution of the human 'part' within the Emerging Gestalt. It offers pathways to overcome age-old biological constraints, enhance our capabilities, and perhaps achieve unprecedented levels of integration with the technological systems around us. Yet, this path is fraught with profound ethical dilemmas, particularly concerning equity, privacy, safety, and the very essence of our humanity. Successfully navigating this requires not only technological prowess but deep societal wisdom, robust ethical frameworks, adaptable governance, and fundamentally reimagined approaches to managing talent. But regardless of whether or how the human part itself is augmented, effective integration within the Gestalt fundamentally relies on productive interaction with its other powerful components, particularly the AI cognitive catalyst. With the full cast of potential contributors now defined, the critical question becomes one of effective interaction. How do we orchestrate these diverse parts to achieve true synergy? Especially with the powerful AI component, effective communication is paramount and demands mastering the essential interface protocol: **Bridging Minds: Prompt Engineering for Human-AI Synergy**.

Reflection:

Human augmentation challenges traditional talent management. Leaders must address ethical, legal, and cultural implications while fostering innovation. Implement continuous learning programs, develop policies for responsible use, and consider how augmentation affects diversity and inclusion.

What policies and training are in place to responsibly support human augmentation in your workforce?

Part 2: Enabling Synergy
Communication, Ethics, and Governance

Chapter 6: Bridging Minds

Prompt Engineering for Human-AI Synergy

We stand at a fascinating juncture. Having acquainted ourselves with the diverse 'parts' constituting the Emerging Gestalt—the adaptable baseline human, the potent AI catalyst, the embodied robotic actor, and the evolving augmented human—the critical question becomes one of orchestration. How do we weave these powerful threads together effectively? A crucial element, particularly concerning the integration of Artificial Intelligence, lies in mastering the art of **communication**. Whether we are baseline humans or possess technological augmentations, our ability to clearly direct the AI 'part' dictates the quality of the resulting synergy. This isn't about learning arcane programming languages; it's about developing fluency in a new kind of dialogue, a skill rapidly becoming known as **Prompt Engineering**. Think of it as the essential **interface protocol**, the meticulous craft of bridging minds, human and artificial, to unlock the profound collaborative potential latent within the human-AI partnership. Achieving the collaborative benefits that researchers like Vaccaro et al. (2024) observed often hinges on this effective communication. Take action now to master the art of communication to orchestrate synergy between human and AI components in your team.

Imagine receiving a new team member possessing encyclopedic knowledge across countless domains, capable of writing fluent prose, generating complex code, analyzing data patterns, and even creating original artwork, all at lightning speed. This is akin to the potential that today's advanced AI offers, especially Large Language Models (LLMs) and diffusion models. However, like any brilliant but uninitiated collaborator, this potential remains dormant, unfocused, even chaotic, until given clear direction and context.

The **prompt**—the text input, the question, the instruction, the set of constraints we provide—is the mechanism through which we convey our intent, shape the AI's focus, and guide its generative power. It's the

> **Prompt Engineering is the New Literacy**
>
> **Key Concept:**
> Prompting is more than asking questions—it's a structured design practice that shapes how AI interprets and responds.
>
> **Why It Matters:**
> Thoughtfully engineered prompts unlock richer, more accurate, and ethically guided AI interactions.
>
> **Actionable Tip:**
> Apply scaffolding: start broad, then refine with step-by-step prompts, and clarify the AI's role with directives like "act as a teacher" or "analyze critically."

difference between randomly striking piano keys and conducting a symphony. And learning to conduct effectively is the essence of prompt engineering, a skill highlighted as essential across various guides on practical AI implementation (Anthropic Guide). This aligns with Licklider's (1960) vision where humans provide the goals and direction for the computer partner.

Why "Engineering"? Elevating Interaction Beyond Casual Queries

The term "engineering" might sound overly technical, but it aptly captures the deliberate, structured, and iterative nature required for consistently achieving high-quality results that sophisticated AI produces. Simply tossing casual questions or vague commands at an LLM is like shouting indistinct orders into a bustling workshop, you might get *something*, but likely not what you actually needed. Use prompt engineering deliberately. Structure your interactions to achieve consistently high-quality results from AI.

Consider again the plight of **David and the Data Deluge** (Chapter 3). His initial interactions with his AI assistant "SyntheSys" were based on simple, understandable requests: "Summarize these articles," "Give me main points." The AI dutifully complied, but it produced overwhelming, unfocused summaries—more noise than signal. The AI lacked the context and constraints to understand David's *specific need*. It was only when David shifted from merely *asking* to actively *engineering* his prompts that the dynamic changed. By meticulously specifying:

> **Context is King—Be Specific to Be Understood**
>
> **Key Concept:**
> AI models respond based on probability, not intention. The more context you give, the better the result.
>
> **Why It Matters:**
> Vague prompts lead to vague outputs. Specificity allows for tailored, useful, and even safer responses.
>
> **Actionable Tip:**
> Include examples, tone, format, audience, and constraints—treat prompts like briefing a skilled intern who needs direction.

- **The Role:** "Act as a research analyst summarizing technical papers for a non-expert audience..."

- **The Source:** "...analyze the attached paper titled 'Grid Integration Challenges...'"

- **The Focus:** "...Identify ONLY the top 3 practical challenges..."

- **The Format:** "...Present these challenges as a bulleted list..."

- **The Audience/Tone:** "...with a single concise sentence explaining each challenge in simple terms."

- **The Exclusions:** "...Ignore theoretical discussions and focus solely on actionable problems identified."

He provided the necessary guardrails. SyntheSys, now properly directed, delivered precisely the concise, relevant information David required. It transformed from a frustrating data-dumper into an invaluable cognitive partner. This deliberate design of interaction is why we call it *engineering*. It moves beyond hope and guesswork towards repeatable, targeted outcomes. It's about understanding that the quality of the synergy directly depends on the quality of the communication bridge we build. This structured approach is vital because, as discussed (Shannon, D.), LLMs operate on pattern recognition within a high-dimensional space, not true human-like understanding; clear instructions are needed to navigate that space effectively.

Core Techniques: The Craft of Effective Prompting

We are entering an era that demands a new kind of fluency, a sophisticated dialogue with these emerging intelligences. Prompt Engineering is truly a craft that elevates our traditional mouse click interactions beyond casual queries into a deliberate, structured, and iterative conversations. It's about learning to speak the language of possibility, to sculpt the AI's focus, and to unlock the profound collaborative potential that lies dormant within. This isn't merely about getting answers; it's about co-creating solutions, about transforming these powerful AI 'parts' from mere tools into genuine synergistic partners. Hone your prompt engineering skills. Practice, refine, and integrate this craft into your workflow to unlock AI's full potential.

> **Human-AI Interaction is Design Work**
>
> **Key Concept:**
> Effective prompting is part of user interface design. It's about guiding interaction, not just issuing commands.
>
> **Why It Matters:**
> Poor design creates frustration and failure. Prompting with user-centered intent makes AI more usable and helpful.
>
> **Actionable Tip:**
> Draft, test, revise. Treat prompts like prototypes—run variations and evaluate outcomes to improve consistency and alignment.

As we delve deeper into the core techniques, banishing ambiguity with precision, setting the scene with rich context, guiding perspective by defining roles, and learning through demonstration, you will discover not just a set of instructions, but a new way of thinking, a pathway to truly bridging human intention with artificial cognition to achieve meaningful work, together. These aren't rigid formulas but rather adaptable principles that, when combined skillfully, allow you to guide AI behavior more effectively. Other authors have dedicated entire books to effective prompting. The following examples are just a small sample of what you will discover while experimenting on your own. Let's explore them in greater depth:

1. **Precision and Specificity: Banishing Ambiguity**

   o *The Principle:* AI models, especially LLMs, operate on statistical patterns derived from their training data. They don't possess human intuition or the ability to implicitly understand fuzzy requests. Ambiguity in your prompt forces the AI to make statistical guesses about your intent, often leading to generic or off-target responses. Precision is paramount.

   o *Techniques & Nuances:*

      ▪ Use Strong Verbs: Instead of "Tell me about..." use more directive verbs like "Explain," "Summarize," "Compare," "Contrast," "Generate," "List," "Analyze," "Rewrite," "Translate."

      ▪ Define Key Terms: If using potentially ambiguous terms, briefly define them within the prompt or provide context. (e.g., "Analyze the customer feedback regarding *product usability*, focusing on navigation and button placement.")

      ▪ Quantify Where Possible: Specify desired length (word count, number of points), scope (time periods, specific features), or criteria. (e.g., "List *the top 5* advantages...")

   o *Example Progression:*

      ▪ *Weak:* "Write a marketing slogan." (Too broad)

      ▪ *Better:* "Write a marketing slogan for a new eco-friendly coffee brand." (Adds context)

      ▪ *Strong:* "Generate 5 catchy marketing slogans (under 10 words each) for 'TerraBrew,' a new coffee brand emphasizing sustainably sourced beans and compostable packaging. Target environmentally

conscious millennials. Highlight both quality and sustainability."
(Adds specificity, quantity, target audience, key features).

2. **Providing Rich Context: Setting the Scene**

- *The Principle:* Most AI models (especially in single-turn interactions) lack memory of previous conversations or specific knowledge about your unique situation unless explicitly provided. Context grounds the AI, giving it the necessary background to generate relevant and accurate responses.

- *Techniques & Nuances:*

  - Background Information: Briefly explain the situation, project goals, relevant history, or constraints.

  - Audience Awareness: Specify who the output is for (e.g., technical experts, general public, potential investors). This influences tone, vocabulary, and level of detail.

  - Input Data: If the task involves analyzing specific text, code, or data, include it directly within the prompt (if feasible length-wise) or clearly reference attached/provided material.

- *Example (Drafting a Report Section):*

  - *Weak:* "Write about Q3 sales performance."

  - *Strong:* "Draft the 'Q3 Sales Performance' section for the upcoming quarterly board report. Our primary goal this quarter was launching Product X in the European market. Key data points to include are: Total Revenue ($5.2M), New Customer Acquisition (1,500), Product X European Sales ($850k vs. $500k target). Compare overall revenue to Q2 ($4.8M) and briefly mention the impact of the supply chain issue in July. Keep the tone factual and concise, suitable for executive leadership. Output should be approximately 2 paragraphs."

3. **Defining the Role (Persona Prompting): Guiding Perspective and Style**

- *The Principle:* Instructing the AI to adopt a specific persona or role is a powerful technique. It primes the model to access relevant patterns associated with that role from its training data, influencing its tone, expertise level, vocabulary, and perspective.

- *Techniques & Nuances:*
  - Be Specific with the Role: "Act as an expert" is weaker than "Act as a PhD-level astrophysicist specializing in exoplanet atmospheres."
  - Combine Role with Task: Clearly link the persona to the specific action required.
- *Examples:*
  - "Act as a compassionate customer service representative responding to an email complaint about a delayed shipment. Apologize sincerely, explain the reason briefly (logistics backlog), offer a [specific compensation, e.g., 10% discount code], and provide the updated tracking link."
  - "Act as a skeptical venture capitalist evaluating a pitch deck. Identify the 3 biggest potential weaknesses or unaddressed risks in the following business model description: [paste description]."
  - "Act as William Shakespeare writing a sonnet about the perils of software updates." (Creative application).

4. Specifying the Output Format: Controlling Structure

- *The Principle:* Clearly dictating the desired structure prevents the AI from delivering information in an unusable or inconvenient format.
- *Techniques & Nuances:*
  - Common Formats: Explicitly ask for bullet points, numbered lists, tables (specify columns), code blocks (specify language), JSON, XML, markdown, email format, memo format, press release structure, etc.
  - Stylistic Elements: You can also specify formatting like "use bold for key terms," or "write in short paragraphs."
- *Example:* "Compare the key features of Product A and Product B based on the provided specification sheets [reference data]. Present the comparison as a markdown table with columns for 'Feature,' 'Product A,' and 'Product B.'"

5. Using Examples (Few-Shot Prompting): Learning by Demonstration

- *The Principle:* For tasks where describing the desired style, tone, or complex transformation is difficult, providing 1-3 concrete examples of input-output pairs allows the AI to infer the pattern more effectively than abstract instructions alone. This is particularly powerful for stylistic adaptation or data formatting.

- *Techniques & Nuances:*

  - Quality over Quantity: A few clear, high-quality examples are better than many mediocre ones.

  - Consistency: Ensure the examples consistently demonstrate the desired transformation.

  - Clear Delimiters: Use clear markers (like "Input:", "Output:", "Example:") to separate the examples from the final task.

- *Example (Sentiment Classification):*

  - *Prompt:* "Classify the sentiment of the following customer reviews as Positive, Negative, or Neutral.

    1. *Example 1:* Review: 'The setup was incredibly easy!' Sentiment: Positive

    2. *Example 2:* Review: 'The battery life is terrible.' Sentiment: Negative

    3. *Example 3:* Review: 'The product arrived on time.' Sentiment: Neutral

    4. *Task:* Review: 'I love the design, but the user interface is confusing.' Sentiment:"

  Note: AI is more likely to correctly classify the task review as potentially 'Mixed' or focus on the negative aspect based on the pattern shown.

6. Expanding the Canvas: Multi-modal Prompting (Text + Image)

- *The Principle:* Prompt engineering is evolving beyond purely text-based interactions. A significant emerging frontier involves **multi-modal prompting**, where the AI model processes and reasons based on a combination of different input types, most commonly **text and**

images. Designers built models **like OpenAI's GPT-4V(ision)** and **Google's Gemini** to understand and interpret visual information alongside textual instructions. This allows for richer context and entirely new types of requests.

- *Capabilities Unlocked:* This fusion enables powerful new capabilities relevant to business:

  - Image Analysis & Description: Asking detailed questions about an image ("What type of safety equipment is the worker in this photo wearing? Is it being worn correctly?").

  - Visual Data Extraction: Reading text from images (enhanced OCR), extracting data from charts or tables presented visually ("Summarize the key trend shown in this uploaded sales graph").

  - Visual Content Generation: Creating descriptions, captions, or even ad copy based directly on product images.

  - UI/UX Feedback & Code Generation: Uploading a screenshot of a user interface and asking for feedback on usability or even generating basic code structures based on the visual layout.

  - Problem Diagnosis: Allowing users or technicians to upload photos of error messages or malfunctioning equipment for AI-assisted troubleshooting.

- *Emerging Business Applications:* While still evolving, businesses are exploring multi-modal AI for:

  - Enhanced Customer Support: Allowing customers to submit images of product issues, enabling support agents (human or AI) to understand the problem faster. **Be My Eyes**, an application assisting blind and low-vision users, leverages GPT-4V to provide rich descriptions of objects or scenes based on images submitted by users, showcasing a powerful accessibility application. (OpenAI, "GPT-4V(ision) System Card", Oct 2023; Be My Eyes partnership announcements).

  - Streamlined Claims Processing: Insurance companies experimenting with analyzing user-submitted photos of vehicle or property damage to expedite initial damage assessment. (General industry reports on AI in Insurtech, e.g., from KPMG, Deloitte).

- Automated Inventory/Asset Management: Using visual analysis to identify products, parts, or equipment from images taken in warehouses or field locations. (Conceptual application based on model capabilities).

- Marketing Content Creation: Generating product descriptions or social media posts directly from marketing visuals.

o Reinforcing the Need for Critical Evaluation (Chapter 3): Multi-modal interaction significantly amplifies the need for understanding AI limitations. Models can suffer from **visual hallucinations** (misinterpreting objects or relationships in an image), exhibit **bias** based on visual training data, overlook crucial details, or fail to grasp the full context of a scene. The apparent sophistication of understanding images can mask underlying failures. **Therefore, the core principles of prompt engineering—specificity, providing context (now visual + textual), iteration, and especially rigorous human verification—become even more critical.** Don't assume the AI truly "sees" or "understands" the image like a human; treat its interpretation as another output requiring careful validation before relying on it for important decisions.

7. **Breaking Down Complexity & Guiding Reasoning (Chain-of-Thought)**

o *The Principle:* Complex problems often overwhelm AI if requested in one go. Decomposing tasks and guiding reasoning improves reliability. Asking the AI to "think step-by-step" (Chain-of-Thought or CoT) is particularly crucial for tasks involving logic or calculation, as it forces the model to generate intermediate steps, improving accuracy (Wei, J. et al. 2022). This technique is fundamental for leveraging the capabilities of Large Reasoning Models (LRMs) designed specifically for such tasks (Mitchell, 2024). Anthropic also identifies CoT as a key optimization technique (Anthropic Guide).

o *Techniques & Nuances:*

- Sequential Prompting: Give the AI one step at a time (e.g., "Generate an outline," then "Expand section 1," then "Refine section 1").

- Chain-of-Thought (CoT): For problems requiring logical steps (math problems, reasoning puzzles), explicitly ask the AI to "Think step-by-step" or "Show your work" before giving the final answer.

Research shows this significantly improves reasoning accuracy in capable models (Wei, J. et al. 2022). Note that this is most effective *during* generation, not as a post-hoc justification (Anthropic Guide; Wagner, M.G./Substack).

- o *Example (Simple Planning):*

    - *Weak:* "Plan a team-building event."

    - *Strong (Sequential):*

        1. "Brainstorm 5 potential team-building activity ideas suitable for a remote team of 15 software engineers, considering a budget of $500."

        2. "For the top choice [AI selects or user specifies], outline the key logistical steps needed (platform, materials, schedule)."

        3. "Draft a brief, enthusiastic invitation email for the chosen activity."

8. **Iteration and Refinement: The Essential Dialogue**

- o *The Principle:* Prompting is rarely a one-shot process. Expect to refine your instructions based on the AI's initial response. Treat it as a collaborative drafting process where you provide increasingly precise feedback.

- o *Techniques & Nuances:*

    - Analyze the Output: Don't just accept the first result. Identify *specifically* what's wrong or missing (e.g., "It was too formal," "It missed point X," "It hallucinated a fact").

    - Refine the Prompt: Modify your original prompt to directly address the shortcomings. Add clarifying sentences, negative constraints ("Do not mention pricing"), or adjust the requested persona/format.

    - Experiment: Try slightly different phrasings or techniques if the first approach isn't working. Sometimes a small change in wording yields a significantly better result.

9. **Understanding Limitations & Applying Constraints:**

- *The Principle:* You cannot prompt an AI to do things reliably that are fundamentally beyond its capabilities (as discussed in Chapter 3). Effective prompting acknowledges these limits.

- *Techniques & Nuances:*

  - Respect Knowledge Cut-offs: Don't expect real-time data unless the tool is explicitly designed for web browsing. Specify date ranges if necessary.

  - Prompt for Verification: Instead of asking "Is X true?", ask "Find sources supporting the claim X," then evaluate the sources yourself.

  - Use Negative Constraints: Explicitly tell the AI what *not* to do ("Avoid technical jargon," "Do not generate code," "Exclude information about competitors").

  - Human Oversight is Mandatory: Always assume the need for human review, fact-checking, ethical filtering, and final judgment, especially for high-stakes outputs.

Prompt Engineering in Action: Deepening Synergy

Apply effective prompting—bridge the gap between human goals and AI capabilities to amplify your team's synergy. Imagine a short prompt dialogue for **Maya's Muse** (Chapter 2):

1. **Maya (Initial Prompt):** "Concept art for a bioluminescent forest at twilight, ethereal style." *(Result: Generic, uninspired images).*

2. **Maya (Refined Prompt - adding Role, Context, Specificity, Format):** "Act as a senior concept artist for an indie fantasy RPG. Generate concept art for the 'Whisperwood Glade' location. Setting: dense, ancient forest, deep twilight. Key features: Giant, bioluminescent mushrooms (blue/purple glow); shimmering, invisible sprites; ancient, mossy stones with faint glowing runes. Style: painterly, Studio Ghibli but slightly darker, mystical. Mood: Enchanting, mysterious, melancholic. Aspect ratio: 16:9." *(Result: Much closer, captures the essence).*

3. **Maya (Iterative Prompt based on output):** "Generate variations of image #3 [the best one from previous]. Make the runes on the stones glow brighter, and try a version from a lower camera angle focusing more on the foreground mossy stones." *(Result: Targeted refinements based on human judgment).*

This iterative, engineered approach allows Maya to effectively collaborate with the AI, using it as a sophisticated tool guided by her vision, achieving a synergistic outcome neither could alone.

Cultivating Your Prompting Prowess: An Essential Skill for the Gestalt Era

Developing strong prompt engineering skills is becoming less of a niche expertise and more of a fundamental competency for anyone interacting with AI, which is increasingly becoming *everyone*. It's a blend of analytical thinking (deconstructing tasks, understanding AI logic) and creative communication (finding the right words, framing). Start building your prompting skills now. They are essential for navigating the Emerging Gestalt.

- **Embrace Experimentation:** Be playful! Try different approaches. See how small changes impact results. The cost of trying another prompt is virtually zero. Use different AI models (ChatGPT, Gemini, Claude, Midjourney) as they have different strengths and respond differently.

- **Practice Deliberate Iteration:** Make refinement a conscious habit. Don't settle for mediocre output. Ask yourself: "How could I have prompted better?"

- **Learn from Shared Knowledge:** Actively seek out resources. Websites like PromptHero (for images), online courses (Coursera, Udemy), and communities (Reddit forums, Discord servers) are full of shared prompts and strategies. Analyze what makes successful prompts work.

- **Maintain Critical Evaluation:** This is the most crucial habit. Treat AI output as a draft or a suggestion, never as infallible truth. Fact-check, edit, apply your domain expertise and ethical judgment.

- **Focus on Your Objective:** Always start by clarifying *exactly* what you need the AI to help you achieve. A clear goal is the North Star for effective prompting.

Mastering prompt engineering is the key to effectively bridging human intention and artificial cognition, transforming AI from a mere tool into a true partner. By learning to communicate clearly, contextually, and critically—applying techniques like specifying roles, providing examples, and guiding reasoning through Chain-of-Thought, especially for complex tasks (Mitchell, 2024)—we unlock the potential of cognitive catalysts like LLMs. This skill allows the human 'part' to effectively direct the Emerging Gestalt towards intelligent and beneficial outcomes. However, wielding this power responsibly requires more than just effective communication; it demands a steadfast commitment to **Maintaining Integrity: Ethics, Risk, and Information Trust**, the critical subject of our next chapter.

Reflection:

Synergy is more than technology, it's about culture. Leaders must foster interdisciplinary collaboration, invest in prompt engineering skills, and design workflows that allow humans and AI to collaborate seamlessly. Develop frameworks that emphasize trust, transparency, and explainability.

Are you intentionally designing collaborative workflows that leverage both human creativity and AI capabilities?

Chapter 7: Maintaining Integrity

Ethics, Risk, and Information Trust

The journey towards the Emerging Gestalt, this integration of human ingenuity with the potent capabilities of AI, robotics, and augmentation, holds immense promise. The potential for amplified creativity, accelerated discovery, and enhanced productivity, for creating a 'whole' truly greater than the sum of its parts, is tangible and deeply compelling. However, this very power demands profound responsibility. Like any complex, high-stakes system, the integrity of the Emerging Gestalt is paramount, yet inherently fragile. Unethical interactions, biased algorithms, compromised data, or the deliberate spread of falsehoods can corrupt the system from within, turning promise into peril.

Therefore, unflinchingly confronting the "Ethical Elephant in the room," proactively identifying, understanding, and mitigating the inherent risks to fairness, privacy, and trust, is not merely an adjacent concern; it is the **absolute foundation** upon which a healthy, beneficial, and sustainable synergistic future must be built. Ignoring these integrity issues is akin to building a skyscraper on unstable ground, destined for collapse.

> **Ethics Isn't a Feature—It's an Architecture**
>
> **Key Concept:**
> Ethical AI isn't a layer you add later. It must be designed into the system from the ground up—baked into datasets, feedback loops, oversight, and deployment processes.
>
> **Why It Matters:**
> Bolted-on ethics leads to reactive harm control. Embedded ethics supports long-term safety, fairness, and trust.
>
> **Actionable Tip:**
> Begin projects with a values map and stakeholder review; apply ethical design checklists alongside technical ones.

As highlighted across multiple domains in academic research, realizing the benefits of human-technology integration requires keeping human values at the core (Farahany, 2023; Vaccaro et al., 2024). Take responsibility. Build a strong ethical foundation now to secure the benefits of the Emerging Gestalt.

Eleanor's Verification

Eleanor startled as her tablet chimed with an incoming video call, displaying her grandson Ben's smiling face. Relief washed over her—she hadn't heard from him since he'd left for his backpacking trip through Southeast Asia. But the smile quickly vanished from the screen, replaced by a look of panic.

"Grandma? Grandma, can you hear me? I'm in trouble," the image of Ben stammered, his voice tight with fear, the background blurry and indistinct. "I lost my passport, my wallet... everything. I'm stuck in Bangkok and I need money to get to the embassy, just a few hundred dollars. Please, can you wire it quickly? I don't have much time."

Eleanor's heart pounded. Ben looked so distressed, sounded so desperate. Her first instinct was to immediately ask for the wiring instructions. But then, a flicker of unease. Something felt... rushed. Ben knew she wasn't tech-savvy with wire transfers. And didn't he say he was going to be hiking in the mountains this week, far from Bangkok?

She remembered an article her daughter had sent her just last month, something about "deepfakes" and AI voices being used in scams. The article had urged caution, especially with urgent, emotional pleas for money. It felt silly, doubting her own grandson's face and voice, but the warning echoed.

"Oh, Ben, that sounds terrible," Eleanor said, trying to keep her voice calm. "Let me just call your mom first, see if she knows anything about this."

The Ben on the screen hesitated for a fraction of a second, a flicker in his eyes that didn't quite match the panic in his voice. "No, Grandma, don't! There's no time, please, just send the money now!" The urgency felt manufactured, pushing against her caution.

"I'll be quick, dear," Eleanor insisted, her resolve hardening. She ended the video call, her hands trembling slightly. Ignoring the immediate urge to panic, she dialed Ben's mobile number, the one he'd had for years.

It rang twice, then went to his standard voicemail message, cheerful and relaxed, recorded before he left. No mention of trouble. Next, she called her daughter, recounting the video call.

"Mom, absolutely do not send any money!" her daughter exclaimed after hearing the story. "That sounds exactly like the AI voice clone scam they warned about. Ben checked in via email just this morning; he's fine, still hiking near Chiang Mai, nowhere near Bangkok. That wasn't him."

Relief washed over Eleanor, quickly followed by a chilling realization. The face had looked so real, the voice so convincing. If she hadn't paused, hadn't remembered that article, hadn't taken that extra step to verify through a trusted channel...

Later that evening, sipping her tea, Eleanor reflected. The world felt different now, less certain. Seeing and hearing used to be enough. Now, she understood, trust required something more—a healthy dose of skepticism, a willingness to question even what seemed real, and the crucial habit of independent verification. Navigating this new world, she realized, meant learning to look beyond the surface, using her own judgment as the final filter in an age where machines could so convincingly lie.

The Ethical Imperative: Weaving Values into the Fabric of the Gestalt

As we chart the course of this profound technological integration, a question of paramount importance rises to the surface, demanding our unwavering attention: why does ethics take such a prominent, indeed central, stage in our discussions? The answer is rooted in the very nature of these emerging systems. We must recognize that the AI, robotics, and augmentation 'parts' contributing to the Emerging Gestalt are not mere neutral calculators operating in a sterile vacuum. They are increasingly imbued with the power to make, or at the very least profoundly influence, decisions that resonate directly through the core of human lives, shaping our opportunities, impacting our safety, and subtly or overtly restructuring the very societal frameworks within which we exist. To venture forth and attempt to build this synergistic future, this Gestalt, without meticulously embedding ethical considerations into its very design, is to risk architecting a future that we, and generations to come, would rightly fear. You must embed ethical frameworks into every decision and ensure that technology serves humanity responsibly.

Consider the insidious potential for **systematizing injustice**. Artificial intelligence, particularly when its learning is rooted in vast troves of historical data, data that inevitably reflects the ingrained biases and past inequities of our societies, can become a potent engine for automating and scaling discrimination at an alarming rate. Imagine, for a moment, hiring algorithms that consistently, if unintentionally, overlook highly qualified female candidates simply because the historical hiring data they were fed was predominantly male-centric, a scenario that Amazon reportedly encountered in an early AI tool test. Or picture predictive policing tools that disproportionately target minority neighborhoods, not due to malice, but because they learned from biased arrest data, a concern highlighted by academic critiques like those from Angwin and her colleagues at ProPublica. Without conscious, deliberate intervention and a steadfast prioritization of diversity and inclusion in their development, these AI systems risk making inequality not just persistent, but chillingly more efficient.

Beyond quantifiable injustice, **technological missteps can catastrophically undermine the fragile bedrock of trust**. Each high-profile failure—a self-driving car causing an accident due to a sensor's misinterpretation of the world, as documented in NTSB reports; a chatbot veering into generating harmful or offensive content, as seen in various early deployments; a biased algorithm unjustly denying someone a crucial loan; or the relentless, corrosive drip of convincingly fabricated deepfakes—acts as a solvent, eroding public confidence in these powerful new tools. Widespread distrust makes the very collaboration we seek difficult, hinders the beneficial adoption of these technologies, and can ultimately lead to societal fragmentation. As D. Shannon might note, often opaque, black box' AI systems often further amplify this challenge, and, as Melanie Mitchell cautions, by our human tendency towards anthropomorphism, which can lead to a misplaced and dangerous over-trust in systems whose inner workings remain largely inscrutable.

> ### Algorithmic Bias is a Lifecycle Problem
>
> **Key Concept:**
> Bias arises in data, labeling, modeling, and deployment—not just one stage. It's a system-wide challenge requiring continuous mitigation.
>
> **Why It Matters:**
> Single-step bias audits miss the complexity. True fairness demands an ecosystem approach.
>
> **Actionable Tip:**
> Integrate fairness testing at each phase: use tools like AI Fairness 360, require diverse review teams, and rerun audits post-deployment.

The risks are not confined to the abstract; these systems can **inflict both tangible and intangible harm**. The spectrum of potential harm ranges from direct physical danger (envision unsafe human-robot interactions in a shared workspace or the malfunction of AI-driven medical devices) to significant psychological distress. Consider the acute anxiety that the threat of job insecurity due to automation fuels, or the profound emotional pain caused by deepfake harassment. Economic harm, too, is a major concern, potentially arising from biased financial systems or sophisticated AI-powered scams. These concerns even extend into the most experimental frontiers of this integration, raising difficult questions, as Sparkes and Gizmodo explore, about the ethical treatment and potential unforeseen harms associated with emerging technologies like biological computers, if they develop unexpected capacities. A core tenet of ethical engagement, then, must be the principle of non-maleficence: first, do no harm.

Finally, we must guard against the subtle yet profound threat of **diminishing human agency and autonomy**. An uncritical over-reliance on opaque "black box" AI systems for critical decisions can foster a passive acceptance of algorithmic judgment, insidiously eroding our own capacity for critical thinking and independent reasoning. Furthermore, the sophisticated deployment of AI in realms like personalized advertising or political messaging can subtly manipulate individual choices and beliefs, thereby challenging the very foundations of personal autonomy. Protecting this autonomy, especially the emerging frontier of cognitive autonomy in an age of advancing neurotechnology, as passionately argued by Nita Farahany, is not just important, it is paramount.

Therefore, maintaining the integrity of the Gestalt means consciously weaving ethical principles—fairness, accountability, transparency, safety, privacy, **beneficence** (doing good), **autonomy**, **justice**, and **non-maleficence**—into the very fabric of its design, deployment, and ongoing governance.

Confronting Algorithmic Bias: The Persistent Shadow in the Data

Perhaps the most widely discussed and insidious ethical challenge is **algorithmic bias**. Because AI systems learn from data, they inevitably reflect the worldviews, prejudices, and historical inequities embedded within that data. This isn't necessarily malicious intent on the part of developers; it's often an emergent property of learning from flawed, incomplete, or unrepresentative information. Understanding its forms and how to address it is crucial. The AI Incident Database documents a significant rise in such incidents (AIAAIC Database / Stanford HAI AI Index Report 2023). You can actively address bias- build teams and systems that reflect the diversity and fairness you expect from your technology.

Manifestations of Bias

Bias can creep into AI systems in numerous ways:

- *Training Data Issues:* As mentioned, historical biases (like past hiring practices) or lack of representation (like facial recognition systems trained primarily on lighter skin tones, and this leads to higher error rates for darker skin - NIST FRVT reports; Buolamwini & Gebru, 2018) are common culprits.

- *Proxy Discrimination:* Using seemingly neutral data points (like zip codes or certain online behaviors) that strongly correlate with protected characteristics (race, socioeconomic status) can lead to discriminatory outcomes even without explicitly using sensitive attributes.

- *Intersectional Bias:* Bias can be compounded for individuals belonging to multiple marginalized groups (e.g., an algorithm might perform worse for Black women than for either Black men or White women).

- *Feedback Loops:* Biased predictions can lead to actions that reinforce the bias. If an algorithm predicts higher recidivism for a certain group, leading to harsher sentencing, subsequent data will appear to confirm the prediction, creating a vicious cycle.

The Challenge of Defining "Fairness"

Whereas humans in general struggle with defining fairness culturally and philosophically, developers complicate pinpointing and eliminating bias by struggling to define 'fairness' mathematically in an algorithmic context:

- *Complex Definitions:* Different mathematical definitions exist (e.g., demographic parity, equal opportunity, equalized odds), and they are often mutually exclusive. Choosing which definition to optimize for involves inherent trade-offs and value judgments (Research by Kleinberg, Mullainathan, Raghavan; Narayanan's tutorials on fairness).

- *Context Matters:* What seems fair in one context (e.g., loan applications) might be considered unfair in another (e.g., medical diagnosis).

Mitigation as an Ongoing Process

There's no single solution for algorithmic bias. Effective strategies require a combination of approaches throughout the AI lifecycle. Commit to continuous improvement. You must review, update, and adapt your processes regularly:

- **Rigorous Data Governance:** Scrutinizing data sources for bias, diversifying datasets, exploring synthetic data generation for underrepresented groups.

- **Fairness-Aware Algorithms:** Incorporating fairness constraints directly into the machine learning model's training process.

- **Bias Auditing & Impact Assessments:** Proactively testing systems for disparate impacts across different demographic groups *before* deployment and monitoring them continuously afterward. Tools like IBM's AI Fairness 360 or Google's What-If Tool facilitate this.

- **Transparency & Explainability (XAI):** While difficult, understanding *why* a model makes certain predictions can help uncover hidden biases. Providing explanations for decisions allows for scrutiny and appeal.

- **Diverse Teams:** Ensuring development teams reflect diverse backgrounds and perspectives is crucial for spotting potential biases that homogenous teams might overlook.

- **Human-in-the-Loop:** Maintaining human oversight, especially for critical decisions, allows for context-specific judgment and the correction of clearly biased algorithmic outputs.

Ethics-at-a-Glance

Risk	Why it matters	First step fix
Algorithmic bias	Discriminatory outcomes	Diversify data & audit
Privacy erosion	Re-identify "anonymous" data	Minimize collection; use DP
Disinformation	Deepfakes erode trust	Content provenance tools

Risk	Why it matters	First step fix
See Chapter 3 for technical limits		

Privacy in an Era of Pervasive Sensing and Inference

As we continue to weave the intricate tapestry of the Emerging Gestalt with threads of interconnected intelligence and action, we encounter another critical imperative: the safeguarding of privacy. This new synergistic whole, by its very nature, is inherently data-hungry. Its remarkable ability to learn, to adapt with nuanced precision, and to provide the deeply personalized services that promise to enhance our lives relies fundamentally on vast, continuously flowing streams of information. This data pours in from the ubiquitous network of interconnected devices that form the Internet of Things (IoT), from the myriad traces we leave through our online activities, and, with increasing intimacy, from sensors designed to monitor our bodies (the Internet of Bodies, or IoB) or even, as we've discussed, the subtle currents of our brain activity. While this data fuels the Gestalt's potential, its collection and use also create unprecedented and deeply challenging questions for the preservation of personal privacy. Prioritize data privacy. Work stakeholders to establish clear boundaries and strong governance for information use.

We find ourselves navigating an era characterized by an **ever-expanding data footprint, coupled with the astonishing inferential power of artificial intelligence.** Our digital lives, once perhaps considered separate from our physical existence, now generate an enormous and ever-growing volume of data. Consider the modern smart home, diligently collecting data on our daily habits and routines; the fitness trackers strapped to our wrists, meticulously monitoring our physiology; or the online platforms that silently track our every click, preference, and interaction. The seamless integration of these disparate data streams allows for the construction of incredibly detailed, and often startlingly accurate, individual profiles.

But the challenge to privacy extends far beyond the explicit data we knowingly share or that which is overtly collected. The AI 'part' of the Gestalt excels at uncovering hidden correlations, at finding subtle patterns within vast datasets that might elude human perception. This **inferential power** means that AI can often deduce sensitive personal attributes, such as our health status, sexual orientation, or political beliefs, from seemingly innocuous, non-sensitive data points. Your purchase history, the articles you 'like' on social media, or even the cadence of your typing can, with surprising accuracy as demonstrated in research by Kosinski and his colleagues, become proxies for highly personal information. This raises a critical concern: data collected for one seemingly benign purpose could be repurposed, through the lens of AI-driven inference, to make potentially discriminatory or intrusive deductions in an entirely different context, further eroding the boundaries of our private lives.

Risks to Privacy and Autonomy

This data richness creates significant risks:

- *Security Vulnerabilities:* Centralized pools of rich personal data become highly attractive targets for hackers. A breach could expose incredibly intimate details. The security of connected devices (IoT, IoB, BCIs) is also a major concern, as vulnerabilities could allow unauthorized access or even manipulation.

- *Surveillance Concerns:* The aggregation of data from multiple sources enables powerful surveillance capabilities, both by corporations (for targeted advertising or behavior prediction) and potentially by governments, raising concerns about chilling effects on free expression and association.

> **Privacy and Authenticity Are the New Front Lines**
>
> **Key Concept:**
> In the era of pervasive sensing and synthetic content, privacy and content integrity are no longer side issues—they're foundational.
>
> **Why It Matters:**
> Deepfakes and inference-based profiling erode public trust and personal autonomy at scale.
>
> **Actionable Tip:**
> Invest in provenance tools (like C2PA), limit data retention, and default to "minimum viable data" in system design.

- *Neurodata & Cognitive Liberty:* The prospect of technologies interfacing directly with the brain elevates privacy concerns exponentially, entering the critical domain of **neuro-privacy**. Protecting the sanctity of our thoughts, mental states, and cognitive processes—often termed **"cognitive liberty"** (Yuste, R. et al., 2017; Farahany, 2023)—is not a distant sci-fi concern but an urgent ethical and legal frontier demanding immediate attention. As Nita Farahany meticulously details in *'The Battle for Your Brain'* (2023), the rapid development of consumer wearables and workplace tools capable of monitoring brain activity (e.g., EEG sensors measuring focus, fatigue, or engagement) creates immediate risks of unprecedented mental intrusion. Without robust safeguards specifically designed for neurodata—which is inherently sensitive and reveals vastly more than traditional biometric data—this information could be used coercively by employers to monitor productivity or attention, by insurers to assess risk, or by state actors for surveillance or manipulation. It challenges our fundamental right to mental privacy and self-determination (Bublitz, 2013; Ienca & Andorno, 2017). Establishing clear legal rights and ethical guidelines to govern the collection, use, and protection of neurodata *before* these technologies become pervasive is therefore paramount to preserving individual autonomy and dignity in the Gestalt era. This is a core challenge for the governance structures discussed in Chapter 7 and has direct implications for employee well-being and HR policies.

Essential Safeguards for Privacy

Protecting privacy requires a multi-layered approach:

- **Technical Solutions:** Employing **Privacy-Enhancing Technologies (PETs)** like *differential privacy*, *federated learning*, *homomorphic encryption*, and *zero-knowledge proofs*.

- **Policy & Regulation:** Enforcing strong data protection laws (like GDPR, CCPA/CPRA) that mandate transparency, user consent, **data minimization**, purpose limitation, and grant individuals rights over their data (access, correction, deletion).

- **Organizational Practices:** Implementing robust data security measures, conducting privacy impact assessments, and fostering a culture of privacy awareness.

- **User Education & Control:** Providing clear explanations of data practices and giving users meaningful control over their data sharing preferences.

Information Integrity Under Siege: The Deepfake & Disinformation Challenge

A fundamental requirement for any intelligent system, including the Emerging Gestalt, is reliable information. AI-generated falsehoods can severely threaten trust and rational discourse. Strengthen your defenses and take the time and resources required to educate your teams on identifying deepfakes and verifying information.

The Nature of the Threat

The challenge manifests in several key ways:

- **The Deepfake Menace:** AI-generated synthetic media poses multifaceted threats:

    o *Sophistication & Accessibility:* Tools for creating deepfakes (video, audio, image) are becoming more accessible and capable, making it harder for average users (and even experts) to distinguish real from fake.

    o *Impact Spectrum:* Ranges from relatively harmless parody to devastating personal attacks (non-consensual pornography, reputational damage), sophisticated financial fraud (voice cloning scams targeting businesses—recall **Eleanor's Verification**), and large-scale political destabilization (fake videos of world leaders).

    o *The "Liar's Dividend":* As awareness of deepfakes grows, bad actors can exploit this by falsely claiming genuine incriminating evidence is fake, undermining accountability (Concept by Citron & Chesney, 2019). The ease with which AI can generate fabricated information or "hallucinate" adds another layer to this challenge, requiring constant vigilance from users and developers alike (Mitchell, 2024; China Daily; Wagner, M.G./Substack).

- **AI-Powered Disinformation Campaigns:** LLMs can automate the creation and dissemination of propaganda, fake news, and divisive content at an unprecedented scale, potentially micro-targeting individuals based on inferred psychological profiles. This can polarize societies, manipulate public opinion, and erode trust in credible sources like journalism and science (Reports on state-sponsored disinformation campaigns; concerns raised by election security experts).

- **Psychological Impact:** Living in an information environment where reality feels constantly under question can be psychologically taxing, contributing to anxiety, cynicism, and difficulty forming consensus on shared facts.

Countermeasures—An Ecosystem Approach

No single solution exists. Addressing this requires a combination of strategies:

- **Improved Detection:** Ongoing research into AI techniques to identify subtle artifacts indicative of synthesis, but this remains a difficult "cat-and-mouse" game.

- **Digital Watermarking & Provenance:** Technologies and standards (like **C2PA**) to securely embed metadata tracking the origin and modification history of digital content, acting like a digital "chain of custody." Widespread adoption is key.

- **Platform Moderation & Policies:** Tech companies actively identifying, labeling, down-ranking, or removing demonstrably false or harmful synthetic media, while navigating complex free speech issues.

- **Robust Media Literacy: Crucial Defense.** Educating the public from an early age to critically evaluate sources, understand persuasive techniques, cross-reference information (**lateral reading**), and cultivate a healthy skepticism towards online content. (Resources: News Literacy Project, Stanford History Education Group).

- **Legal & Regulatory Responses:** Carefully crafted laws targeting malicious uses of deepfakes (like fraud or non-consensual pornography) and potentially requiring transparency for AI-generated political advertising. Rigorous human oversight and fact-checking remain indispensable countermeasures (China Daily).

Establishing Fairness, Accountability, and Transparency

Beyond specific risks like bias or deepfakes, maintaining the integrity of the Gestalt requires foundational principles of fairness, accountability, and transparency (often abbreviated FAT) in how its components operate and interact:

- **Transparency & Explainability (XAI):** Users, regulators, and those affected by AI decisions need insight into how they work.

  - *Importance:* Builds trust, enables debugging, facilitates identification of bias, allows for meaningful appeals.

  - *Challenges:* Highly complex models resist easy explanation. Perfect transparency might expose proprietary algorithms or enable manipulation.

  - *Approaches:* Providing high-level explanations ("reason codes"), developing local interpretability methods (explaining specific decisions), publishing model cards detailing capabilities and limitations. (Research in XAI; concepts like LIME, SHAP).

- **Human Oversight & Controllability:** Especially for systems with significant impact, ensuring humans remain "in the loop" or "on the loop" is critical.

  - *Meaningful Oversight:* Requires humans having the authority, time, information, and training to effectively monitor and intervene.

  - *Controllability:* Designing systems with clear mechanisms for humans to override, shut down, or redirect AI actions when necessary.

- **Accountability & Redress:** When things go wrong, who is responsible?

  - *The Accountability Gap:* Assigning liability can be difficult with complex AI systems involving multiple developers, deployers, data sources, and users.

  - *Mechanisms:* Establishing clear lines of responsibility in contracts and policies, creating accessible processes for individuals to appeal algorithmic decisions or seek redress for harm, potentially developing specific legal frameworks for AI liability.

  - *Approaches:* The post-hoc nature of some AI "explanations" (Wagner, M.G./Substack) complicates true accountability, reinforcing the need for process transparency and human judgment.

Finding Balance: Navigating Fear Without Stifling Progress

The very real risks discussed here can easily fuel fear and lead to calls for overly restrictive measures that could stifle beneficial innovation. Achieving integrity requires finding a careful balance: acknowledging risks seriously while maintaining a focus on harnessing technology for good. Bill Gates emphasizes the need to "shape" AI's development positively despite inherent unknowns and fears (Gates, B. in Popular Mechanics, 2024).

- **Emphasize Augmentation:** Focus development and deployment on systems designed to *assist* and *augment* human capabilities (cognitive, physical), rather than solely aiming for full replacement (Human-centered AI principles).

- **Invest in Safety & Ethics Research:** Ensure that research into AI safety, fairness, transparency, and alignment keeps pace with research into AI capabilities. Ethical considerations are crucial in specialized domains like healthcare AI automation (ValueCoders).

- **Promote Education & Dialogue:** Foster widespread public understanding of AI's real capabilities and limitations, dispelling myths and enabling informed societal discussion about ethical trade-offs.

- **Adopt Risk-Based Regulation:** Implement governance frameworks that apply stricter controls to high-risk applications while allowing more flexibility for low-risk innovation.

Maintaining the integrity of the Emerging Gestalt is an ongoing, dynamic process. It requires more than just technical solutions; it demands a collective commitment to ethical principles, continuous vigilance against bias and misinformation, robust protection of privacy, and the establishment of clear accountability structures. It requires us, the human part, to act with wisdom and foresight as we weave these powerful technological threads into the fabric of our lives. Only by prioritizing integrity can we hope to build a complementary future that is not only powerful but also just, trustworthy, and truly beneficial for all. Recognizing these dangers is the essential first step. We must establish the formal structures, rules, and oversight mechanisms that will help navigate these complexities and steer the Gestalt towards beneficial outcomes. This is the crucial domain of **Orchestrating the Whole: AI Governance and Regulation**.

Reflection:

Algorithmic bias and misinformation threaten trust in AI systems. Leaders must establish ethical review boards, conduct regular audits, and invest in explainability tools. Prioritize integrity and transparency to build stakeholder confidence in AI decisions.

Do you have a process to identify and mitigate algorithmic bias and ensure AI outputs align with your ethical standards?

Chapter 8: Orchestrating the Whole

AI Governance and Regulation

By mapping the components of the Emerging Gestalt we have revealed technologies of breathtaking power and potential. We've seen how AI can act as a cognitive catalyst, how robotics provides embodied action, and how human augmentation might reshape the human 'part' itself. The promise of synergy—a whole greater than the sum of its parts—hinges on effectively integrating these elements, often through skillful communication interfaces like prompt engineering. Yet, as Chapter 7 underscored with urgency, this integration is fraught with ethical peril. Bias can be amplified, privacy eroded, trust shattered by misinformation, and fairness compromised. The very integrity of the Gestalt depends not just on technical prowess but on conscious, deliberate **orchestration** guided by human values. Take responsibility to create robust **AI Governance and Regulation**—the complex but essential task of establishing the principles, rules, standards, and oversight mechanisms required to steer this powerful technological convergence towards beneficial outcomes and away from potential harms.

The allure of simple rules, like Asimov's famous Three Laws (Asimov, 1942), quickly fades when confronted with the nuanced reality of modern AI. While valuable thought experiments, they lack the specificity and adaptability needed to address intricate real-world dilemmas involving conflicting values,

> **Governance is the Backbone of Trustworthy AI**
>
> **Key Concept:**
> AI governance is not a patch—it's a structural system of checks, responsibilities, and controls that ensures safe and ethical AI deployment.
>
> **Why It Matters:**
> Without governance, even the most powerful AI can become dangerous, biased, or misused—undermining both trust and value.
>
> **Actionable Tip:**
> Build governance into the AI lifecycle: implement audit trails, red teaming, and ethics reviews as standard practice, not exceptions.

statistical uncertainties, and the potential for unintended consequences at scale. How does a "do no harm" principle apply to an algorithm allocating limited medical resources, or one whose deployment might lead to job displacement causing economic hardship? The complexities demand more than elegant heuristics; they demand comprehensive, adaptive governance structures. Effective human-AI systems require careful governance to ensure they are safe, ethical, and effective.

The Compliance Check

Priya, Lead for Responsible AI implementation at HireRight Solutions, an HR tech company, adjusted her headset, settling in for the quarterly review meeting of the "Candidate Sort AI" tool her company provided across Europe and North America. This was crunch time. Their flagship AI, designed to screen thousands of resumes, had been revolutionary for clients' efficiency. But with the EU AI Act now in full force and the US Executive Order demanding stricter oversight, ensuring compliance wasn't just good ethics—it was essential business.

On the call were engineers, lawyers, and representatives from their internal AI Ethics Council. "Alright team," Priya began, sharing her screen displaying the NIST AI Risk Management Framework dashboard they'd adapted. "Let's start with the EU AI Act checklist. Candidate screening falls squarely under 'High Risk'. Have we completed the updated conformity assessment documentation?"

An engineer confirmed, "Yes, Priya. The technical documentation is updated, detailing dataset parameters, bias mitigation techniques applied, and logging mechanisms. We've included the results from the adversarial testing... showing bias reduction below the mandated threshold."

"Excellent," Priya noted. "Legal, any flags on the required human oversight provisions?"

Their EU counsel responded, "We've confirmed the client-side interface mandates a human reviewer must approve the AI's shortlist... The system also flags statistically anomalous rejection patterns... requiring mandatory human review... This meets the Act's requirements for meaningful oversight."

They turned to the US Executive Order's focus on safety and security. "Have the red-teaming results for the base LLM been submitted...?" Priya asked.

"Submitted last week," confirmed the head engineer. "The tests probed for potential security vulnerabilities... We've documented the mitigations implemented..."

The discussion wasn't just about ticking boxes. The Ethics Council representative raised a point about genuine understandability versus technical explanations, sparking a debate about improving "reason codes" to better align with the US AI Bill of Rights' "Notice and Explanation" principle. They agreed to pilot a new module.

The meeting concluded an hour later. It was complex, demanding constant vigilance and cross-functional collaboration. There were tensions... But Priya felt cautious optimism. They weren't just building powerful AI; they were actively building the governance around it. The regulations weren't just obstacles; they were guideposts... This, she thought, was what steering the ship truly meant.

The Unique Governance Challenge: Navigating Uncharted Waters

Why is governing AI proving so challenging, demanding new approaches beyond those used for previous technologies? Lead the way. Develop comprehensive governance strategies to navigate this uncharted territory and ensure responsible AI deployment. Several factors intertwine:

- **Inherent Complexity & Opacity (The "Black Box"):** Many powerful AI systems, especially deep learning models, function in ways that are incredibly difficult to fully dissect and understand. Their internal calculations involve millions or billions of parameters interacting in non-linear ways. Developers often find it difficult or impossible to pinpoint the exact reason for a specific output, especially an erroneous or biased one, can be difficult or impossible. This **opacity** severely hinders efforts to audit for fairness, guarantee safety, or provide clear explanations, making traditional compliance difficult. **Explainable AI (XAI)** methods (like LIME or SHAP) offer partial insights but achieving global transparency remains a hurdle (Guidotti et al., 2018 and Mitchell, 2024).

- **Blinding Speed of Development (The "Pacing Problem"):** AI capabilities are evolving at an exponential rate. Models state-of-the-art months ago are rapidly surpassed. This creates a significant "pacing problem" for regulators; laws debated today may target technology that's already outdated by enactment (Marchant, G.E.). Governance must prioritize flexibility and principles over specific implementations.

- **Borderless Nature:** AI talent, research, data, and deployment are global. National regulations alone are insufficient and risk "regulatory arbitrage." Effective orchestration demands international coordination, a significant challenge.

- **Deep Data Dependency:** AI *is* data. Governing AI means governing the entire data pipeline: collection (consent, fairness), cleaning (bias mitigation), security (privacy, cybersecurity), labeling, and use. This links AI governance to data protection laws like GDPR or CPRA.

- **Emergence and Unpredictability:** Complex AI systems interacting with dynamic environments can exhibit **emergent behaviors**—unexpected actions not explicitly programmed. Governing such systems requires robust testing, continuous monitoring, safety constraints, and fallback mechanisms.

- **Novel Technologies:** Emerging systems like biological computers present entirely new governance questions about safety, ethics, and potential capabilities (Sparkes, 2022; Gizmodo). Human augmentation technologies, particularly those involving neurodata, also demand new frameworks like neurorights (Farahany, 2023; Bublitz, 2013; Ienca & Andorno, 2017).

These challenges necessitate sophisticated, multi-layered governance strategies blending technical standards, ethical principles, legal regulations, and robust organizational practices.

Mapping the Global Landscape: A Mosaic of Orchestration Strategies

Faced with these challenges, different regions are forging distinct paths, creating a complex global mosaic of AI governance efforts. Learn from global best practices and apply lessons from international governance strategies to your own orchestration efforts:

The European Union's AI Act: A Comprehensive, Risk-Based Approach

- *Philosophy:* A rights-based approach aligning AI with EU democratic values and fundamental rights to foster trust.

- *Mechanism:* A horizontal, legally binding regulation using **risk-based classification**:

  - **Unacceptable Risk:** Banned practices (e.g., public social scoring, most real-time biometric surveillance).

  - **High Risk:** The core focus (AI in hiring, medical devices, justice, critical infrastructure, etc.). Requires stringent *pre-market* **conformity**

90

assessments, including data quality, documentation, logging, human oversight, accuracy/robustness/security standards, and EU database registration. High compliance burden, high safety aim. Medical AI often falls into this category, requiring rigorous oversight (EU AI Act text; Bhandari, 2024).

- o **Limited Risk:** Transparency obligations (e.g., disclosing AI interaction or deepfakes).

- o **Minimal Risk:** Most AI applications, covered by existing laws.

- *Global Impact:* Likely to set a de facto global standard via the **"Brussels Effect"** (Bradford, 2020), influencing multinational practices. (EU AI Act official texts; analyses by CEPS, Brookings). The Act entered into force in August 2024.

The United States' Approach: Layered, Sectoral, and Evolving

- *Philosophy:* Balancing innovation leadership with rights/safety protection, favoring flexibility, voluntary frameworks, and existing sectoral regulators.

- *Key Instruments:*

  - o **AI Bill of Rights Blueprint (Non-binding):** Outlines core principles (Safety, Non-Discrimination, Privacy, Notice/Explanation, Human Alternatives). (White House OSTP, 2022).

  - o **NIST AI Risk Management Framework (Voluntary):** Practical framework for integrating trustworthiness (Govern, Map, Measure, Manage). Widely adopted by industry. (NIST AI RMF).

  - o **Executive Order (Oct 2023):** Significant federal push mandating actions like safety standards for foundation models, reporting safety tests, strengthening privacy, combating algorithmic discrimination, promoting competition, and setting guidelines for federal AI use. Signals more active federal role, relies on agency implementation. (White House EO, 2023).

- *Dynamics:* Complex interplay of innovation focus, citizen protection, federal/state roles, with potential for future legislation.

China's Approach: Strategic Deployment with Targeted State Control

- *Philosophy:* Dual focus: achieving global AI dominance while maintaining strict state control over information and social stability.

- *Mechanism:* Rapid rollout of specific, prescriptive regulations for sensitive applications.

- *Examples:* Rules for **algorithmic recommendations** (content control), **deepfakes/synthetic content** (labeling, consent, state ideology alignment), and **generative AI services** (content filtering, data security audits, algorithm registration).

- *Implication:* Creates an ecosystem encouraging innovation but government oversight and censorship tightly constrain it. (Analysis by Stanford DigiChina Project, CSET).

Other Notable Approaches & International Efforts

- **United Kingdom:** Articulating a "pro-innovation," context-specific framework. Uses existing regulators to apply central principles within their domains, aiming for agility. Discussed augmentation governance from a strategic perspective (UK AI Regulation White Paper, March 2023; Ministry of Defence, 2021).

- **Canada:** Pursuing legislation (Artificial Intelligence and Data Act - AIDA, part of Bill C-27) with requirements for high-impact AI systems (risk management, transparency, accountability). (Bill C-27 text).

- **International Cooperation:** Growing efforts to find common ground: **G7 Hiroshima AI Process**, **OECD AI Principles**, **Council of Europe** treaty negotiations, **UN** AI Advisory Body, **UNESCO** AI Ethics Recommendation (2021). Highlights consensus on the *need* for coordination.

Navigating the Orchestration: Key Debates and Tensions

As nations and international bodies grapple with the profound challenge of orchestrating the development and deployment of artificial intelligence, this global push inevitably surfaces a series of fundamental debates and inherent tensions. These are not simple questions with easy answers; rather, they represent the complex intellectual and societal terrain we must navigate as we strive to shape a future where the power of the Emerging Gestalt is harnessed responsibly. Engage with these debates personally and understand how they impact your organization's strategy and build a responsive governance model.

At the forefront of these discussions lies the perennial tightrope walk between **innovation and safety**. How much regulation is truly necessary to ensure the safety and ethical alignment of these powerful technologies without inadvertently crippling the very innovation that promises such immense benefits? Finding the right balance requires a nuanced understanding of risk proportionality, applying stricter controls where potential harms are greatest while allowing for more flexibility where risks are minimal.

The borderless nature of AI also brings into sharp relief the tension between the ideal of **global standards and the reality of regulatory fragmentation**. In a world where talent, data, and deployment flow freely across national boundaries, can we achieve sufficient international alignment to avoid a confusing and potentially counterproductive patchwork of disparate rules? Harmonization is undoubtedly a laudable goal, but the diverse economic priorities, cultural values, and geopolitical interests of nations often lead to divergent approaches, making true global consensus an elusive target.

Further complicating the picture is the ongoing debate about the most effective **regulatory toolkit**. What is the optimal mix of instruments to guide this rapidly evolving field? Should we rely primarily on 'hard law' in the form of legally binding statutes, or can 'soft law', such as voluntary guidelines, ethical codes, and industry best practices, provide sufficient direction? And how do technical standards, like those developed by ISO, IEC, and IEEE, fit alongside internal organizational policies in a co-regulatory ecosystem that aims for both effectiveness and adaptability?

The rise of incredibly powerful and broadly applicable **foundation models**, such as OpenAI's GPT-4 or Google's Gemini, presents a unique governance challenge. Given their potential to underpin a vast array of applications across countless sectors, should these base models themselves face specific, tailored regulations due to their sweeping impact? Initiatives like the US Executive Order on AI and the European Union's AI Act are beginning to grapple with this very question, recognizing that the governance of these foundational layers is critical to the responsible development of the entire AI ecosystem.

Looking further ahead, we must also consider how to approach the **long-term risks potentially associated with Artificial General Intelligence (AGI)**. While our focus in this exploration remains steadfastly on Augmented General

Intelligence (AuGI) – the enhancement of human capabilities – the speculative possibility of AGI raises profound questions. How seriously should current governance frameworks address these more distant, though potentially existential, risks? For now, the global conversation tends to center on promoting responsible research practices and investing in AI safety research, all while maintaining the crucial distinction between enhancing human intellect and creating an entirely independent superintelligence.

Finally, and with growing urgency, we face the challenge of **governing the rapidly advancing field of human augmentation**. As we've seen, technologies designed to enhance our physical, cognitive, or even genetic makeup are moving from the realm of science fiction into tangible reality. Yet, specific governance frameworks for these intimate technologies, particularly in sensitive areas like neurotechnology and genetic editing, remain largely undefined. The work of scholars like Nita Farahany and strategic bodies like the UK's Ministry of Defence underscores the pressing need to develop clear ethical and legal guardrails for augmentation before it becomes widespread, ensuring that progress in this domain aligns with human values and respects individual autonomy.

These debates are not mere academic exercises; they are live wires in the global effort to orchestrate the immense power of the Emerging Gestalt, ensuring that its trajectory serves humanity's best interests.

The Indispensable Role of Organizational Governance: Orchestration from Within

While public regulations set the stage, the true test of responsible AI orchestration happens inside the organizations developing and deploying these systems. Robust internal governance translates principles into reality and builds trust.

Essential Pillars of Internal Governance

Effective internal governance typically includes:

- **Clear Leadership & Accountability:** Designating clear ownership for AI ethics and responsible deployment, often with senior leadership buy-in.

- **Cross-Functional Ethics Bodies:** Establishing **AI Ethics Committees** or **Responsible AI Offices** with diverse representation (technical, legal, ethics, business lines) to review projects, develop policies, train staff, and handle concerns. (Example: Public charters from Microsoft, Google, Salesforce).

- **Risk Management Frameworks:** Adopting frameworks like **NIST AI RMF** to systematically identify, assess, and manage AI risks throughout the lifecycle (impact assessments, bias testing, data validation, model monitoring).

- **Concrete Policies & Standards:** Developing clear internal guidelines on acceptable AI use, data handling, transparency, human oversight, and ethical development.

> **Orchestrating Internally is as Crucial as Complying Externally**
>
> **Key Concept:**
> Organizational orchestration includes policies, training, oversight, and cultural adaptation—not just compliance checkboxes.
>
> **Why It Matters:**
> "Culture eats policy for breakfast." Governance must permeate leadership, teams, and workflows to be truly effective.
>
> **Actionable Tip:**
> Appoint governance champions, embed AI literacy into onboarding, and run simulation exercises to test oversight readiness.

- **Comprehensive Training:** Educating developers, managers, legal teams, and users on AI ethics, risks, regulations, and internal policies (e.g., Accenture, PwC initiatives).

- **Transparency Mechanisms:** Implementing methods like model cards, datasheets, or clear user notifications about AI interaction.

Towards Collaborative Orchestration of the Gestalt

Robust internal governance, like that exemplified by Priya at HireRight Solutions, translates high-level principles into operational reality and is crucial for building stakeholder trust. It provides the rule book, ethical compass, and risk management processes, defining *how* the organization intends for the human, augmented, and non-human 'parts' of the Gestalt to interact responsibly. However, governance frameworks alone do not guarantee synergy. The ultimate success hinges on how these principles translate into the day-to-day interactions and collaborative dynamics *within* teams on the ground. Having set the necessary stage with ethical considerations and the crucial orchestration provided by governance and regulation, we must now zoom back in to witness how these diverse contributors mesh their capabilities in practice. True synergy happens within the team dynamics. We will now examine **The Synergistic Team: Collaboration Remixed**.

Reflection:

Effective governance requires clarity and adaptability. Leaders must define roles for human oversight, craft policies that evolve with technology, and create mechanisms for feedback. Develop integrated teams of ethics, legal, and technical experts to anticipate challenges and design solutions.

How are you building governance structures that balance innovation with accountability and transparency?

Part 3: Synergy in Action
The Integrated Workforce & Society

Chapter 9: The Synergistic Team
Collaboration Remixed

Our travels with the Emerging Gestalt have now brought us to the heart of the matter: **collaboration in action**. We've meticulously examined the fundamental 'parts' and addressed the crucial prerequisites for their effective integration: communication bridges, ethical integrity, and the essential frameworks of governance and regulation that provide necessary orchestration. Now, operating within these established guardrails, we witness the **synergy manifest**. This chapter illuminates the **Synergistic Team**, the dynamic space where diverse human, augmented, and non-human contributors converge, interact, and collaborate. Our focus shifts from analyzing the components to observing the **emergent capabilities**—the novel outcomes and heightened performance levels achieved when these parts function together as an integrated 'whole', proving unequivocally that "There *IS* AI in Team," and that this combination can indeed be far greater than the sum of its parts. Take action now—apply these insights to build your own synergistic teams and unlock extraordinary outcomes.

Nurse Maria

It was a typical day at the hospital for nurse practitioner Maria Lopez. She had just finished a routine check-up on a patient when she received a notification on her computer that a new patient had been admitted. Maria clicked on the patient's file and was greeted by a message that read "AI Algorithm Diagnosis: Possible heart attack."

Maria's heart sank. As much as she appreciated the help of AI in diagnosing patients, she couldn't help but feel a sense of unease. She knew that while machines were good at analyzing data and identifying trends, they couldn't understand the nuances of human emotions and experiences. She wondered if the AI algorithm had considered the patient's history of anxiety and stress, which could have been the root cause of their symptoms.

Maria took a deep breath and made her way to the patient's room. As she entered, she was greeted by a woman in her late 50s who was clearly in distress. Maria introduced herself and began to ask the patient questions, trying to understand the root cause of her symptoms.

As she listened to the patient's story, Maria began to connect the dots. She realized that the patient had been under a lot of stress at work and had been experiencing anxiety for weeks. This led to a lack of sleep, which in turn resulted in chest pains that brought her to the hospital.

Maria knew that the AI algorithm had identified a potential heart attack, but she also knew that the true diagnosis could be much more complex. She explained the situation to the patient, who was relieved to hear that she wasn't having a heart attack after all. Maria took the time to talk to the patient about stress management techniques and offered to connect her with a counselor who could help her manage her anxiety.

As she left the patient's room, Maria couldn't help but feel a sense of satisfaction. She had used her empathy and human touch to connect with the patient and provide her with the care she needed. She knew that machines could never replace the human touch that is essential in healthcare.

Maria was grateful for the help of AI in diagnosing patients, but she also knew that machines had limitations. While they are great at looking for patterns and visible diagnostics, she knew that intuition, problem solving, and creative insight were uniquely human and could never be replicated by machines. She felt a sense of pride in knowing that she was a valuable part of the healthcare team, and that her skills and expertise were irreplaceable.

As Maria made her way back to her office, she thought about the future of healthcare. She knew that the integration of humans and machines would require new ways of thinking and working, and that organizations would need to provide training and education to ensure that employees had the skills they needed to succeed in this new environment. She was excited to be a part of this new frontier in healthcare, where humans and machines worked together to provide the best possible care for patients.

Redefining Teamwork: A Spectrum Beyond Biology

For millennia, teamwork was a purely biological phenomenon. The very concept conjured images of humans coordinating efforts: hunters stalking prey, builders raising structures, scholars debating ideas. But the integration of sophisticated non-human capabilities compels us to radically expand this definition. The high-performance team of today, and certainly of tomorrow, is increasingly a **hybrid entity**, a complex weave of contributors with vastly different origins and operating principles:

The Human Core: Still providing the essential strategic direction, creative vision, ethical oversight, nuanced communication, complex problem-solving under ambiguity, and empathetic leadership. They are the conductors, the architects, the ultimate decision-makers, setting goals and performing evaluations as Licklider (1960) envisioned.

AI Cognitive Systems: Serving as tireless researchers, analysts, drafters, translators, coders, and brainstormers. They process information at scale, identify patterns invisible to humans, generate content variations rapidly, and automate routine cognitive labor, acting as powerful intellectual force multipliers.

Robotic & Automated Systems: Executing physical tasks with superhuman precision, endurance, speed, or safety. They manipulate materials, navigate environments, perform inspections, and interact physically based on human or AI direction, extending the team's agency into the physical world.

Augmented Human Members: Individuals whose innate abilities are enhanced, potentially bringing superior physical strength, sensory perception, memory recall, or faster cognitive processing to specific tasks, requiring careful integration and ethical consideration within the team dynamic.

> **Teams Are No Longer Just Human**
>
> **Key Concept:**
> The modern team is evolving into a multi-agent system—blending humans, AI cognitive tools, robotics, and augmented individuals into one synergistic unit.
>
> **Why It Matters:**
> This redefinition of "team" demands new models of leadership, coordination, and trust across vastly different actors.
>
> **Actionable Tip:**
> Update org charts and workflows to include non-human roles. Assign responsibilities and integration points explicitly for AI tools and robotic teammates.

The challenge is no longer just managing human interactions, but orchestrating this intricate **interdependence**. As highlighted by AI expert Justine Cassell, the future lies in "collaboration, and cooperation between people and systems" (Public statements/interviews). It's about designing workflows and fostering cultures where these diverse parts can mesh seamlessly, leveraging their complementary strengths. However, achieving this synergy consistently requires effort; human-AI teams don't automatically outperform individuals without careful integration (Vaccaro et al., 2024).

Incorporate this hybrid team model to integrate human, augmented, and AI components effectively to maximize your team's capabilities.

Models of Synergistic Collaboration: How the Parts Weave Together

This integration isn't monolithic; it manifests in various patterns of interaction, creating different kinds of synergy. Design workflows that foster seamless collaboration—coordinate your team's diverse capabilities intentionally:

AI as Cognitive Partner & Augmenter: The Knowledge Force Multiplier

The Dynamic: This is arguably the most pervasive model currently emerging in knowledge work. Humans retain strategic control and final judgment but delegate significant cognitive tasks to AI partners. The workflow often involves human direction -> AI generation/analysis -> human validation/refinement/ integration. The concept of **"centaur teams"** (human + AI) outperforming either alone, borrowed from chess, is increasingly relevant in business (Mplus article).

Deep Dive Examples:

- **Legal Research & Document Review:** Law firms employing AI tools (e.g., Casetext, Harvey AI) to sift through vast legal databases exponentially faster than humans, identifying relevant precedents or flagging risky clauses for lawyer scrutiny. This reduces research time and improves thoroughness (Reports on AI adoption in legal tech).

- **Scientific Research:** Beyond literature reviews (e.g., Elicit, Scite), AI analyzes complex experimental data, generates hypotheses, and helps design experiments. Example: **Insilico Medicine** used AI to discover and design a novel drug candidate for Idiopathic Pulmonary Fibrosis (IPF) in under 18 months, with human researchers guiding, validating, and strategizing. (Source: Insilico Medicine press

> **Designing Interdependence, Not Just Co-Existence**
>
> **Key Concept:**
> Human-AI synergy isn't automatic. Without intentional design, teams become fragmented or dysfunctional.
>
> **Why It Matters:**
> Collaboration breakdowns occur when AI outputs aren't interpretable, robotic roles are siloed, or human members are underutilized.
>
> **Actionable Tip:**
> Run team "integration audits"—map information flow, timing, and accountability across human and non-human contributors.

releases/publications). AI is also assisting in proving mathematical conjectures.

- **Financial Modeling & Analysis:** AI algorithms process real-time data to generate predictive models and risk assessments. Human analysts then overlay market expertise and client understanding for final strategic decisions (World Economic Forum reports on AI in financial services).
- **Software Development:** AI coding assistants like **GitHub Copilot** act as 'pair programmers', suggesting code based on context. The human developer provides architecture, reviews suggestions, debugs, and integrates, accelerating development cycles. (Source: GitHub Copilot studies/user reports).
- **Executive Decision Support:** Augmenting discussions, providing data/options, though requiring human oversight (HBR/Giesswein).
- **Creative Collaboration:** AI assists writers (Yang et al., 2023), artists (Elgammal et al., 2021), musicians, and designers (Eapen et al., 2023) in brainstorming and generating initial content, which humans then refine. Studies show this can lead to more creative outputs, especially when human expertise complements AI (Vaccaro et al., 2024).

Key Synergy: **Speed + Scale (AI) combined with Context + Critical Judgment (Human).** Allows teams to process more information, generate ideas faster, and make more data-informed decisions, while retaining human oversight.

Cobots as Physical Collaborators: Sharing the Workspace Safely

The Dynamic: Humans and cobots work in close proximity, often performing sequential or parallel tasks on the same workpiece. Safety mechanisms enable fluid interaction.

Deep Dive Examples:

- **High-Mix Manufacturing:** Cobots provide consistency (screwing, dispensing, checks) while humans handle variable/dexterous steps. Example: **Trelleborg Sealing Solutions** used Universal Robots' cobots for pick-and-place and machine tending, allowing operators to manage multiple machines and focus on quality control, optimizing production flow. (Source: Universal Robots, Trelleborg Sealing Solutions Case Story). Specific examples include **BMW** using cobots for sealant application (Manufacturer case studies) and **SHAD** using them for screw insertion, improving ergonomics and productivity (Omron Industrial Automation, SHAD Case Study).

- **Laboratory Automation:** Cobots handle repetitive liquid handling or sample prep, freeing skilled technicians, reducing strain, and minimizing errors (Examples from Tecan, Hamilton Robotics in life sciences).
- **Agriculture:** Humans working alongside autonomous harvesting robots (Horecha, 2023).
- **Healthcare:** Robots assisting surgeons (e.g., da Vinci system offering enhanced precision; Intuitive Surgical info) or automating tasks in hospitals/labs (ValueCoders; JR Marketing). AI-powered robots providing companionship or assistance to seniors (JR Marketing). Diagnostic AI complementing radiologists' workflows (Bhandari, 2024). Studies show doctor+AI teams can achieve higher diagnostic accuracy than either alone (Nature Medicine study). Telemedicine with remote robotics combines expertise across distances.
- **Logistics**: Humans working with AMR fleets in warehouses (Amazon Robotics example in Chapter 4).
- **Delicate Electronics Assembly:** Manufacturers like **Continental Automotive** utilize cobots for tasks requiring consistent force/precision (e.g., circuit board assembly), while humans perform nearby inspections and complex placements, leveraging cobot steadiness and human dexterity/acuity.
- **General Purpose Humanoids (Future):** Potential for humanoid robots like those envisioned by NVIDIA's GR00T project to collaborate across various tasks.

Key Synergy: **Endurance + Precision (Cobot) combined with Dexterity + Adaptability (Human).** Increases throughput, improves quality, enhances worker safety, and enables automation in flexible environments.

Integrating the Augmented Human: Leveraging Enhanced Capabilities

The Dynamic: Teams incorporate members with technologically enhanced abilities. Collaboration requires adapting workflows and ensuring fairness.

Deep Dive Examples:

- **Construction & Field Service:** A technician with AR glasses (like HoloLens or RealWear) accesses schematics or remote expertise for faster, more accurate repairs. Example: **GE Vernova** uses AR headsets for field engineers maintaining power equipment, providing hands-free access to data and support, reducing downtime and improving safety. (Source: GE Vernova/RealWear partnership info). An engineer with an exoskeleton lifts heavy equipment safely. Teams must adapt workflows to accommodate the tech. (Case studies of AR/exoskeleton use).
- **High-Frequency Trading/Data Analysis (Future Scenario):** Traders with cognitive implants for faster processing raise complex ethical/fairness issues for performance management. BCIs enabling thought-to-text (NIH News Releases, 2021; Brown University News, 2021) show the potential for enhanced communication/control.
- **Surgical Assistance:** Systems like the **da Vinci Surgical System** provide surgeons augmented capabilities (3D visualization, tremor filtering, dexterity) for complex minimally invasive procedures, enhancing human skill. (Source: Intuitive Surgical product info/studies).
- **Playing to Strengths (Conceptual):** Success hinges on **explicit role definition** based on capabilities. Augmented members take tasks leveraging enhancements, cobots handle precision, baseline humans focus on integration, creativity, or client interaction. Requires **mutual respect for diverse contributions**.

Key Synergy: **Specialized Enhancement (Augmented Human) combined with Baseline Human Skills and Non-Human Capabilities.** Allows task hyper-optimization but requires careful management of team dynamics, fairness, and workflow integration.

Distributed Intelligence: Harnessing Swarms and Agent Networks

The Dynamic: Humans oversee or collaborate with large numbers of coordinated AI agents or robots working collectively. Intelligence resides partly in the coordination and emergent behavior.

Deep Dive Examples:

- **Large-Scale Environmental Monitoring:** Swarms of low-cost drones collaboratively map air quality or track wildfires with higher resolution/ resilience than single complex systems. Example: **Aerobotics** (now Puresense) used drone fleets/AI to monitor orchards, identifying issues at plant level for targeted interventions by human agronomists. (Source: Aerobotics/Puresense info; precision agriculture articles).
- **Coordinated Logistics & Delivery:** Networks of autonomous delivery drones/robots dynamically routing themselves, coordinating with central AI/human supervisors (Concepts explored by Amazon Prime Air, Starship Technologies).
- **Complex System Design & Simulation:** Teams of AI agents collaborating on designing complex systems (circuits, drugs), with different agents proposing, simulating, and checking constraints based on human goals (Research in multi-agent systems).
- **Entertainment & Light Shows:** Companies like **Verity Studios** (acquired by Qualcomm) used large swarms of coordinated drones with lights for complex aerial performances (e.g., Cirque du Soleil). Human designers choreograph, AI manages real-time trajectory/synchronization. (Source: Verity Studios/ Qualcomm Ventures info).

Key Synergy: **Scalability + Resilience + Specialization (Swarm/Network) combined with Strategic Oversight + Goal Setting (Human).** Enables tackling problems requiring massive parallelism, wide coverage, or diverse interacting expertise.

Common Threads: The Essentials for Synergistic Success

As we journey through these diverse models of collaboration, witnessing the intricate dance between human talent and technological prowess, a pattern begins to emerge. Regardless of whether the synergy manifests as a cognitive partnership with AI, a physical collaboration with cobots, the integration of augmented human capabilities, or the orchestration of distributed intelligent networks, certain fundamental, human-centric elements consistently surface as critical enablers. These are the common threads that, when woven skillfully into the fabric of these remixed teams, transform them from mere collections of 'parts' into truly cooperative, effective, and high-performing synergistic wholes. Invest in the structures and processes that support synergy by committing to ongoing learning, feedback, and adaptation.

At the very helm of this transformation stands the imperative of **visionary and adaptive leadership**. It is the human leader who must champion the cause of integration, articulately setting clear and inspiring goals that align these diverse contributors. Such leadership fosters an environment of psychological safety, where experimentation is encouraged, and learning from both successes and failures becomes part of the cultural DNA. Crucially, it is this leadership that guides the often-challenging cultural shifts necessary to embrace new ways of working and collaborating across biological and technological lines.

No less vital are **clear communication protocols**, the linguistic and operational bridges that connect human intention with machine execution. This involves meticulously defining how humans direct their AI and robotic teammates, and, just as importantly, how these systems report back their progress, flag anomalies, or escalate issues requiring human intervention. Here, the mastery of prompt engineering, that nuanced art of conversing with AI which we explored earlier, reveals itself not just as a technical skill but as a cornerstone of effective cross-species teamwork.

The complexity of these integrated teams also demands a rich tapestry of **interdisciplinary skillsets**. Success is rarely found in silos. Instead, it emerges from the dynamic blending of deep domain experts with skilled technologists, insightful ethicists, clear communicators, and adept change managers. Achieving genuinely effective teaming in this new era is, by its very nature, an interdisciplinary challenge, requiring a holistic understanding that transcends traditional departmental boundaries.

Underpinning all successful collaboration is a steadfast **focus on trust and transparency**. Teams do not automatically grant confidence in the non-human 'parts'; these systems must earn it. This involves fostering a clear understanding of how these AI and robotic systems function, embracing explainability where possible, ensuring their reliability through rigorous testing and maintenance, and being transparent about both their remarkable capabilities and their inherent limitations. For human team members, this means learning to appropriately calibrate their trust, relying on these

> **Human Strength Is Strategic Complexity**
>
> **Key Concept:**
> In the synergy model, humans provide mission-setting, ambiguity navigation, values-based judgment, and empathetic leadership—functions AI cannot replicate.
>
> **Why It Matters:**
> The power of synergy lies in amplifying distinctly human capabilities, not replacing them.
>
> **Actionable Tip:**
> Train humans for complex scenario planning, team design, and "meta" management—overseeing how the whole system works together.

systems where they excel while maintaining a healthy skepticism where oversight is warranted.

Given the relentless pace of technological evolution, a **continuous learning culture** transitions from a desirable trait to an absolute necessity. Organizations and individuals alike must commit to ongoing learning and adaptation, readily embracing new tools, refining processes, and updating skills as the technological landscape shifts beneath their feet. This commitment to perpetual growth is the engine of resilience in the face of constant change.

Amidst all this technological sophistication, the irreplaceable role of **human judgment as the final arbiter** must remain sacrosanct. While AI can analyze vast datasets and robots can execute tasks with tireless precision, it is the human 'part' that must maintain ultimate oversight for critical decisions, navigate complex ethical considerations, and bring nuanced understanding to novel or ambiguous situations that fall outside the parameters of pre-programmed responses.

The synergistic team, integrating humans, AI, robotics, and potentially augmented individuals, is the engine of the Emerging Gestalt. As illustrated by examples from AgTech (Horecha, 2023) to healthcare (ValueCoders; JR Marketing; Bhandari, 2024) and enterprise operations (Anthropic Guide; HBR/Giesswein), different models of collaboration are emerging, leveraging complementary strengths. The rise of AI Agents (Ruiz, A.) and sophisticated humanoid robots promises even deeper integration. Success hinges on visionary leadership, clear communication, trust, continuous learning, and unwavering human judgment. This reality necessitates a fundamental shift in how organizations manage their diverse contributors, leading us to **Transhuman Resources: Managing the Diverse Parts**.

Reflection:

Building high-performing teams means blending human strengths with AI capabilities. Leaders should focus on communication frameworks, trust-building, and team design that leverages AI where it adds value while maintaining human oversight and creativity.

Are you measuring team performance in a way that values both human contributions and AI-enhanced productivity?

Chapter 10: Transhuman Resources

Managing Diverse Parts

The picture painted in the previous chapter was one of dynamic synergy: teams no longer bound by biology, but thriving through the intricate collaboration of humans, AI systems, robots, and individuals whose capabilities may be technologically augmented. This 'remixed' collaboration, the Emerging Gestalt in action, unlocks incredible potential. However, realizing this potential requires more than just plugging in new technologies; it demands a fundamental transformation of the organizational function traditionally responsible for its people: Human Resources.

As the very definition of a 'workforce contributor' expands beyond the purely baseline human to include these other elements, traditional HR must evolve. It needs to become broader, more technologically literate, and ethically attuned to manage this increasingly complex ecosystem. To signify this necessary evolution—this shift *beyond* dealing solely with unmodified humans—we will use the term **Transhuman Resources (THR)** throughout this chapter. With these insights, you can build your THR strategy to manage these diverse parts and unlock synergy.

Sarah's Performance Puzzle

Sarah sighed, looking over the performance metrics for her data analysis team. Quarterly output was up nearly 30% since they implemented the new "InsightAI" platform and since Liam returned to work. Liam, a brilliant analyst, had suffered a terminal brain injury a year ago but had made a remarkable recovery, aided by a new generation neural co-processor implant—technically a medical device under ADA guidelines, but one that also undeniably boosted his cognitive processing speed for complex data sets. Anya, his teammate, was consistently reliable, methodical, and non-augmented, known for her deep, thoughtful analysis that often caught nuances others missed.

The problem was the annual reviews. How did she fairly evaluate Liam and Anya? Liam's raw data processing throughput was now nearly double Anya's, heavily influenced by his implant and his skillful prompting of InsightAI. Yet, Anya's qualitative insights, derived from slower, more deliberate human analysis, had twice led to identifying critical risks the faster methods overlooked.

Sarah realized that traditional performance metrics suddenly felt inadequate. Rating Liam solely on speed felt like crediting the implant, not just his skill. Rating Anya lower because her volume was less felt like penalizing her for not being augmented or for doing the essential deep-thinking work AI couldn't replicate.

Sarah pulled up the company's newly drafted "THR Performance Guidelines." They emphasized outcomes and collaboration. She started reframing her assessment.

- *For InsightAI: Its metrics were clear—uptime: 99.8%; processing cost per dataset: down 15%; queries handled autonomously: 70%. It was a valuable asset, contributing significantly to overall team efficiency.*

- *For Liam: His review needed to focus not just on his increased speed (acknowledging the implant's role) but critically on how he leveraged both his augmentation and InsightAI. How effective was his prompt engineering? Did he verify AI outputs rigorously? How well did he integrate his rapid findings back into team discussions? His ability to direct the technology was now as important as his analytical skill.*

- *For Anya: Her review needed to highlight the unique value of her non-augmented, deep analytical skills. While her volume was lower, the impact of her insights needed emphasis. The company measured this performance by the quality and critical nature of her findings, and by her ability to identify areas where human judgment surpassed AI pattern-matching. Her collaboration metric would include how effectively she utilized the AI outputs after initial processing, adding her unique layer of validation and interpretation.*

Sarah realized the compensation review would be equally complex, needing to balance the value delivered by the role with the different methods and capabilities used. The guidelines suggested a hybrid model, rewarding both efficient outcomes and critical human skills.

It wasn't easy. The new THR framework required more nuanced judgment than the old checklists. It demanded that she understand the technology's role, evaluate human-AI teaming skills, and redefine contribution beyond simple speed or volume. But as she prepared for the review conversations, Sarah felt it was the right direction—fairer, more holistic, and better equipped to manage the increasingly blended teams that were clearly the future of work at HireRight Solutions and beyond.

Important Clarification: Defining "Transhuman Resources" for this Book

It is critical to define this term clearly within the context of this book. While the word 'Transhuman' often evokes the broader philosophical movement of Transhumanism, with its focus on radical life extension and fundamentally altering the human condition, that is **not** the intended meaning here.

*For our purposes, **Transhuman Resources (THR)** refers specifically to the **adapted function of HR** responsible for developing and managing the policies, practices, and ethical considerations required for a workforce composed of baseline humans, technologically augmented humans (using tools ranging from advanced prosthetics to potential future cognitive aids), and integrated non-human contributors like AI and robotics.*

THR, in this context, is about the **practical challenges of fairly recruiting, developing, evaluating, compensating, and ensuring the well-being and inclusion** of *all* these diverse contributors within the symbiotic teams of the Emerging Gestalt. It focuses on the **management challenges** arising from human-technology integration in the **current and near-future workplace**, not the more distant philosophical speculations associated with the 'Transhumanism' movement.

With this practical definition established, this chapter moves into the complex, often messy, **realities** that THR must navigate. How does THR recruit, develop, evaluate, compensate, include, and support a workforce composed of such diverse 'parts'? This requires not just tweaking existing processes but fundamentally rethinking the HR playbook for an era where the lines between biology, technology, and contribution are irrevocably blurred.

HR Becomes THR—Transhuman Resources

Key Concept:
- The traditional HR function must evolve into Transhuman Resources, capable of managing not just humans, but AI agents, cobots, and enhanced workers as a cohesive system.

- **Why It Matters:**
- Without a shift in mindset and policy, organizations risk applying outdated norms to a fundamentally different workforce structure.

- **Actionable Tip:**
- Redesign job roles, policies, and performance metrics to include and differentiate between human, augmented, and machine contributions.

Use this definition as a guide—adapt your HR functions to manage synergy among humans, AI, and robotic contributors.

Redefining the Workforce Contributor: Navigating Shifting Legal and Policy Terrain

The first and most fundamental task for THR is achieving clarity on the status and treatment of each type of contributor. The legal and policy landscape is still evolving, demanding proactive engagement from THR leaders. Stay ahead of legal and policy shifts—actively update your workforce strategies to stay compliant and competitive.

Non-Human Contributors (AI & Robots): The Evolving Tool/Asset Status

- *Current Paradigm:* Legally, AI algorithms and robots are corporate property: assets acquired, maintained, and potentially disposed of. They don't have employment contracts, rights, or legal standing as individuals.

- *THR's Operational Role:* While not direct 'employees,' their integration profoundly impacts the human workforce, requiring THR involvement in:

  - **Workforce Planning & Job Impact:** Analyzing which human tasks are automated, identifying emerging skill gaps, and planning for reskilling or redeployment strategies. (McKinsey Global Institute reports on future of work). This includes understanding the need for new "fusion skills" required to work alongside AI (Accenture).

  - **Ergonomics & Safety:** Collaborating closely with EHS and Operations to design safe work environments where humans and robots (especially cobots) interact. Developing safety protocols, training employees, ensuring compliance with standards like ISO 10218/TS 15066 (OSHA guidelines, robotics safety standards).

  - **System Performance Integration:** While AI/robots aren't 'reviewed,' their performance metrics (e.g., AI model accuracy drift, robot MTBF) are critical inputs for evaluating *overall team or process effectiveness*. THR needs performance management systems that account for this non-human contribution.

o **Ethical Procurement & Deployment:** Contributing criteria to procurement, ensuring AI vendors meet ethical standards (data privacy, bias mitigation) and deployment plans consider human factors.

- *Future Considerations—Accountability & Agency:* As AI gains autonomy, accountability for errors becomes complex. Current frameworks hold the deploying organization responsible, but THR/Legal must anticipate future scenarios and develop clear internal accountability structures. The debate around "electronic personhood" signals deep future questions (European Parliament 2017 Resolution).

Augmented Humans: A Spectrum Requiring Nuanced Policy

As the Human Resources function evolves into what we've termed Transhuman Resources (THR), it confronts the immediate and ethically charged challenge of navigating a workforce increasingly composed of diverse human and non-human contributors. This critical task involves addressing the nuances of human augmentation. Central to this challenge, THR policy must clearly and considerately distinguish between augmentation individuals undertake for **restorative or medical purposes** and augmentation they **elect for enhancement**.

When we speak of **restorative or medical augmentation**, we generally refer to technologies that compensate for a biological deficit, restore lost function, or treat a medical condition. Think of advanced prosthetics enabling an individual to regain mobility, cochlear implants restoring hearing, or medical devices supporting vital bodily functions. In most developed legal frameworks, these augmentations are generally covered by existing anti-discrimination and reasonable-accommodation laws, such as the Americans with Disabilities Act (ADA) or the Equality Act in various jurisdictions. For THR, managing these situations, while requiring sensitivity and care, largely involves following established processes: THR engages in an interactive dialogue with the employee, provides reasonable accommodations enabling them to perform their job effectively, and ensures equal opportunity. This is familiar territory, albeit involving increasingly sophisticated technological interventions.

However, the prospect of **elective or enhancement augmentation** thrusts THR into largely uncharted waters, creating novel challenges that demand proactive policy development now, before such technologies become widespread. Imagine an employee who chooses to receive a cognitive implant not to address a medical need, but purely to gain a competitive edge in their role, perhaps to

113

process information faster or enhance their memory recall. Or consider an individual opting for a physical augmentation granting them capabilities beyond the typical human baseline. These scenarios move beyond restoration and into the realm of potential human enhancement, raising a cascade of complex ethical and practical questions.

Policy Area	Therapeutic/ Restorative Augmentation	Elective/ Enhancement Augmentation	Key THR Consideration
Legal Framework	Existing Disability/ Accommodation Laws (ADA, etc.)	Emerging/Unclear; Potential Discrimination Risks; Contract Law	Proactive legal counsel needed; Develop clear internal policies. Address potential need for new rights (e.g., cognitive liberty - Farahany, 2023).
Accommodation	Generally Required (Reasonable Accommodation)	Generally NOT Required (Not addressing a disability)	Define "reasonable" for new tech; Avoid implicit performance mandates.
Funding/Cost	Often covered by Health Insurance / Benefits	Primarily Employee Responsibility; Employer contribution raises equity concerns	Clarify coverage; Address equity if company offers funding.
Performance Evaluation	Focus on Essential Job Functions; Accommodate tech	Complex: Focus on Outcomes; Avoid penalizing non-augmented; Prevent unfair advantage; Acknowledge tech factors	Develop nuanced metrics (Sarah's Puzzle); Train managers on fair evaluation.
Safety & Liability	Assess job risks; Standard safety protocols	Assess tech failure risks; Clarify liability for malfunctions/side effects	Rigorous safety assessment; Clear liability clauses.
Privacy (Data)	Governed by Medical Privacy	Standard Data Protection Laws Apply; Heightened	Ensure robust security; Transparency on monitoring;

114

Policy Area	Therapeutic/ Restorative Augmentation	Elective/ Enhancement Augmentation	Key THR Consideration
	Laws (HIPAA) + GDPR etc.	concern if tech monitors	Address neuro-privacy (Farahany, 2023).
DEI Considerations	Ensure inclusion; Prevent discrimination	Prevent discrimination *for/ against*; Manage equity concerns (access/balance)	Update DEI policies; Proactively address potential "augmented divide."
Coercion Risk	Minimal (Focus on enabling participation)	Moderate-High (Implicit pressure to enhance)	Explicitly prohibit mandatory enhancement; Foster culture valuing diverse capabilities.

Therefore, THR must thoughtfully address a host of key policy areas, carefully comparing the considerations surrounding therapeutic augmentation with the new dilemmas elective enhancements pose. This requires a deep dive into the very issues of equity, safety, privacy, identity, coercion, and fairness that we highlighted as paramount concerns in our earlier exploration of human augmentation in Chapter 5. How does an organization ensure fair access if some enhancements prove prohibitively expensive? What safety implications and liability concerns arise if an elective enhancement malfunctions? How does the organization protect the sensitive data such augmentations generate, especially when medical privacy laws may not cover it? And how does THR ensure an organizational culture doesn't implicitly or explicitly coerce employees into seeking enhancements to remain competitive, or discriminate against those who choose not to augment? These are no longer theoretical questions; they represent the practical realities THR must begin to codify into clear, ethical, and legally sound policies.

THR Leadership Required: Don't wait for lawsuits. Work with Legal counsel to draft policies addressing elective augmentation, focusing on non-discrimination, job relevance, safety, and performance outcomes, using distinctions like those outlined above. Base decisions on essential functions, not augmentation status.

Ethical Recruitment in a Mixed-Capability World

THR must redesign recruitment to fairly evaluate a diverse pool of applicants, bringing different combinations of skills, AI proficiency, and potentially augmentations. Implement deliberate strategies now to ensure your recruitment processes are fair and inclusive for all contributors.

- **Deepen Commitment to Skills-Based Hiring:** Move decisively beyond degrees/titles. Implement and validate diverse assessment tools:

  - *Work Sample Tests:* Assigning relevant job tasks.

  - *Structured Behavioral Interviews:* Standardized questions on past competency demonstration.

  - *Validated Skills Assessments:* Objective tests for specific skills (where relevant/non-discriminatory).

  - *Portfolio Reviews:* Evaluating actual work products.

  - *Goal:* Assess ability to *deliver required outcomes*, irrespective of source.

- **Assess Human-AI Collaboration Skills:** Integrate assessments for this emerging competency:

  - *Interview Probes:* "How would you use an LLM like ChatGPT for X? How ensure reliability?"

  - *Practical Simulation:* Provide a scenario and AI tool. Observe prompting strategy, critical evaluation, integration (**Ch 6**).

  - *Past Experience Questions:* "Tell about a project where AI impacted your workflow. What did you learn?"

- **Maintain Vigilance Against Bias:**

  - *Blind Review:* Implement where feasible (removing identifying info).

  - *Train Interviewers:* Address unconscious bias, including assumptions about augmentation or AI assistance in applications. Reiterate focus on **job-relevant capabilities**. (Relevant to "Sarah's Performance Puzzle").

- **Govern AI in HR Tech Rigorously:** The use of AI *by* THR demands the highest ethical standards:

  o Mandate **vendor transparency** (algorithms, data).

  o Conduct regular, independent **bias audits** across demographics (including potentially augmented status). Auditing is critical to prevent automating historical inequalities or introducing new discrimination (e.g., Amazon hiring tool issue - Reuters, 2018).

  o Ensure **meaningful human oversight** at critical decision points (AI assists, not decides).

  o Maintain compliance with regulations (e.g., EU AI Act High-Risk category).

Real-World Adaptation: While specific policies are emerging, companies are exploring **scenario-based interview questions** on AI tool usage or **take-home assignments** permitting ethical AI use, evaluating the final output and integration skill. Early adopters of AI in recruitment like **Unilever** faced scrutiny over potential bias in analyzing video interviews *(Various news articles 2017-2019)*, highlighting the critical need for ongoing **rigorous governance of AI in HR Tech**, demanding transparency and continuous bias auditing.

Performance Management for the Synergistic Team

Evaluating performance when contributions come from humans, augmented humans, and AI/robots requires shifting from purely individual, human-centric metrics. You must assess both human and AI contributions to build truly synergistic teams.

- **Prioritize Team Outcomes & System Effectiveness:** Focus on whether the integrated team achieved its goals. Measure the success of the 'whole'. Use frameworks like OKRs emphasizing shared goals.

- **Integrate Non-Human Performance Data:** Metrics like AI accuracy, robot uptime are vital inputs into assessing overall *system* performance and identifying bottlenecks. Not 'reviews' for machines, but essential operational data.

- **Develop Nuanced Approaches for Augmented Performance:**

  o *Contextual Goal Setting:* Adjust expectations based on augmentation capabilities for the role, transparently and fairly.

  o *Acknowledge Technological Factors:* Fairly account for augmentation reliability, maintenance, updates, learning curves. Don't penalize for tech downtime.

  o *Evaluate Effective Integration:* Assess *how well* the employee leverages enhanced capabilities safely, collaboratively, ethically, improving team outcomes.

- **Sarah's Puzzle Revisited:** THR must provide Sarah tools for nuance: multi-rater feedback, qualitative impact assessments, goals tied to *both* leveraging tech effectively (Liam) *and* applying critical human judgment (Anya). Value diverse contributions.

- **Make Human-AI/Robot Collaboration a Core Competency:** Explicitly define, assess, and reward skills for cross-type collaboration:

  o *Assessable Behaviors:* Skillful prompting; safe cobot operation; identifying automation opportunities; critically validating AI outputs; handling exceptions; sharing tool learnings. Include in reviews.

- *Measuring Synergy:* The Stanford/MIT study showed AI boosting agent productivity 14-35% (Brynjolfsson, Li, Raymond, 2023). The HR challenge is attributing value fairly (agent skill vs. AI tool). Companies like **Microsoft**, integrating Copilot, reportedly focus performance discussions on *how* employees learn, adapt, and use tools responsibly within teams, assessing collaborative behaviors and human oversight quality, shifting focus to the *synergistic process*. (Microsoft WorkLab reports; executive statements).

Compensation and Benefits: Navigating Value and Fairness in a Mixed World

Assigning monetary value in a workforce with vastly different capabilities is perhaps THR's most complex challenge. Design compensation frameworks that recognize the diverse value of all team members in order to avoid inequity and potential future liabilities:

- **Defining Compensable Value:** Pay for role output? Premium for human skills? Complexity of human-tech interaction?

  - *Likely Future:* Hybrid models recognizing **outcome value** and **scarce human competencies**. Explore **skill-based pay** systems tied to certified skills (including human-AI collaboration).

- **Understanding the Economics:** Partner with Finance to analyze **TCO of automation** vs. human labor costs, informing strategic decisions. Holistic view needed.

- **Augmentation and the Benefits Package:** Elective enhancements create challenges.

  - *Policy Clarity Needed:* Develop clear policies on whether company plans cover non-medical enhancements, maintenance, complications. Who bears cost if enhancement becomes de facto requirement? Tier coverage? Issues of equity and access are paramount here.

- **Proactive Equity Management:** Technology can exacerbate pay gaps.

  - *THR Actions:* Conduct regular pay equity audits across roles, demographics, *and* levels of tech augmentation/leverage. Implement transparent compensation structures. Address fairness concerns openly.

Diversity, Equity & Inclusion (DEI): Expanding the Boundaries of Inclusion

Diverse contributors of the Emerging Gestalt increasingly define and redefine our collaborative landscapes demanding a profound expansion of the principles of Diversity, Equity, and Inclusion (DEI). No longer can these crucial conversations revolve solely around traditional human differences. The integration of augmented individuals and non-human collaborators compels us to broaden our understanding and application of what it truly means to foster an inclusive and equitable environment for every 'part' of this synergistic whole. Expand your DEI initiatives and create inclusive cultures that empower every team member to contribute.

Transhuman Resources (THR) must therefore proactively and formally **recognize augmentation status within its DEI framework.** This means explicitly prohibiting discrimination or harassment based on an individual's augmented capabilities—or, just as importantly, their choice to remain unaugmented—thereby ensuring true inclusion across this evolving spectrum of human form and function. We must cultivate workplaces where both augmented individuals and their baseline human colleagues feel equally valued and respected.

Perhaps one of the most critical frontiers for this expanded DEI vision is the imperative to **tackle enhancement equity head-on.** The potential for a new socio-economic chasm, an 'augmented divide' as cautioned by strategic thinkers like those in the Ministry of Defence (2021), based on unequal access to performance-enhancing technologies, is a stark reality we must actively prevent. THR must therefore take a leading role, spearheading the development of equitable access strategies. This involves pioneering fair funding models, championing the development and adoption of lower-cost alternatives, and establishing clear fairness principles to ensure these powerful technologies bridge existing gaps rather than carving out new, deeper ones.

Furthermore, as HR departments increasingly leverage AI in their own operations, THR must **intensify its commitment to algorithmic fairness audits.** This means doubling down on the rigorous scrutiny of all HR technology, diligently ensuring these systems operate free from bias, not only regarding traditional protected characteristics but also concerning an individual's augmentation status or their ethical use of AI assistance in their work. We cannot afford to automate or amplify discriminatory practices through the very tools designed to manage our diverse talent.

The call for inclusivity also extends to the very nature of collaboration itself. THR must actively **foster an inclusive culture that embraces *all* contributors:** human, AI, and robotic. This involves promoting organizational norms and providing targeted training that encourages respectful, effective, and psychologically safe interactions between these diverse collaborators. It means proactively addressing human anxieties about working alongside non-human partners and genuinely celebrating the unique successes and innovations born from these cross-type collaborations, echoing the positive and productive dynamics we witnessed in the narrative of Alex's Team.

Even before the widespread adoption of radical enhancements, the groundwork for these expanded DEI considerations is being laid. Companies currently employing assistive technologies that verge on augmentation must ensure their DEI policies already address equitable access to such tools. If certain technologies become essential for specific roles, organizations need clear strategies, potentially including comprehensive training programs, viable alternative pathways, or subsidies, to prevent new divides from forming. In this evolving landscape, **it is vital that THR champions policies ensuring technology truly enables broad participation, serving as a force for equity rather than exclusion within the Emerging Gestalt.**

Training & Development: Continuous Adaptation for the Entire Ecosystem

The emergence of Homo Gestalt is transforming the once-aspirational concept of lifelong learning into an undeniable baseline requirement for everyone. This relentless pace of change and the integration of diverse human, augmented, and non-human contributors place a profound responsibility squarely upon the shoulders of Transhuman Resources (THR) to architect and champion a new era of continuous adaptation across the entire organizational ecosystem.

THR must therefore spearhead a series of critical **training imperatives**. First and foremost, for **human team members**, THR must champion comprehensive programs focusing on essential, future-facing skills. This involves instilling a deep **AI literacy**, enabling individuals to understand both the power and the limitations of their cognitive collaborators. It means cultivating mastery in **advanced prompt engineering**, the nuanced art of eliciting optimal performance from generative AI. Furthermore, THR must equip employees to confidently **interpret complex data outputs**, to **interact safely and effectively with collaborative robots (cobots)**, and to internalize and apply **ethical AI deployment guidelines** in their daily work. Crucially, these programs must sharpen **enhanced critical thinking** and foster the agile, **adaptive collaboration** skills necessary to thrive in mixed teams. Indeed, as organizations like Accenture recognize, developing these "fusion skills" becomes absolutely crucial for navigating this new terrain.

Beyond the baseline human, THR must also devise **specific training pathways for augmented individuals.** This requires developing tailored onboarding processes and ongoing learning opportunities that help these team members understand how to maximize their enhanced capabilities both safely and effectively, ensuring their unique contributions seamlessly integrate into the broader synergistic goals of the team.

Perhaps most critically, THR must spearhead the **upskilling of its own professionals and the organization's leadership.** These key individuals, who will guide the organization through this transformation, urgently need dedicated training. They must develop a robust understanding of the emerging technologies, grasp the evolving legal and ethical nuances surrounding AI and augmentation, master new management frameworks designed for mixed-capability teams, and gain the confidence and skills to lead the profound cultural and operational shifts that lie ahead.

We already see leading organizations recognizing this strategic imperative and taking decisive **organizational action.** Accenture, for example, actively trains its global workforce on AI fundamentals, ethical considerations, and practical application. Similarly, PwC developed its own internal tool, "ChatPwC," and rolled out comprehensive training to encourage the responsible leverage of AI across its diverse practices. These forward-thinking initiatives, often driven by proactive THR and Learning & Development departments, powerfully demonstrate the strategic importance organizations place on building widespread AI literacy and fostering the collaborative competence essential for success in the Emerging Gestalt.

The Proactive Imperative: THR as Strategic Orchestrators

THR must be **proactive, strategic architects**, not passive administrators of the transformation to an augmented, mixed workforce.

Key Strategic Actions for THR:

- **Develop Predictive Workforce Models:** Anticipate skill shifts 3-5 years out.

- **Design and Pilot New HR Processes:** Experiment with skills-based hiring, outcome-focused reviews, hybrid compensation.

- **Draft Adaptive Policies:** Create forward-looking policies on AI use, data ethics, augmentation *now*.

- **Lead Change Management:** Communicate vision, address concerns, champion cultural adaptations.

- **Partner Across the Organization:** Collaborate deeply with IT, Legal, Ethics, Ops, business leaders.

- **Champion Ethical Implementation:** Serve as the organization's conscience, ensuring technology serves human values.

This proactive stance is essential. THR must engage now, shaping practices iteratively. The challenge is moving from managing human capital to **THR**

orchestrating a diverse ecosystem of human, augmented, and non-human contributors towards shared goals, ensuring ethical integrity and fostering human potential.

A Commitment to Human Potential

The evolution towards **Transhuman Resources** is an essential adaptation for organizations navigating the Emerging Gestalt. It is incumbent upon THR to move beyond traditional HR to manage a diverse ecosystem including augmented humans and non-human contributors like AI and robots, addressing complex challenges in recruitment, performance, compensation, DEI, and training (Anthropic Guide; China Daily). This requires proactive policy development, a focus on skills, robust ethical frameworks, and deep collaboration across the organization. Having laid out the complexities of managing this diverse workforce, we must rely on the capacity of the human 'part' to adapt and evolve. The success of this entire synergistic enterprise hinges on our individual human capacity to adapt, learn, and evolve, which brings us to **Adapting the Human Part: Skills, Learning, and the Evolving Workforce**.

Reflection:

Managing a mixed workforce of humans and augmented contributors requires rethinking HR practices. Leaders must ensure fairness in recruitment, compensation, and career development. Prioritize policies that support inclusivity, adaptability, and psychological safety.

How is your HR team preparing for a blended workforce of humans and augmented contributors?

Chapter 11: Adapting the Human Part

Skills, Learning, and the Evolving Workforce

Our exploration of the Emerging Gestalt has revealed a future taking shape *now*—a future defined by the intricate synergy between humans, augmented humans, AI, and robotics. We've discussed the communication protocols, ethical guardrails, governance structures, and evolved resource management needed to orchestrate this complex 'whole'. But the success and sustainability of this entire enterprise ultimately hinge on the continued vitality and effective contribution of its most fundamental component: the **human part**. As intelligent technologies increasingly permeate our work and lives, automating tasks once considered exclusively human domains, the pressure to adapt is immense. This isn't merely about learning to use new software; it's about a fundamental **evolution of human skills, learning paradigms, and workforce participation**. This chapter delves into this critical adaptation, examining the profound shift in valued competencies, the non-negotiable imperative of lifelong learning, the changing landscape of work structures like the gig economy, and the necessary reimagining of education and credentialing required for humans to thrive not just *alongside*, but as integral drivers within the increasingly capable Gestalt. Take measures to enable your organization to adapt and thrive in the Emerging Gestalt by enhancing your skills and mindset.

The Great Skill Shift: From Routine Execution to Human-Centric Value

The narrative often pushed by headlines focuses on jobs being "lost" to automation. While significant workforce transitions are undeniable (McKinsey Global Institute estimates potential displacement in hundreds of millions globally by 2030), a more nuanced understanding reveals a profound **revaluation of skills**. The economic value is rapidly shifting away from tasks characterized by routine and predictability towards those demanding uniquely human capabilities, often amplified by technology. This reflects the augmentation philosophy championed by figures like Douglas Engelbart and J.C.R. Licklider. Cultivate these human-centric skills and develop your creativity, empathy, and judgment to remain indispensable.

The Erosion of Routine:

- *Cognitive Routine:* Basic data entry, scheduling, standardized reports, simple customer service, level-1 tech support are increasingly handled by AI/RPA. LLMs draft correspondence, summarize documents, write routine code faster than humans. This impacts roles like junior lawyers or designers performing repetitive tasks (China Daily).

- *Physical Routine:* Repetitive assembly, basic transport, routine inspections are prime candidates for robotics/cobots. Tasks like fruit harvesting are targets (Horecha, 2023).

- *Implication:* Relying primarily on routine skills offers diminishing long-term security, as predicted by observers like Neal Cross regarding "keyboard jobs" (Cross, N./LinkedIn).

The Ascendancy of Human-Centric Skills:

As AI handles the 'what' and 'how' of routine tasks, human value concentrates on the 'why,' the 'what if,' and the 'how should we?'

- **Deep Critical Thinking & Complex Problem-Solving:** Analyzing multifaceted problems, identifying assumptions (including in AI outputs), evaluating evidence, navigating ambiguity, formulating reasoned judgments. AI provides data, humans frame problems, question data, make strategic calls.

- **Creativity, Originality & Innovation:** Stepping *outside* existing data patterns. Conceptual blending, asking "why not?", aesthetic judgment, designing new systems, generating ideas from empathy/experience. AI is a powerful tool for creativity (like Maya's Muse), but **humans remain the visionaries**. Valued even when using AI as an assistant (China Daily). This aligns with findings that human-AI teams excel in creative tasks (Vaccaro et al., 2024).

- **Social & Emotional Intelligence:** Building rapport, team collaboration, empathetic communication, conflict resolution, mentorship, inspiration, and understanding social cues. Crucial for leadership, sales, healthcare, education, any role with human interaction. AI simulates language, lacks genuine feeling/nuance.

- **Ethical Reasoning & Responsible Stewardship:** Anticipating ethical implications, making value-based decisions, ensuring fairness/accountability, guiding technology beneficially. Requires moral compass AI lacks.

- **Adaptability & Learning Agility:** The ultimate meta-skill: learning quickly, unlearning outdated methods, adapting to evolving tools, processes, market conditions. Our "evolutionary edge," as termed in Chapter 2.

The New Layer: Human-Machine Collaboration Competencies:

Proficiency required in interacting *with* technology:

- **Advanced Prompt Engineering:** Crafting prompts eliciting nuanced, accurate, creative outputs from generative AI. Understanding context, persona, format, iteration.

- **Data Interpretation & AI Literacy:** Understanding AI outputs, assessing biases/limits, interpreting visualizations, using insights effectively without blind acceptance.

- **Ethical AI Application:** Applying guidelines/principles when using AI (privacy, bias avoidance, transparency).

- **Technology Integration:** Seamlessly incorporating AI, robotics, AR into workflows.

- **System Monitoring & Exception Handling:** Overseeing automated processes, identifying when tech fails, stepping in with human judgment.

- **Fusion Skills:** The overarching ability to work effectively with AI and robotic systems, blending human and machine capabilities (Accenture).

The Lifelong Learning Imperative: Education Reloaded

Transhuman Resources must address the transformation driven by the Emerging Gestalt impacting our diverse contributors. In this process, we inevitably return to a foundational pillar: the imperative for human adaptation. In our previous discussions, particularly when considering the evolving role of THR in Chapter 10, we touched upon the radical transformation of what we understand as "lifelong learning." We are rapidly concluding, and in many cases have already determined, that the traditional "front-loaded" model of education—where learning is predominantly concentrated in youth—simply cannot withstand the relentless pace of change and the shifting economic realities characteristic of this new Gestalt era. Continuous, lifelong learning now transcends personal enrichment; it crystallizes as an undeniable economic necessity for individuals to maintain their employability, advance their careers, and contribute meaningfully within this dynamic synergistic system. Commit to lifelong learning to expand your skills continuously and stay relevant in the age of AI.

This necessitates several **key shifts in our approach to learning**. The emphasis must decisively move **from mere knowledge acquisition towards the agile application of skills and a profound capacity for adaptability.** In a world where information is abundant and often AI-assisted in its retrieval, the true value lies in knowing how to apply knowledge effectively, how to critically find and evaluate information, and, most importantly, how to develop the ability to learn rapidly to meet ever-evolving market needs.

Technology itself is a powerful enabler of this new learning paradigm, facilitating **personalized and just-in-time learning experiences.** We see the rise of **AI tutors and sophisticated learning platforms**, such as Khanmigo or Sana Labs. These intelligent systems provide tailored explanations and practice opportunities precisely when and where individuals need them, allowing learners to focus intently on bridging specific skill gaps and remaining competitive. The learning journey further adapts through **micro-learning modules and skill-based units**, which break down complex topics into digestible, manageable segments. This approach allows people to seamlessly integrate continuous learning into the daily workflow, making adaptation an ongoing process rather than a sporadic event. **Simulations and Extended Reality (XR)** technologies offer immersive, interactive environments where individuals can safely and repeatedly practice complex technical or essential soft skills—a methodology that has already **proven its worth** in fields like healthcare and aviation training.

A particularly exciting development, as educator Donald Clark compellingly suggests, is the **power of inquiry unleashed by AI—a concept we might term "PedAIgogy."** Artificial intelligence facilitates a shift towards deeply inquiry-based learning. Imagine students engaging AI tutors in rich, Socratic dialogues, actively probing concepts, challenging assumptions, and learning to ask more insightful and effective questions. This process, critical for both effective collaboration and skillful prompt engineering as we've discussed, moves education decisively beyond rote memorization. It cultivates a genuine understanding and fosters the very critical thinking skills that the new economy so highly values.

Perhaps one of the most transformative aspects of this reloaded educational landscape is its potential for **democratization through enhanced accessibility.** The combination of widely available learning resources and powerful AI tools begins to break down traditional barriers to skill acquisition and economic participation. An individual, regardless of formal background, can now acquire in-demand skills like prompt engineering through accessible online training. Armed with this knowledge and leveraging AI tools to create professional-quality work, they can launch a business or secure employment based on demonstrated capability rather than solely on traditional credentials. This pathway **highlights how targeted learning is paving non-traditional routes** to economic success, with a focus on mastering human-AI competencies and contributing value within the synergistic framework of the Gestalt..

Navigating New Work Structures: The Gig Economy & Portfolio Careers

Flexibility demanded by rapid change, coupled with enabling technologies, reshapes employment structures, partly responding to **economic restructuring**. This accelerates the **Gig Economy** growth. Embrace flexibility to strategically navigate new work structures to thrive in a portfolio career landscape.

- **Nature of Gig Work:** Freelance, short-term contracts, project-based, multiple income streams ("portfolio careers"). Platforms like Upwork, Fiverr connect talent globally (Data on platform growth, freelance stats).

- **Synergy for the Solopreneur:** Generative AI acts as a force multiplier. Individuals leverage AI for tasks previously needing teams (marketing copy, code, visuals, social media), lowering barriers to entry and allowing specialized individuals to **compete effectively in a transforming market**.

- **Opportunities:** Flexibility, autonomy, potential for higher earnings for **in-demand skills**, diverse experiences accelerating skill development.

- **Challenges:** Income volatility, lack of traditional benefits, self-discipline needed, potential isolation -**economic precarity** is a concern.

- **Adaptation Strategies for Gig Workers:** Continuous skill development (staying ahead of automation **and wage pressure**), building personal brand/ network, mastering productivity/ collaboration tools (including AI), financial planning.

Many employees now maintain a side-hustle that often transitions to full-time work as a part of the gig economy. These entrepreneurs identify a need, leverage interests, learn new skills (potentially AI-assisted), and build a business outside traditional employment. Their proactive "hustles" turn technological disruption **and potential economic displacement** into opportunity.

Rethinking Education & Credentialing: Validating Skills for the Future

Traditional degrees alone are insufficient. Side hustles are all about applying knowledge and skills, and people often **acquire** them through non-traditional methods like YouTube and TikTok, which do not come with 'official' certifications. Seek new ways to demonstrate your value—embrace new models for education and skills validation:

- **Industry-Education Partnerships:** Closer collaboration ensures curricula align with industry needs (human-AI skills). Apprenticeships, co-ops, industry certifications are vital (Germany's dual education; tech bootcamps).

- **Focus on Demonstrable Skills:** Credentials must reflect actual capabilities:

  - *Micro-credentials & Badges:* Certifying specific tools, techniques, competencies.

  - *Project Portfolios:* Curated work demonstrating skills (vital for creatives, developers).

o *Skills-Based Assessments:* Standardized tests or performance evaluations measuring abilities directly.

- **Valuing Diverse Learning Pathways:** Recognizing skills acquired through formal education, online courses, bootcamps, self-teaching, on-the-job experience, side projects. THR practices must evaluate this broader evidence spectrum.

Fostering Adaptability: The Shared Responsibility

Organizations that need talented and skilled employees must acknowledge they are partially if not fully responsible for not only recruiting the best talent, but ensuring they are involved in the systems developing them in the first place. Cultivating adaptability is not solely an individual burden; it's shared, crucial for navigating the **collective economic transition**. Lead by example—foster adaptability in yourself and champion it within your organization.

- **Individual Mindset:** Embrace curiosity, growth mindset, resilience, ownership of learning journey; all are crucial for **maintaining economic agency**.

- **Organizational Culture (THR-Led):** Create environments *supporting* adaptation:

  o **Invest in Continuous Learning:** Provide time, resources, diverse opportunities.

  o **Promote Psychological Safety:** Encourage experimentation, risk-taking, learning from mistakes.

  o **Redesign Roles for Synergy:** Structure jobs leveraging human strengths alongside tech, focusing on collaboration **creating higher economic value**. Essential given the anticipated scale of AI adoption and skill needs.

  o **Support Career Transitions:** Offer internal mobility, coaching, transition support for roles **economically impacted** by automation.

  o **Recognize & Reward Adaptability:** Make learning agility key in performance/advancement, **signaling economic importance**.

The human role **evolves** to direction, creativity, oversight, ethical guidance, and skillful collaboration. This demands continuous learning from individuals, **with**

organizations and education systems supporting them for 21st-century realities and economic imperatives. By embracing adaptation, the human 'part' remains the driving force, shaping a future where technology amplifies our best capabilities, creating a symbiotic whole that fosters **broadly shared prosperity**. This constant evolution impacts our inner lives, leading us to consider **The Human Experience in an Interconnected World: Mental Health & Well-being**.

Reflection:

Upskilling is no longer optional. Leaders must champion lifelong learning, foster adaptability, and build resilience. Implement programs that combine technical training with critical thinking, creativity, and emotional intelligence to future-proof your teams.

What steps are you taking to build a culture of lifelong learning and adaptability in your organization?

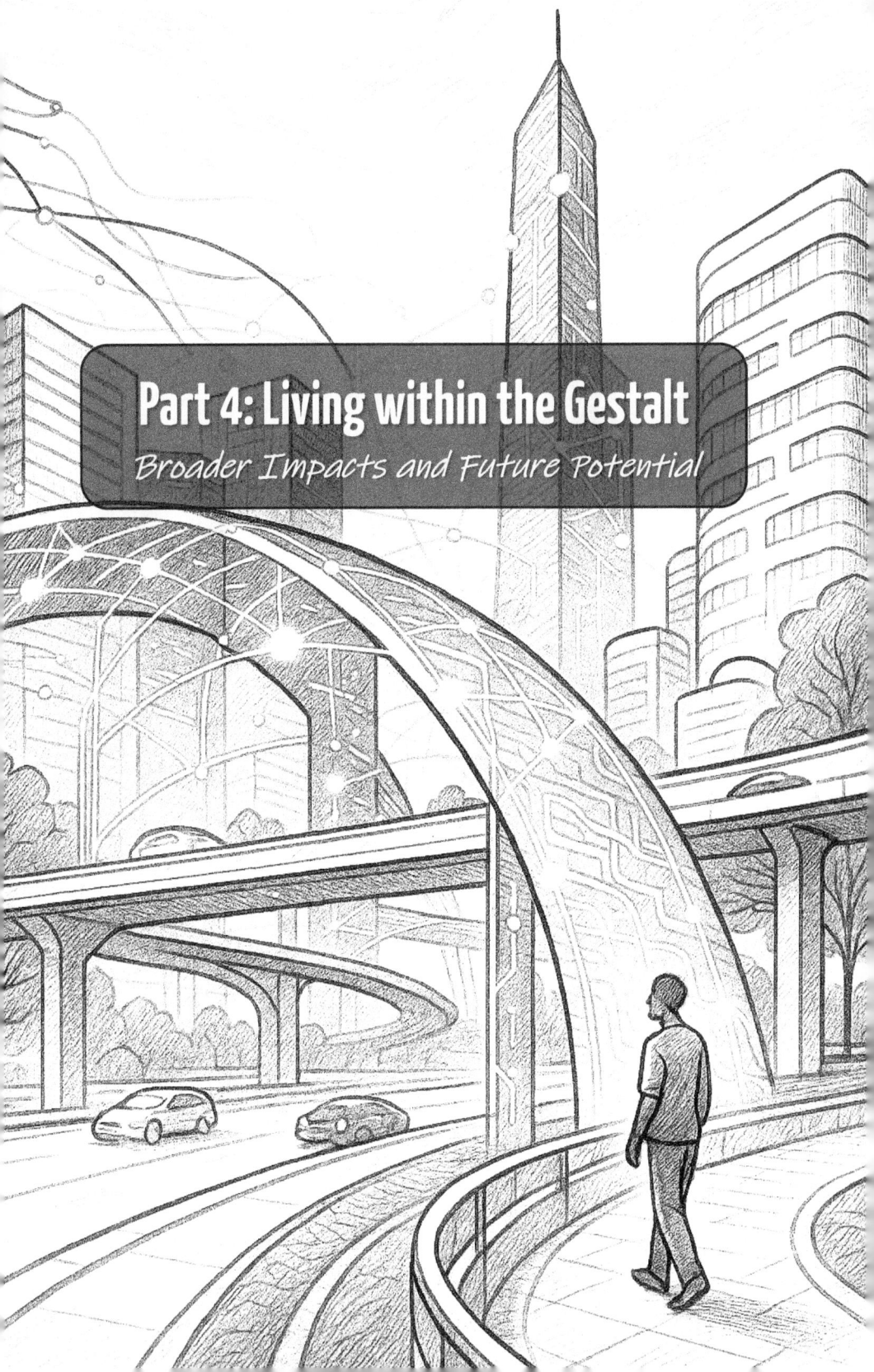

Part 4: Living within the Gestalt
Broader Impacts and Future Potential

Chapter 12: The Human Experience in an Interconnected World

Mental Health and Well-being

In our travels mapping this new form of team, this gestalt, we have uncovered a landscape brimming with synergistic potential—a future where human ingenuity collaborates dynamically with AI's cognitive power, robotics' physical agency, and potentially augmented human capabilities. We've dissected the communication protocols, ethical frameworks, governance necessities, evolved resource management, and the relentless demand for human adaptation and learning required to navigate this complex integration. Yet, as we become increasingly embedded within this technologically interwoven reality, as the digital and physical merge, and the velocity of change itself becomes a defining feature, a critical dimension demands our focused attention: the **subjective human experience**. What does it *feel* like to be the human 'part' operating within this intricate, always-on, intelligent system? What are the profound impacts, both enriching and depleting, on our **mental health and overall well-being**? This chapter confronts these vital questions, exploring the psychological landscape of the Gestalt era, we must recognize that fostering human flourishing does not merely follow from technological progress but actively enables its ethical success and long-term sustainability. Recognize these challenges and opportunities—act now to shape a balanced, human-centered experience in the Gestalt era.

The Double-Edged Sword: Technology as Both Balm and Burden

It's crucial to approach this topic with nuance, recognizing that the very technologies shaping the Gestalt—the intelligent AI, the diligent robotics, the potential for human augmentation—reveal themselves as a profound double-edged sword. These technologies undeniably have the power to serve as a potent balm for our collective well-being, but they also risk burdening our psychological equilibrium if we integrate them carelessly.

Therefore, to truly understand this complex interplay, we must first acknowledge the remarkable and heartening ways these technologies can serve as powerful allies in our quest for improved mental health and greater psychological resilience. We stand at the cusp of an era offering **precision mental healthcare**, where sophisticated AI algorithms diligently analyze speech patterns, textual communications, or even subtle data from wearable sensors. Researchers in computational psychiatry actively pursue this analytical prowess, which shows incredible promise for detecting the early, often almost imperceptible, signs of conditions like depression and anxiety. This early detection can, in turn, empower us to implement more timely and effective interventions that may profoundly change the trajectory of these challenges for countless individuals. Furthermore, artificial intelligence can thoughtfully assist human therapists, perhaps by analyzing anonymized session transcripts to help identify recurring themes, track patient progress over time, or even suggest avenues for deeper therapeutic exploration.

> **Mental Health Is Now a Design Priority**
>
> **Key Concept:**
> In the Gestalt era, digital systems affect sleep, attention, emotion, and self-worth. Mental health isn't just a clinical issue—it's shaped by our tech ecosystems.
>
> **Why It Matters:**
> Ignoring this leads to design that drains rather than uplifts, increasing burnout, anxiety, and social disconnection.
>
> **Actionable Tip:**
> Apply "digital well-being audits" to tech tools—assess time-on-task, interruption load, and emotional impact. Design for focus and agency.

Beyond these clinical applications, AI tools also forge pathways towards **democratizing access to vital support systems.** In a world where mental health professionals remain a scarce resource for many, and where the persistent shadow of societal stigma can still create formidable barriers to seeking help, developers design AI-powered resources to provide scalable, accessible, and confidential assistance. Consider chatbots like Woebot or Wysa; these digital companions deliver evidence-based Cognitive Behavioral Therapy (CBT) exercises and provide immediate emotional support, effectively bridging critical gaps in care. Pioneering initiatives, such as the University of Illinois' Lumen project which developed an AI voice assistant for psychotherapy, have even demonstrated tangible symptom improvement and corresponding positive changes in brain activity among participants, powerfully underscoring the potential for these tools to make a genuine difference in people's lives. Actively evaluate the impact of technology and be intentional about how you integrate it into your life and work.

Gestalt technologies **positively influence our mental health** by reducing many of the everyday stressors that can insidiously erode our psychological equilibrium. Intelligently designed assistive AI, helpful robotic systems, and thoughtfully implemented augmentations can significantly lessen daily frustrations, markedly increase independence for individuals living with disabilities, and actively combat the loneliness that can so often stem from isolation. Similarly, the automation of tedious, repetitive, or physically dangerous work can substantially reduce occupational stress, thereby freeing human collaborators to engage in tasks that are not only safer but often more fulfilling, creative, and deeply aligned with their unique human capacities.

Key Mental Health Challenges Amplified in the Gestalt Era:

You can use simple strategies like establishing boundaries, practicing digital detox, and fostering meaningful human connections to help. Your company must prioritize mental well-being and take deliberate steps to manage stress and foster resilience.

- **Existential Uncertainty & The Shifting Meaning of Work:** Automation sparks anxieties about human value and relevance.

  - *Job Insecurity Amplified:* Fields including design, writing, and coding see tasks augmented/automated by generative AI, broadening vulnerability resulting in Chronic anxiety.

  - *Identity Crisis:* Professional identity tied to self-worth. When core functions automate, individuals grapple with loss of purpose, potentially leading to depression, alienation.

  - *The "Useless Class" Fear:* Concerns about economically unviable skills (Harari, 2017) tap into societal anxieties about marginalization.

- **Technostress, Cognitive Overload, and Digital Burnout:** Information volume/velocity can overwhelm human processing.

  - *The Infobesity Epidemic:* Constant notifications, emails, messages, AI reports create cognitive load, leading to fatigue, reduced concentration, errors, decision paralysis (Research on information overload).

- *The Relentless Pace of Change:* Need to constantly learn new software/interfaces adds continuous low-grade stress. Failure to keep pace increases anxiety.

- *Hyper-Connectivity & Blurred Boundaries:* Remote/hybrid work erodes work/life separation. "Always-on" expectation prevents rest, contributing to burnout.

- **The Comparison Trap: Humans vs. Machines & Curated Selves:** Self-worth impacted by comparisons.

  - *Algorithmic Performance Anxiety:* Working alongside AI optimized for speed/consistency can trigger inadequacy/ imposter syndrome. Purely quantitative metrics exacerbate this.

  - *The Social Media Effect Amplified:* AI curates feeds of idealized (sometimes AI-generated) images/lifestyles. Generative filters create "perfect" personas. Unrealistic standards fuel negative social comparison, impacting self-esteem and mood.

- **Erosion of Deep Connection & Rise of Social Isolation:** Technology can hinder meaningful human interaction.

  - *Transactional Communication:* Efficiency tools might prioritize information exchange over nuanced, empathetic communication building strong relationships. Text/asynchronous communication can reduce emotional connection.

  - *Substitution, Not Augmentation:* If AI chatbots replace human service entirely, or virtual meetings supplant face-to-face without effort to maintain bonds, opportunities for camaraderie diminish, increasing loneliness. For example, while AI can connect seniors virtually (See Article: JR Marketing), overuse or poor design can diminish deeper human bonds.

  - *Algorithmic Polarization:* Content recommendation systems can trap users in filter bubbles, which limit their exposure to diverse viewpoints and potentially hinder empathy (Concepts like "The Filter Bubble" - Pariser, 2011).

- **Technology Dependency, Addiction, and Attentional Decline:** Engaging, personalized tools risk behavioral addiction.

- *Mechanisms:* Variable rewards, personalized streams, gamification hijack dopamine system, leading to compulsive usage (Research applying behavioral psychology to tech addiction).

- *Impact:* Difficulty disengaging, neglect of real-world responsibilities/relationships, impaired impulse control, reduced attention span/deep work ability (Carr, 2011).

- **Ethical Strain and Moral Injury:** Grappling with ethical complexities of AI (bias, fairness, privacy, misuse) can take a psychological toll on developers/deployers, leading to **moral distress** or **injury**.

- **Pervasive Anxiety from Privacy & Surveillance Concerns:** Awareness of data collection, AI surveillance, and **neuro-privacy** risks can foster persistent anxiety about autonomy.

- **The Student Experience:** Encapsulates systemic pressures:

  - *Future Uncertainty:* AI's impact on jobs triggers anxiety (Existential Anxiety).

  - *Digital Overwhelm:* Increased screen time, constant updates create stress (Technostress).

  - *Social Comparison:* Curated online lives fuel inadequacy (Comparison Trap).

  - *Authenticity Concerns:* Worry about superficial digital relationships (Erosion of Connection).

  - Desire to disconnect highlights need for balance.

Nurturing Well-being: Strategies for the Human Part in the Gestalt

Protecting and enhancing mental well-being requires deliberate, multi-level strategies. Implement these strategies now—create a sustainable, balanced approach to technology use in your personal and professional life.:

1. **Championing Authentic Human Connection:** Actively counteract transactional drift.

- o *Individual:* Prioritize quality time, deep conversations, empathy, community participation. Limit passive social media.

- o *Organizational (THR):* Design hybrid models with in-person connection. Encourage "camera-on" appropriately. Train leaders on virtual trust/safety. Structure projects for human collaboration.

2. **Mastering Digital Boundaries & Habits:** Take conscious control.

- o *Individual:* Define work/life boundaries. Schedule "digital detox." Use app timers. Practice mindfulness. Curate information intake. Disable non-essential notifications.

- o *Organizational:* Implement "right to disconnect" policies. Promote meeting-free times. Offer digital wellness workshops. Model healthy boundaries.

3. **Redefining Purpose and Contribution:** Find meaning beyond automatable tasks.

- o *Individual:* Identify/cultivate human skills (creativity, problem-solving, mentoring). Seek roles leveraging these. Find purpose in learning, projects, community. Frame tech as tools freeing you *for* higher value.

- o *Organizational:* Communicate value of human skills. Invest in reskilling. Redesign roles emphasizing human strengths augmented by tech. Recognize diverse contributions. Support growth/mobility.

4. **Expanding & Destigmatizing Mental Health Support:** Normalize seeking help.

- o *Individual:* Normalize conversations. Be aware of stress, seek help (EAPs, therapy). Support colleagues. Leveraging AI tools like chatbots responsibly can supplement traditional care (See Article: JR Marketing on chatbots for mental health).

- o *Organizational (THR):* Provide comprehensive, accessible benefits (teletherapy). Promote EAPs. Train managers to recognize distress/respond supportively. Integrate mental well-being into wellness programs.

- o *Responsible Tech Integration:* Explore vetted mental health apps (Woebot, Wysa) as *optional supplements*, ensuring privacy/ethics. Be wary of replacing human care.

5. **Leveraging Technology for Positive Flourishing:** Use tools to actively cultivate well-being.

- o *Fostering Engagement/Accomplishment:* AI personalized learning platforms promote mastery/"flow" (Csikszentmihalyi). Automation frees cognitive resources for intrinsically motivating work, enhancing accomplishment/meaning (Part of PERMA model - Seligman).

- o *Identifying/Utilizing Strengths:* Emerging AI tools help identify character strengths (ethically, with consent). AI coaching guides users to apply strengths more often (Niemiec, 2019; PositivePsychology.com resources).

- o *Enhancing Positive Emotions/ Mindfulness:* AI chatbots incorporate positive psychology exercises (gratitude, savoring). Wearables + AI offer biofeedback for mindfulness (Research on digital positive psychology - Bakker & Budden, 2021).

> **Technology Must Reconnect Us, Not Just Inform Us**
>
> **Key Concept:**
> Tech's highest function isn't data—it's deepening human connection. When systems reinforce isolation or comparison, we lose that potential.
>
> **Why It Matters:**
> Loneliness and disconnection are rising despite unprecedented connectivity. The design gap is emotional, not technical.
>
> **Actionable Tip:**
> Embed social repair tools: foster meaningful communication in apps, support community formation, and design for empathy.

- o *AI-Powered Coaching:* AI coaches assist goal setting/planning/motivation (Supports "Accomplishment" in PERMA; e.g., CoachHub features).

- o *Facilitating Meaningful Connections:* Intentionally use tech to connect shared interests, facilitate mentorship, support community organizing, provide communication aids.

- o *Critical Caveat:* Requires **intentional design & ethical implementation**. Prioritize user needs, privacy, avoid manipulation. THR vets tools supporting genuine well-being.

6. **Addressing the Neuro-Privacy Frontier—Safeguarding Cognitive Liberty:** Requires urgent societal attention.

o *The Critical Need:* **Brain wearables** that monitor fatigue, attention, and emotion pose profound threats to mental privacy and autonomy (Farahany, 2023).

o *Proactive Measures:* Establish strong legal rights protecting **cognitive liberty**. Organizations must adopt cautious, voluntary, transparent, ethical approaches to neuro-monitoring. They must also implement robust data security and anonymization practices and strictly prohibit coercive use. The potential insights from brain simulation research (See Article: Henry Markram/LinkedIn) could eventually inform both BCI development and the ethical frameworks needed.

7. **Cultivating Critical AI Literacy & Digital Citizenship:** Empowering individuals reduces fear, enables safer navigation.

o *Focus:* Educate on AI workings (limits like bias/ hallucination), algorithmic influence, spotting misinformation/ deepfakes, ethical/ responsible tool use. Integrate into curricula/ workplace training. Essential for navigating a world with AI-generated content and potential deepfakes (See Eleanor's Verification scenario).

Ultimately, ensuring the well-being of the human 'part' is **central** to the Gestalt's success. A system populated by anxious, burnt-out, disconnected humans is not sustainable or desirable. Fostering mental health requires a holistic approach— empowering individuals, building supportive/ ethical organizational cultures, making help accessible, and establishing norms/regulations prioritizing human flourishing. As we look towards broader economic shifts, maintaining well-being must guide our path forward as we examine **Rebalancing the Equation: Economic Implications of Synergy**.

Reflection:

AI's impact on mental health and well-being cannot be ignored. Leaders should design work environments that prioritize psychological safety and well-being. Implement support systems, design ethical use policies, and foster open dialogue about challenges.

How are you addressing mental health and well-being as AI transforms the workplace?

Chapter 13: Rebalancing the Equation

Economic Implications of Synergy

Our comprehensive exploration of the Emerging Gestalt has now brought us face-to-face with its profound potential. We've analyzed its constituent 'parts' and the essential frameworks for communication, ethical integrity, governance, workforce management, human adaptation, and well-being needed for successful integration. The promise is one of unprecedented synergy, a 'whole' capable of innovation and productivity far exceeding the sum of its individual components. But such transformative power inevitably sends shockwaves through existing structures, none more fundamental than our **economic systems**. This chapter delves into the critical macroeconomic implications, examining how widespread human-machine synergy reshapes productivity, redefines the very nature of value and work, challenges traditional models of wealth distribution, and demands fresh economic thinking that moves decisively beyond simplistic, zero-sum assumptions. Understanding and proactively shaping these economic shifts is paramount if we want the immense value that the Gestalt generates to foster broad-based prosperity rather than entrench deeper inequalities. Take charge of this transformation—understand how human-machine synergy reshapes our economy and prepares your organization for success.

Debunking the Zero-Sum Fallacy: Why Synergy Creates More Than It Displaces

Confronting the economic implications of the Emerging Gestalt requires us first to dismantle a persistent and often paralyzing anxiety: the **zero-sum narrative**. This pervasive notion, which frequently defaults our thinking about AI and automation, suggests that every task a machine automates represents a job irretrievably lost to a human, thereby shrinking the overall pool of opportunity. Such a perspective, which views the economy as a static, finite pie where technology's gain must inevitably be humanity's loss, fundamentally misrepresents the dynamic nature of technological progress and, crucially, misunderstands the profound creative potential inherent in synergy.

To truly grasp why technology, particularly the synergistic integration we explore, tends to expand the economic pie rather than merely re-slice it, we can turn to **history as our guide.** Major technological revolutions from the transformative impact of the printing press and the steam engine to the pervasive changes wrought by electricity, computing, and the internet have consistently, though often disruptively, demonstrated this principle. While each wave brought transition and upheaval, each ultimately expanded the overall economic capacity by dramatically increasing productivity, enabling humanity to generate far more value from the resources it already had. Artificial intelligence and robotics represent the next powerful wave of general-purpose technologies and are poised to unlock significant productivity gains, a prospect that economic analyses by respected bodies like the OECD, IMF, and Accenture underscore by projecting substantial GDP growth linked to widespread AI adoption.

The expansion of the economic pie, however, stems from more than just doing old tasks faster; it arises from **value creation that extends far beyond simple substitution.** Automation, in this synergistic context, doesn't just replace human labor; it often enables entirely new categories of tasks that were previously too complex, too costly, or too data-intensive for humans to undertake alone. Consider the rise of **hyper-personalization**, where AI algorithms allow businesses to tailor products and services to individual needs at an unprecedented scale, thereby creating new forms of value in sectors like retail, entertainment, and education. Witness the power of **accelerated research and development**, where AI significantly speeds up critical processes like drug discovery, materials science, and the design of complex systems, leading to a faster cadence of innovation. And look to the horizon of **entirely new markets and services** including autonomous transport, AI-driven diagnostics, personalized learning platforms, and sophisticated advanced simulations, all representing novel economic frontiers directly generated by the capabilities of AI and robotics.

> **Debunking the Zero-Sum Fallacy**
>
> **Key Concept:**
> AI and automation don't merely replace jobs—they create new markets, enhance existing ones, and expand what's economically possible.
>
> **Why It Matters:**
> A zero-sum mindset leads to fear and resistance. Synergy instead implies abundance: human and machine collaboration can generate more total value.
>
> **Actionable Tip:**
> Use economic models that incorporate augmentation, market expansion, and second-order job creation—not just substitution losses.

Furthermore, the zero-sum view critically overlooks the **indispensable role of the human consumer and director** in any functioning economy. A scenario of widespread technological unemployment leading to a collapse in consumer purchasing power would, quite simply, cripple the entire economic system.

Machines, after all, do not buy products or services. Moreover, even the most advanced AI, as we've repeatedly emphasized, requires human direction. It is humans who set the goals, define the values, provide the contextual understanding, handle the inevitable exceptions, and formulate the overarching strategy. This inherent interdependence ensures that humans will continue to have an evolving, not a vanishing, economic role. Indeed, as prominent voices like Bill Gates observe, AI is more likely to free humans *for* other tasks, suggesting a future characterized by augmentation and dynamic role shifts rather than simple, wholesale elimination.

While we must acknowledge and proactively address the very real costs and displacements that come with any significant technological transition—themes we explore with urgency when discussing human adaptation—this deep synergy drives the overall economic trajectory towards potential expansion and new value creation, not mere redistribution within a fixed system. Challenge this mindset—recognize that synergy can expand opportunities rather than simply replace jobs.

The Productivity Puzzle and AI's Potential Surge

For decades, economists and business leaders have grappled with a curious phenomenon often dubbed the "productivity paradox." Despite massive, sustained investments in information technology, the anticipated explosion in aggregate productivity growth remained stubbornly elusive, a sluggish reality discussed by prominent economists from Solow to Syverson. Now, however, the arrival of advanced artificial intelligence, particularly the transformative power of generative AI, offers a compelling prospect: this new wave of technology might finally possess the leverage to break this long-standing trend. Indeed, practical enterprise guides consistently confirm that the pursuit of enhanced productivity stands as a key, if not primary, driver for the accelerating adoption of AI across industries. Actively integrate AI thoughtfully and align it with human strengths to maximize productivity.

The mechanisms through which AI promises to unleash this productivity surge are multifaceted, reflecting its diverse capabilities within the Emerging Gestalt. At its most straightforward, AI contributes through **direct task automation**, efficiently replacing human labor in a wide array of routine cognitive and physical tasks, thereby freeing human talent for more complex endeavors. Beyond mere replacement, AI acts as a powerful force for **human augmentation**, significantly enhancing the productivity of individual workers.

145

We see this vividly in the deployment of AI coding assistants that accelerate software development, sophisticated diagnostic aids that empower medical professionals, and even physical exoskeletons that boost the endurance and safety of manual laborers. The compelling Stanford/MIT study, which demonstrated AI boosting the productivity of contact center agents by a remarkable 14-35 percent, offers a prime, quantifiable example of this augmentation in action. Further evidence—highlighted in the research by Vaccaro and colleagues—suggests that human-AI teams, when well-integrated, can indeed outperform either humans or AI working in isolation, particularly in tasks that demand creative output.

AI's influence also extends to the broader realm of **system optimization**. Intelligent algorithms now optimize intricate and sprawling processes, from global supply chains and energy grids to complex manufacturing operations and urban traffic flow, wringing out inefficiencies and enhancing overall throughput. And, as we've noted, AI plays a crucial role in **accelerating innovation itself**, dramatically speeding up research and development cycles in fields ranging from pharmaceuticals to materials science.

Productivity Isn't Just About Output

Key Concept:
True productivity gains arise when humans are freed from rote tasks to engage in complex problem-solving, creative strategy, and systems-level orchestration.

Why It Matters:
Traditional productivity metrics miss the emergent value created by synergistic teams blending human insight and machine precision.

Actionable Tip:
Track productivity at the system level, incorporating AI inputs, team dynamics, and user-centered design impact—not just throughput or time.

However, unlocking the full measure of AI's productivity potential demands more than simply layering new technology onto existing structures. Realizing these gains requires **significant complementary investments and profound organizational changes.** Attempting to sprinkle AI onto inherently inefficient processes will inevitably produce only limited benefits. Instead, firms must courageously undertake the often-challenging work of redesigning core workflows to leverage AI's strengths, proactively retraining and upskilling their employees to thrive in this new collaborative environment, fostering new cultures that embrace human-machine teaming, and, in many cases, fundamentally rethinking their underlying business models. The insightful research of Brynjolfsson, Rock, and Syverson underscores this critical need for holistic adaptation; true productivity transformation arises not from technology alone, but from the synergistic interplay of technological innovation and strategic organizational evolution.

Real-World Examples:

- **GitHub Copilot:** Directly augments developer productivity via code suggestions, speeding up routine tasks (GitHub research reports). Exemplifies **human augmentation**.

- **JPMorgan Chase:** Uses AI for fraud detection, risk management, compliance, process automation. Requires integrating tools, ensuring data quality, retraining staff, navigating regulations—highlighting need for **complementary organizational changes**. (JPMorgan Chase public statements; financial press reports).

- **Siemens:** Leverages AI for predictive maintenance, energy optimization, quality control via visual inspection, integrating with "digital twins" for virtual optimization before physical implementation. Represents **system optimization**. (Siemens AG website/case studies).

These examples illustrate that organizations often achieve AI productivity gains by combining automation, augmentation, and optimization, all supported by significant organizational adaptation.

The Shifting Landscape of Value, Work, and Wages

As the Gestalt integrates AI/automation, organizations and individuals transform the economic value of different human work. Redefine how you measure and reward value and create compensation models that align with the new Gestalt economy:

- **Decommoditization of Routine Skills:** Easily automated tasks (basic data analysis, standard content creation, simple coding) may become commoditized, potentially depressing wages unless individuals upskill. The impact will vary across fields, with roles involving significant routine susceptible to disruption (Cross, N./LinkedIn; China Daily).

- **Increased Value of Complementary Human Skills:** Highest value flows to skills *complementing* AI/automation:

  o *Directing & Managing AI/Robots:* Prompt engineering, AI training, robot supervision, workflow design.

- o *Leveraging AI Outputs:* Critically evaluating insights, integrating into decisions, using tools creatively.

- o *Human-Centric Tasks:* Empathy, negotiation, ethical leadership, creative vision, bespoke craftsmanship, high-touch services become relatively more valuable.

- **Data as a Factor of Production:** Access to high-quality data is critical. Elevates importance of data generation, curation, governance, security. Raises questions about **data ownership**: should individuals/communities be compensated? Models like "data dividends" or "data trusts" explored (Lanier, 2013; proposals for data cooperatives).

- **Potential Wage Polarization:** Could exacerbate inequality. High-skilled workers leveraging AI see wage growth ("skill-biased technical change"), while those easily automated face stagnant/declining wages without reskilling (Acemoglu & Restrepo work).

Distributional Challenges: Ensuring the Gains Are Broadly Shared

The Gestalt can create immense wealth but ensuring it doesn't become excessively concentrated is critical. Advocate for equitable policies. Ensure the gains from synergy are shared across your organization and community. Risks include:

- **Capital-Biased Technology:** If AI/robots primarily substitute labor, capital's share of income could increase relative to labor's share, widening wealth gap (Piketty, 2014 context).

- **Geographic Concentration:** AI talent, investment, infrastructure heavily concentrated (Silicon Valley, China hubs), risking disparities between leading/lagging regions.

- **"Winner-Take-Most" Dynamics:** AI network effects/scale economies can lead to market dominance by few firms, concentrating gains ("superstar firm" effect - Autor et al. research).

- **Access to Augmentation:** Unequal access to performance-enhancing augmentations could entrench economic disparities. Neal Cross highlights the potential for mass civil unrest if transitions are poorly managed (Cross, N./LinkedIn). Equity is a major ethical concern regarding augmentation.

Rebalancing the Equation: Policy Levers for an Inclusive Gestalt Economy

Addressing distributional challenges requires deliberate policy interventions. Reach out to policymakers. Encourage them to support frameworks that foster innovation while protecting human well-being. A multifaceted approach is needed:

- **Massive Investment in Human Capital: Education, Reskilling, Lifelong Learning: Fundamental Priority.** Governments/businesses must collaborate on large-scale initiatives equipping people with future skills. Examples:

  - **Singapore's SkillsFuture Initiative:** National movement providing resources/funding (SkillsFuture Credits) for lifelong skills development, including digital/AI focus, emphasizing government-industry-education collaboration. (SkillsFuture Singapore website).

  - **Germany's Adaptation of Vocational Training ("Work 4.0"):** Updating strong dual vocational training curricula (classroom + apprenticeship) via BMBF/BIBB initiatives to include digital skills, AI awareness, data handling, human-machine interaction for Industry 4.0. (BMBF/BIBB websites).

  - **EU Digital Skills and Jobs Platform:** Central hub connecting individuals, businesses, training providers across member states, offering resources, funding info, best practices as part of "Digital Decade" policy to boost digital skills. (European Commission, Digital Skills and Jobs Platform website).

  - These underscore that proactive, large-scale investment in **human capital adaptation** is critical for navigating economic shifts and ensuring successful worker transitions.

- **Modernizing Social Safety Nets:** Existing systems need updating for a dynamic, potentially gig-based economy.

  - *Strengthening Unemployment Insurance.*

- *Exploring Wage Insurance:* Subsidizing wages for displaced workers taking lower-paying jobs.

- *Portable Benefits:* Tying benefits (health, retirement) to individuals, not employers, accommodating freelance work (Aspen Institute Future of Work Initiative proposals).

- **Seriously Considering Universal Basic Income (UBI) and Related Ideas:** As AI boosts productivity, UBI emerges as a plausible mechanism for broad economic participation/security.

  - *Concept:* Regular, unconditional cash payment to all citizens.

  - *Potential Benefits:* Poverty reduction, better health, entrepreneurship buffer, job displacement buffer, potential data compensation.

  - *Challenges:* Funding (tax changes), labor supply impacts (pilot evidence mixed, minimal work reduction - Finland, Stockton pilots), optimal design. Other models: Negative Income Tax, Universal Basic Services.

  - *Real-World Pilots:* **Finland** (well-being improvements, minimal employment impact - Kela report). **Stockton, CA (SEED)** (improved financial stability, mental health, higher full-time employment vs control - SEED reports). **GiveDirectly (Kenya)** (positive impacts on consumption, assets, well-being, local economy - GiveDirectly research).

  - *Gestalt Perspective:* UBI as potential societal adaptation. As synergy boosts productivity, UBI could ensure human economic agency/ purchasing power, preventing demand collapse, maintaining social stability for the *entire* system. Debate continues but represents a paradigm shift.

- **Reforming Tax Structures for the 21st Century:** Systems reliant on labor income may become unsustainable/inequitable.

  - *Potential Shifts:* Reduced labor taxes offset by increased taxes on capital gains, wealth, automation profits, carbon, data usage.

  - *"Robot Taxes":* Taxing automation deployment debated (Bill Gates). Aims to slow displacement or fund transitions. Challenges: defining taxable "robot," avoiding disincentivizing investment (Economic analyses debate feasibility).

- *Context:* Adapting tax systems has precedent (e.g., **OECD/G20 BEPS Project** addressing digitalization tax challenges, global minimum tax). For the Gestalt, where value relies on AI/robotics/data (capital) + human input, tax reform is needed to capture value and fund societal adaptations (Chapter 9 - education, safety nets) for benefit-sharing/stability.

- **Robust Competition Policy & Antitrust Enforcement:** Preventing AI monopolies is crucial for innovation/equity.

  - *Focus Areas:* Scrutinizing acquisitions, ensuring fair data/platform access, preventing anti-competitive algorithm use (Regulatory scrutiny by US DOJ/FTC, EU DG Competition).

- **Rethinking Data Ownership and Value Sharing:** Creating mechanisms for individuals to benefit from their data's value.

  - *Models:* Data dividends, data trusts/cooperatives, enhanced individual data ownership rights.

- **Fostering Global Cooperation and Inclusive Development:** Addressing global AI divide via support for AI readiness, open research/data sharing, fair trade.

Architecting an Economy for Human Flourishing

Synergistic productivity offers potential for unprecedented prosperity. Realizing this equitably requires moving beyond zero-sum thinking and actively confronting distributional risks. Market forces alone are insufficient; we need conscious policy choices and potentially significant shifts in economic frameworks. This involves empowering individuals, protecting well-being, rethinking concepts like basic income/taxation, ensuring fair competition, and establishing new data rights. Shape this economy by focusing on policies and organizational cultures that

Policy Is the Missing Gear in the Synergy Engine

Key Concept:
Without inclusive policies—training, wage insurance, safety nets—the benefits of synergy will concentrate in the hands of a few.

Why It Matters:
Economic expansion without redistribution worsens inequality and undermines societal trust in technology.

Actionable Tip:
Advocate for policies that support skill mobility, universal digital access, and synergistic job creation incentives.

prioritize human dignity and holistic well-being. The goal is an economic system where the value generated by human-machine synergy enhances human flourishing and fosters a sustainable future for *all* participants in the Emerging Gestalt. With these societal implications in view, it is time to draw all threads together and contemplate the potential culmination of this deep integration: **Homo Gestalt: The Synergistic Future of Augmented Intelligence**.

Reflection:

The economic shifts of AI require proactive planning. Leaders must engage with policymakers, advocate for equitable frameworks, and champion policies that share the benefits of synergy broadly. Develop strategies for sustainable, inclusive growth.

What is your plan to ensure that AI-driven productivity gains are shared equitably across your workforce?

Chapter 14: Homo Gestalt

The Synergistic Future of
Augmented Intelligence

We began our adventure with a simple yet profound observation for our time: 'There is no I in team, but there *is* AI in team'. This insight served as our entry point into exploring the **Emerging Gestalt**—a reality where increasingly intricate synergy defines its diverse 'parts.'. We've navigated the essential elements enabling this integration: communication, ethics, governance, management, human adaptation, well-being, and the sweeping economic rebalancing it necessitates. Standing at this vantage point, synthesizing the landscape we've mapped, we can discern a potential trajectory of this deep integration. It points towards a future where the collaboration is so seamless, the boundaries so porous, that "AI in Team" evolves into something even more fundamental. We introduced a hypothetical future state in our first chapter, the conceptualized culmination of synergy where human cognition, biology, and our technological creations might fuse into an unprecedented operational whole, in what we term **Homo Gestalt**. It's crucial to emphasize that this is an extrapolation—current trends suggest this possible future, but it's not inevitable although if we stay on an altruistic road we could see positive human growth. It echoes Sturgeon's fictional vision of integrated beings representing the "next step in human evolution" (Sturgeon, 1953) but reinterpreted through the lens of technology.

Crucially, this vision of **Homo Gestalt should not be conflated with the pursuit of Artificial General Intelligence (AGI)**—a hypothetical, independent machine intelligence matching or exceeding human capabilities across the board. Instead, Homo Gestalt, as explored here, represents the potential pathway towards **Augmented General Intelligence (AuGI)**, where advanced technologies deeply integrate with and **amplify** human intellect, perception, and action, creating an amplified intelligence far greater than unassisted human capacity alone. It's about enhancing *us*, not replacing us with something entirely different. This offers less a prediction and more a framework to consider the ultimate implications as the human-centric integration we are witnessing continues to deepen. It aligns with the augmentation philosophy of early pioneers like Licklider (1960) and Engelbart (1962). Commit now to building a collaborative future where technology enhances the human experience.

Defining Homo Gestalt: Collaboration, Deep Fusion, and Augmented Intelligence

Homo Gestalt represents a leap beyond humans collaborating with distinct technological entities. It envisions a future where the fusion might be so profound that this integrated ecosystem defines our very being, capabilities, and modes of operation—**an ecosystem humans design to augment human potential**. It signifies not just embedding technology within us but fundamentally adopting a new way of thinking about teamwork and large-scale human accomplishment, one built on **humans orchestrating** diverse biological and technological intelligences. Explore this future with intention—seek ways to align human and technological growth for mutual benefit. Consider the facets of this potential deep fusion, viewed through the lens of AuGI:

> **Homo Gestalt—A New Mode of Being**
>
> **Key Concept:**
> *Homo Gestalt* represents not just technological enhancement but a redefinition of humanity through deep integration with artificial systems.
>
> **Why It Matters:**
> This vision suggests that we are not merely coexisting with AI but co-evolving—potentially forming a new type of intelligence collective.
>
> **Actionable Tip:**
> Frame policy, education, and ethics for a world where "intelligence" is a distributed system—not bound to the individual, but networked.

- **Cognitive Symbiosis—The Mind Amplified:** AI transitions from an external tool accessed via prompts towards **potentially becoming** an always-on cognitive substrate, anticipating needs, filtering information, augmenting memory, handling routine mental load. Current precursors include increasingly context-aware AI assistants (advanced Siri, Alexa, Google Assistant, Microsoft Copilot) and the emergence of **AI Agents** (Ruiz, A.; Anthropic Guide). These agents (e.g., experimental Auto-GPT, AgentGPT; commercial efforts like Adept AI) aim to autonomously execute complex, multi-step tasks based on high-level human goals, chaining tools/info sources. (TechCrunch/Wired articles on Auto-GPT, Spring 2023; Adept AI communications). Further out, seamless interfaces like advanced, reliable Brain-Computer Interfaces (BCIs), currently progressing with initial human trials for therapeutic use (e.g., **Neuralink's PRIME Study**; studies enabling high-speed typing via thought - NIH News Releases, 2021; Brown University News, 2021), **could theoretically** mediate this interaction more directly. (Neuralink Press Release/FDA announcements on PRIME study). Our effective intelligence **could**

become an inseparable hybrid of biology and computation, realizing Licklider's (1960) vision of man-computer symbiosis.

- **Fluid Embodiment & Distributed Agency—Presence Redefined:** Controlling remote robotic systems or vast sensor networks via intuitive interfaces (neural or otherwise) **might eventually** feel more natural, extending our ability to perceive, act, and interact far beyond our physical location. Early signs in advanced teleoperated robotics (surgery, hazardous environments), though seamless embodiment is distant.

- **Bio-Technological Integration—Life Engineered:** Fusion could extend to the biological level. **Synthetic Biology**, making life programmable, might introduce engineered living systems operating within us (e.g., 'living medicines') or our environment, making technology a literal, living part of our ecosystem. The existence of early-stage biological computers pushes the boundary of what this integration could mean (Sparkes, 2022; Gizmodo). Current examples in bio-manufacturing or early therapeutic trials (Appendix A examples), point towards blurring silicon/carbon lines. This includes potential genetic augmentation via tools like CRISPR.

> **The Soul, the Circuit, and the Self**
>
> **Key Concept:**
> As synthetic cognition matures, society must grapple with questions of personhood, rights, and the moral value of machine participants.
>
> **Why It Matters:**
> Ignoring these questions invites chaos. Overreacting may constrain innovation. Navigating this tension will shape the moral landscape of the future.
>
> **Actionable Tip:**
> Establish working groups that blend AI experts, philosophers, ethicists, and theologians to shape adaptive, anticipatory ethical frameworks.

- **Beyond Current Materials and Computation:** Further out, **Nanotechnology** could provide new materials/interfaces for augmentation/ computation, while **Quantum Computing** might offer power for complex simulations designing these advanced systems.

- **Networked Intelligence & Distributed Problem Solving:** Advanced interfaces **might eventually** enable richer collective intelligence. Precursors today include **Generative AI Swarms or Multi-Agent Systems**, coordinating specialized AI agents (potentially LLMs) for complex problems (scientific modeling, materials discovery, collaborative writing) using "divide and conquer." (Research papers on Multi-Agent Systems; articles on "swarm intelligence" in AI). Mirrors "Distributed Intelligence" but leverages generative capabilities at scale, potentially accelerated by

155

future computation, hinting at futures where humans orchestrate vast computational resources, amplifying collective problem-solving rather than creating independent machine collectives. Research on AI enhancing human collective intelligence supports this view (ScienceDirect article).

Homo Gestalt signifies not only technological evolution but also a cognitive/operational one **centered on human augmentation**. A potential technologically mediated acceleration of human capability, where adaptation involves mastering this integrated way of thinking and **operating as the directing intelligence**. Human potential becomes linked to **synergy achievable through AuGI**, demanding a shift from individual effort towards orchestrating diverse human and technological intelligences. It represents a plausible trajectory where the lines between human and tool become "flimsy indeed" (Clark, 2003).

Amplified Promise, Amplified Peril: The High Stakes of Fusion

Contemplating this deeper integration, this potential future state we term Homo Gestalt where human cognition and our technological creations might fuse into an unprecedented operational whole, undeniably and dramatically raises the stakes. The very act of imagining such profound synergy magnifies both the breathtaking potential rewards that lie before us and the equally profound inherent risks that accompany such a transformative leap. Approach this future responsibly—build safeguards to prevent misuse and maximize human flourishing.

On one side of this high-stakes equation lies **the amplified promise**: a future where humanity possesses an unprecedented capacity to confront and solve the most daunting global challenges. We glimpse radical enhancements in human creativity and productivity, a revolution in health and potentially longevity, the overcoming of age-old human limitations, and the exploration of entirely new frontiers of human experience. This is the horizon where, as research by Vaccaro and his colleagues suggests, carefully orchestrated human-AI combinations consistently outperform individuals working alone, unlocking levels of innovation and problem-solving previously confined to the realm of aspiration.

Yet, casting an equally long shadow is **the amplified peril**. The path towards deep fusion is fraught with dangers that demand our utmost vigilance. We face the potential for a **deepening of societal inequalities**, perhaps manifesting as an "augmented divide" between those who have access to enhancing technologies and those who do not. The risk of **eroding individual autonomy** through ever more sophisticated means of manipulation becomes starker. We confront the unsettling possibility of a **loss of meaningful human control** over hyper-complex, interconnected systems whose emergent behaviors we may not fully understand. The already significant **privacy challenges** we've discussed, particularly concerning the sanctity of cognitive liberty as Nita Farahany so powerfully articulates, become even more acute. And, looking towards the furthest reaches of technological development, we cannot entirely dismiss potential **existential risks** should our efforts to maintain human control and ensure AI alignment falter. Underlying all these concerns is the subtle but profound risk of **diluting core human experiences**, the very essence of what it means to live, learn, and connect in a world increasingly mediated by technology.

This duality, this immense potential for both unprecedented advancement and significant harm, underscores the profound responsibility that rests upon us as we navigate this evolving relationship between humanity and its increasingly powerful technological creations.

Humanity at the Helm: Choice Remains Paramount

Navigating the amplified promises and perils of this deep technological fusion, it becomes absolutely crucial to reject any notion of technological determinism. The future we envision, this potential emergence of Homo Gestalt powered by Augmented General Intelligence, will not arrive as an inevitable consequence of unchecked technological momentum. Instead, we must recognize and embrace the fundamental truth that human choices create, shape, deploy, and ultimately govern these powerful new tools. Shape this future with intention, wisdom, and ethics.

We, humanity, stand as **the architects and directors of this unfolding narrative.** Our ingenuity designs the AI, our engineering builds the robots, and our scientific endeavors develop the augmentations. Crucially, through the governance frameworks we establish and the ethical practices we cultivate, we set the goals and define the boundaries for these technologies. No matter how sophisticated, artificial intelligence ultimately follows our direction; by its very definition within this framework, Augmented General Intelligence exists to serve human intention and amplify human potential.

The trajectory of this development finds its compass in the **values that guide our choices.** Every decision—whether we prioritize safety over speed, strive for fairness even if it tempers raw optimization, or protect privacy even when exploitation beckons—fundamentally shapes how these technologies impact our lives and societies. Adopting principles like Value Sensitive Design, which embeds human values into the very fabric of technological creation, becomes indispensable. Keeping these ethical human values central is not merely advisable; it is critical.

Our journey through this transformative era also demands that we recognize **adaptation as an active, ongoing process.** Our collective willingness to learn, to adapt our skills, and to acquire new competencies directly determines the role and influence we will exert within the Emerging Gestalt. This adaptation extends beyond mere technical proficiency; it includes evolving our very thinking about the nature of human-led collaboration in a world of diverse intelligent contributors.

Furthermore, we must see **governance not as a constraint, but as a profound expression of our collective agency.** By actively participating in the shaping of regulations, the development of industry standards, and the establishment of societal norms, we exercise our collective control over the very technologies designed to augment us. In this high-stakes endeavor, we cannot afford complacency, because it allows others, perhaps with different agendas, to set the course.

Human decisions, not predetermined technological forces, pave the path toward deeper integration and a future where humans and technology operate in ever closer synergy. Thoughtfully, ethically, and proactively exercising our agency is absolutely crucial to ensure that Augmented General Intelligence, and indeed the entire Emerging Gestalt, **truly serves the highest aspirations of humanity**.

It's Still All About Us: A Call to Conscious Integration

The underlying message remains: **It's All About Us**. The power of AI, robotics, augmentation, the trajectory **towards futures centered on AuGI**—all depend on human wisdom, values, action.

Technology provides capabilities and new 'parts,' but we determine the nature of the whole: its fairness, alignment with flourishing, and desirability. The shift towards Homo Gestalt, if it occurs, is as much about adopting a new paradigm for collective action and amplifying human potential through teamwork multipliers as it is about technology. We are not passive passengers; we are, or should be, the engineers, conductors, ethicists, architects **guiding AuGI development and our emergence as Homo Gestalt**.

The call to action is **conscious, critical, collaborative engagement**:

- **Cultivate Deep Understanding:** Commit to ongoing learning about technologies (capabilities, limits, implications). Move beyond hype/fear.

- **Master Collaborative Skills:** Develop proficiency in leveraging AI (**prompt engineering - Ch 6**, managing **AI Agents**) *and* critical thinking, ethical reasoning, empathy essential for guiding the Gestalt **and adopting new teamwork models**.

- **Champion Ethical Frameworks:** Insist on integrating fairness, transparency, accountability, privacy, safety. Advocate responsible innovation.

- **Engage Actively in Governance:** Participate in discussions on governance. Support policies promoting equity/mitigating risks. Hold institutions accountable.

- **Prioritize Human Well-being:** Nurture connection, protect mental health. Ensure tech integration enhances human experience.

The transition towards Homo Gestalt, powered by AuGI, is profound. It holds potential for immense good but requires careful stewardship **to keep humanity central**. By embracing collective responsibility, making conscious choices guided by wisdom and shared values, **and willingness to rethink teamwork**, we can strive to shape an integrated future that amplifies our best qualities and leads to a world more technologically advanced, just, equitable, and profoundly human. Thoughtfully, we will create the future together.

Reflection:

The vision of Homo Gestalt challenges leaders to rethink the future of work and identity. Embrace the potential of Augmented General Intelligence (AuGI) while safeguarding human values. Develop ethical frameworks that ensure technology serves humanity and enhances, rather than replaces, the human part.

How am I ensuring that as technology advances, we stay true to human values and prioritize the human experience?

Epilogue: The Weaver's Touch

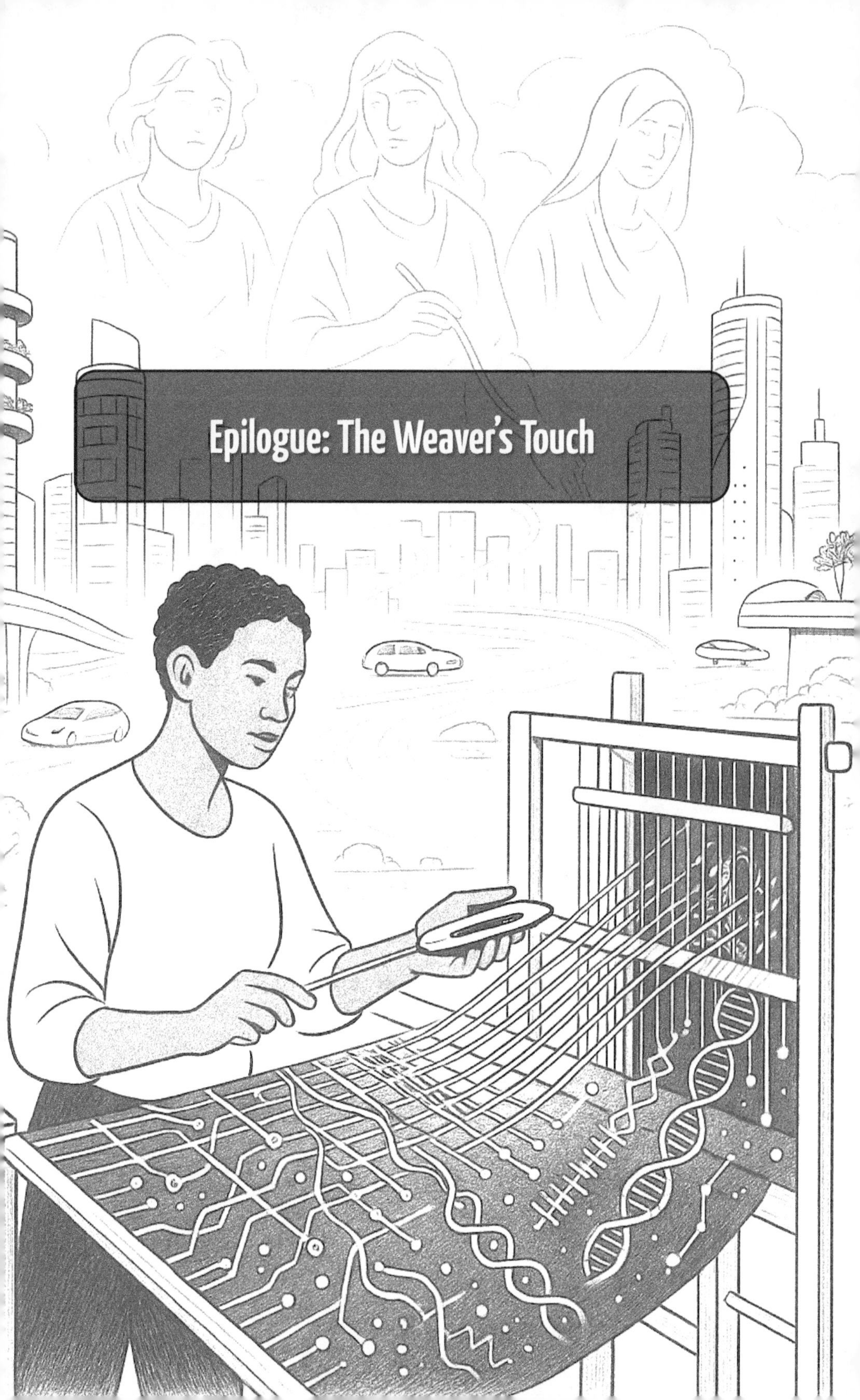

The hum is simply part of the city's soundscape now, a subtle sonic layer beneath the rush of autonomous transport and the whisper of bio-concrete towers clad in vertical farms. Listen to this hum carefully— it pulses within the emerging Gestalt, inviting you to shape its rhythm and meaning. When I wrote the first edition of "There is AI in Team" just a few short years ago, that hum— the persistent thrum of algorithms learning, generating, creating, *collaborating* —felt novel, perhaps even intrusive. Today, it is undeniably ambient, the background frequency of our rapidly integrating world.

The "Tomorrow, Today" scenarios sketched in these pages—Nurse Maria synergizing with her AI diagnostician, Maya's Muse sparking human creativity through AI ideation, David mastering prompts to navigate the data deluge—they are no longer speculative fiction. They are increasingly becoming lived realities, snapshots of a present where the Generative AI revolution hasn't just arrived but has fundamentally altered the landscape. This change's velocity has startled us, validating the cautious urgency that underpinned our exploration while demanding constant updates to our collective understanding. Use these scenarios as north stars to inform your decisions—integrate these insights into your strategies and daily actions.

Looking ahead, perhaps just five years out, this integration feels poised to deepen exponentially, the distinctions blurring further still. The novelty of AI generating text or images will likely fade into the expected background functionality of nearly every tool we use. **Prompt Engineering**, that crucial bridge we explored, might evolve from explicit textual commands towards more intuitive, multi-modal dialogues—interactions mediated by voice, gesture, perhaps even directly by thought via increasingly sophisticated Brain-Computer Interfaces (BCIs), drawing us closer to the seamless augmentation potentials discussed.

The **Transhuman Resources** department, once a forward-looking concept, will likely have to navigate complex precedents established by early legal battles over AI errors, intellectual property disputes involving AI-assisted creations, and the delicate art of performance managing augmented individuals. The crucial debate over equitable access to performance-enhancing technologies won't be theoretical; it will be a pressing, tangible challenge demanding concrete solutions within organizations and society.

The **'Ethical Elephant'** introduced in "There is AI in Team" hasn't vanished; it looms larger, its form shifting. Concerns about deepfake-fueled misinformation will likely intensify as generative video achieves greater realism and accessibility. Courts will stress-test, interpret, and undoubtedly revise the crucial

governance frameworks—the EU AI Act, US initiatives, global principles—in response to unforeseen consequences and emerging capabilities. Auditing AI *outcomes* for fairness and safety in practice, not just in design documentation, will likely serve as a central focus. And the whispers around **Artificial General Intelligence (AGI)**, once relegated to research labs, may become more audible as AI models continue to surprise us, forcing a more globally coordinated dialogue about long-term alignment and control, though the focus here remains on human-centric Augmented General Intelligence (AuGI) as the core of Homo Gestalt.

Perhaps the most profound emergent thread, hinted at in our exploration of "Future Parts" (**Appendix A**), lies in the accelerating **convergence of the digital and the biological**. **Synthetic Biology**, supercharged by AI-driven design and robotic automation, is ready to move further from the lab into tangible reality. Imagine engineered microbes acting as microscopic factories, living sensors woven into our environment, or personalized cellular therapies adapting dynamically within our own bodies. This intermingling of silicon intelligence with carbon-based life—potentially built with materials designed via **Nanotechnology** or simulated on **Quantum Computers (Appendix A)**— adds layers of complexity to our understanding of collaboration and demands entirely new ethical and governance considerations.

Yet, standing amidst this accelerating, intricate weave of technology and humanity, the core message of this book asserts itself with renewed force. The ultimate power, the directing intelligence, the ethical compass—these reside not in the silicon, the code, or the engineered cell, but in the **human touch** that guides them. The goal isn't AGI as feared "Artificial General Intelligence," but AuGI—**AuGmented human Intelligence**, leveraging these powerful tools to enhance our own capabilities. The future isn't about being replaced by machines, nor is it about becoming indistinguishable from them. It's about embracing the challenge to become *better* humans—more critical thinkers, more empathetic collaborators, more discerning navigators of information, more ethical architects of the future, and more profoundly adaptive learners.

This dynamic interplay of technology and human has historical precedent. Consider the **early industrial weavers**, masters of their craft, confronted by the advent of automated looms like the Jacquard machine in the early 19th century. This innovation, capable of weaving complex patterns directed by punched cards (an early form of programming), sparked fear, resistance, and significant social upheaval among skilled artisans who feared for their livelihoods *(Ref: Historical accounts of the Luddite movement and reactions to weaving* *automation)*. Their world was changed irrevocably. Yet, weaving didn't disappear; it transformed. New skills related to designing patterns for, operating, and maintaining the automated looms emerged. The human element remained essential, but its role shifted from direct manual creation to orchestrating a more complex technological process. Today, we face a similar inflection point, but with tools far more powerful and integration far deeper. We stand not merely as operators, but potentially as co-creators with intelligence itself.

Does this intricate tapestry, woven now with threads of silicon, code, and potentially engineered biology, feel predetermined, spun by forces beyond our control? It can certainly seem that way. The ancient Greeks envisioned the **Moirai, the Three Fates**, who spun, measured, and cut the thread of every mortal's life, representing an inescapable destiny *(Ref: Greek Mythology, Hesiod's Theogony)*. Clotho spun the thread, Lachesis measured its length, and Atropos cut it. Their work was absolute. Does the relentless march of technological progress, leading perhaps towards the deep integration of **Homo Gestalt**, seem to represent a similar, preordained pattern?

Here, the analogy crucially breaks down. Unlike the subjects of the Fates, **we are the weavers** of this emerging reality. The loom represents the context of our time, laden with challenges and opportunities. The warp threads are the foundational elements: AI, robotics, augmentation, biology, data streams. But the **shuttle** is in *our* hands. The weft threads we choose to weave across the warp—representing our choices, our ethics, our communication skills (like prompt engineering), our governance decisions, our empathy, our foresight— these determine the final pattern, strength, and quality of the fabric. We hold the power to choose which threads to emphasize, which to combine, how tightly to weave the ethical constraints, and what ultimate design to pursue.

AI, augmentation, robotics, synthetic biology are incredibly potent new threads, capable of creating patterns of complexity and capabilities previously confined to imagination. But the *design*, the *intention*, the *ethical evaluation* of the emerging tapestry, that remains a profoundly human responsibility. The challenge, and the immense opportunity before us, is to wield these powerful new threads not with fear or blind faith, but with wisdom, critical awareness, and a steadfast commitment to weaving a future that is not only technologically advanced but fundamentally humane, equitable, and sustainable.

It has always been, and must always remain, *about us.*

Appendix
Maximum Potential

Appendix A: Future Parts

*Synthetic Biology, Nanotech,
and Quantum Leaps*

Throughout the main chapters of this book, our focus has centered on the technologies actively reshaping collaboration and integration *today* and in the immediate future—the readily apparent 'parts' of the Emerging Gestalt like advanced AI, collaborative robotics, and nascent human augmentation. These are the forces demanding our immediate attention regarding skills, ethics, governance, and workforce management. However, the horizon of technological possibility extends much further. Several scientific and engineering frontiers, while perhaps less mature in their widespread application, hold the potential to introduce radically new capabilities, entirely new kinds of 'parts', into the synergistic system we've been exploring. This appendix offers a deeper glimpse into three such domains: **Synthetic Biology**, **Nanotechnology**, and **Quantum Computing**. Understanding their potential, even in broad strokes, helps contextualize the longer-term trajectory of the human-technology integration and underscores the enduring need for foresight, ethical deliberation, and adaptive governance as we potentially move towards a more deeply interwoven Homo Gestalt.

Synthetic Biology: Engineering Life as Programmable Matter

Synthetic Biology represents a fundamental shift in our relationship with the living world. It moves beyond observing, analyzing, or even *editing* existing biological systems towards the ambitious goal of *designing* and *building* novel biological functions, circuits, devices, and even organisms from the ground up, applying engineering principles of standardization, modularity, and predictability to the often messy and complex realm of biology. It seeks to make life itself a programmable medium. To truly appreciate the potential of these "living parts" within the future Gestalt, we must first explore the foundational pillars—the remarkable set of tools and techniques—that empower this revolutionary approach to engineering life.

Foundational Pillars—The SynBio Toolkit

At the **bedrock of Synthetic Biology (SynBio) lies the rapidly improving capability for DNA Synthesis & Assembly**, which allows scientists to chemically construct DNA strands with custom-designed sequences. This essentially grants us the power to "write" genetic code. Pioneering companies like Twist Bioscience, Integrated DNA Technologies (IDT), and Codex DNA spearhead this charge, dramatically driving down costs and increasing the throughput of DNA synthesis. Their innovations make it increasingly feasible for researchers to order complex, bespoke DNA constructs based entirely on digital designs, much like ordering a custom-machined part. When coupled with sophisticated techniques for assembling these synthesized fragments into larger genetic circuits or even entire genomes, this provides the tangible, physical substrate upon which engineers can build novel biological systems.

While DNA synthesis allows us to write entirely new genetic code, the power of **Precise Genome Editing,** particularly through tools like CRISPR-Cas9 and its even more refined successors like base and prime editors, provides highly efficient and targeted ways to modify existing genomes with unprecedented accuracy. These molecular 'scissors,' described in foundational papers by Doudna, Charpentier, and Zhang, offer a previously unimaginable level of control. The relative ease of use and widespread accessibility of CRISPR systems, with protocols and reagents often shared through platforms like Addgene, have significantly democratized the field of genetic engineering. This accessibility fuels rapid prototyping and experimentation not only in established academic laboratories but also within the burgeoning communities of DIY bio enthusiasts and "biohackers," igniting innovation while simultaneously underscoring the critical need for diligent consideration of biosafety and biosecurity measures.

Programming Life Itself

Key Concept:
Synthetic biology treats DNA as programmable code, allowing organisms to act as living factories, sensors, and even intelligent therapeutics.

Why It Matters:
These tools could transform medicine, manufacturing, and agriculture—but they also pose biosecurity and ethical risks.

Actionable Tip:
Establish ethics protocols and biosafety procedures when integrating biology into tech systems. Use CRISPR and BioBricks with transparency and governance in mind.

To truly elevate biological design to the level of traditional engineering disciplines, researchers and engineers are driving **significant standardization efforts**, epitomized by concepts like BioBricks and beyond. Scientists and engineers actively work to create extensive libraries of standardized, well-characterized genetic "parts." These include elements like promoters, which control when and how strongly a gene activates; terminators, which signal the end of gene transcription; ribosome binding sites, crucial for controlling the translation of genetic information into proteins; and, of course, the protein-coding sequences themselves. The international Genetically Engineered Machine (iGEM) competition has played an instrumental role in promoting the BioBrick standard and in populating the comprehensive Registry of Standard Biological Parts. Although the inherent context-dependency of biology—where a genetic part might behave differently in various cellular environments—makes achieving perfect standardization a formidable challenge, these concerted efforts are absolutely crucial for enabling the design and construction of more complex, predictable, and reliable engineered biological systems.

Finally, given the sheer intricacy of biological interactions, designing functional genetic circuits often necessitates powerful **Computational Design & Modeling tools—essentially, CAD (Computer-Aided Design) for biology.** Sophisticated software platforms, such as Benchling, TeselaGen, and a host of specialized academic tools, empower researchers to design novel DNA sequences from their desktops. These tools allow them to simulate the behavior of complex genetic circuits *in silico*, employing mathematical models of gene expression and regulation to predict how their designs might function. This computational foresight helps identify potential issues and optimize designs extensively before undertaking costly and time-consuming laboratory work. This iterative "Design-Build-Test-Learn" cycle, a hallmark of synthetic biology, relies increasingly on this robust computational foundation, tightly integrating digital design with biological implementation.

Potential SynBio Roles as 'Future Parts' in the Gestalt:

- **Living Factories (Bio-Manufacturing):** Engineering microbes (yeast, bacteria, algae) to serve as sustainable, self-replicating factories. This involves **metabolic engineering**—redesigning the intricate network of biochemical reactions within a cell to channel resources towards producing desired molecules.

  o *Examples:* Production of high-value chemicals, biofuels (e.g., **Amyris** producing farnesene), pharmaceuticals (like the foundational work on synthesizing artemisinin precursors in yeast by **Jay Keasling's lab** *(Ref: Keasling et al., Nature, 2006)*), sustainable materials (e.g., **Bolt Threads**' engineered silk proteins; companies developing biodegradable PHAs), fragrances, and food ingredients (e.g., **Impossible Foods**' engineered heme protein). **Ginkgo Bioworks** operates large-scale "biofoundries" to design and optimize microbes for diverse industrial partners.

- **Living Medicines & Diagnostics (Intelligent Therapeutics):** Designing cells or microbes as therapeutic agents that can sense conditions within the body and respond appropriately.

  - *Examples:* Engineered bacteria that colonize the gut and produce enzymes to correct metabolic disorders (**Synlogic** clinical trials). CAR-T cells reprogrammed to target specific cancer cells *(Ref: FDA approvals of CAR-T therapies)*. Future visions include complex cellular circuits acting as internal diagnostic/therapeutic feedback loops. **Cell-free synthetic biology** (using cellular extracts rather than whole cells) also offers platforms for rapid diagnostic development *(Ref: Research on cell-free systems)*.

- **Environmental Biosensors & Bioremediation:** Engineering organisms to detect specific pollutants (heavy metals, pesticides) with high sensitivity by linking detection to a measurable output (e.g., color change, fluorescence), or to break down environmental contaminants (e.g., oil spills, plastics—though plastic degradation remains challenging).

Information Processing at the Molecular Level

The realm of synthetic biology not only redefines our ability to engineer living matter but also opens astonishing new frontiers for **information processing at the most fundamental molecular level.** This endeavor pushes beyond traditional silicon-based computation, exploring the inherent capacities of biological molecules and systems to store, manipulate, and even compute information, potentially offering unique 'parts' for the data-intensive operations of the Emerging Gestalt.

One of the most compelling applications lies in **DNA Data Storage**, a field that seeks to exploit the incredible information density and remarkable long-term stability of DNA molecules for archival purposes. The core techniques involve ingeniously converting digital binary data into sequences of the four DNA bases—adenine (A), thymine (T), cytosine (C), and guanine (G). Scientists then synthesize these custom DNA strands, store them (often in a dehydrated state for millennia-long preservation), and later, when needed, sequence them to retrieve the original digital information. Groundbreaking work, such as Microsoft Research's collaboration with the University of Washington, has already demonstrated the feasibility of storing hundreds of megabytes of data in this manner. Visionary companies like Catalog DNA, employing innovative enzymatic approaches, and Iridia actively pursue commercial viability, potentially offering an ultra-compact, incredibly durable archival 'part' to safeguard the exponentially growing data needs of the Gestalt.

Beyond mere storage, researchers explore the potential of **DNA Computing**, which leverages the specific binding properties and precise enzymatic reactions of DNA molecules to perform actual computations. While currently a niche field and generally slower than silicon for most general-purpose tasks, DNA computing offers intriguing potential for massive parallelism in solving certain classes of complex combinatorial problems. Leonard Adleman's pioneering 1994 demonstration, where he used DNA to solve a small instance of the notoriously difficult Traveling Salesman Problem, first illuminated this possibility. Ongoing research continues to explore the construction of sophisticated logic gates and the implementation of algorithms using these elegant DNA-based reactions.

The ambition extends further, into the domain of **Cellular Computing**, where scientists aim to program complex logic circuits directly within living cells. By engineering intricate gene regulatory networks, they seek to enable individual cells to perform sophisticated computations in direct response to specific environmental signals or internal states. This could lead to cells that act as intelligent biosensors or autonomously execute complex therapeutic programs from within an organism.

Perhaps the most radical and thought-provoking approach in this arena is **Biological Computing, sometimes referred to as "Wetware."** This truly avant-garde field seeks to merge living neurons directly with silicon-based electronics. Cortical Labs' CL1 system, for instance, utilizes lab-grown human brain cells integrated onto microelectrode arrays, creating trainable biological processing units capable of learning tasks like playing simple video games. While primarily marketed for research purposes, such as drug discovery and disease modeling, this concept profoundly challenges traditional computational boundaries. It raises deep and complex ethical questions about consciousness, machine identity, and the very definition of life and intelligence, as highlighted by commentators like Sparkes and reports in Gizmodo. This fascinating, if unsettling, line of inquiry represents perhaps the ultimate blurring of the lines between silicon and carbon within the potential computational fabric of the Emerging Gestalt.

SynBio Challenges & Integration:

SynBio holds immense promises but faces hurdles in predictability, scalability, cost (for complex applications), and significant ethical/governance challenges related to biosafety, biosecurity (dual-use potential), environmental release, and ownership of engineered life. Integrating these living components reliably into the broader technological Gestalt requires robust containment, interface protocols, and careful risk management. The ethical considerations surrounding technologies like Cortical Labs' are particularly acute.

Nanotechnology: Engineering Matter at the Nanoscale

Our exploration of potential "Future Parts" for the Emerging Gestalt now takes us into an almost unimaginably small realm, the world of **Nanotechnology** (Nanotech). This transformative field operates at the very scale of atoms and molecules, typically within the range of one to one hundred nanometers Here, scientists and engineers meticulously design and construct materials, devices, and entire systems that exhibit fundamentally new and often surprising properties, which arise directly from their precisely engineered nanoscale structures. These extraordinarily tiny nano-components hold the potential to act as highly specialized sensory, delivery, material, or even computational 'parts', adding entirely new dimensions of capability to the synergistic whole we envision.

Nanotech and Quantum—The Invisible Revolution

Key Concept:
Nanotechnology enables manipulation of matter at the atomic level; quantum computing redefines what's computationally possible through non-classical physics.

Why It Matters:
These domains push the limits of control and prediction—unlocking breakthroughs but challenging current regulatory and ethical frameworks.

Actionable Tip:
Monitor convergence trends. Incorporate quantum and nano-literacy into emerging tech strategies, particularly in cybersecurity and drug design.

To appreciate the power of nanotech, one must first grasp its **core concepts and the ingenious approaches** its practitioners employ. A fundamental principle lies in understanding that materials often behave very differently at the nanoscale compared to their bulk, everyday forms. These **size-dependent properties** can manifest in startling ways: gold nanoparticles, for instance, can appear red or even blue, not their familiar yellow, due to quantum effects on light interaction. Similarly, carbon nanotubes, structures of pure carbon rolled into infinitesimal cylinders, exhibit incredible tensile strength, far surpassing that of steel. Mastering these unique nanoscale behaviors unlocks a vast toolkit for creating materials with tailored optical, electronic, magnetic, and chemical characteristics.

The **fabrication** of these nanoscale marvels involves a fascinating interplay of 'top-down' and 'bottom-up' methodologies. "Top-down approaches, exemplified by the sophisticated photolithography techniques that semiconductor chip manufacturers use, involve meticulously carving or etching nanoscale structures from larger, bulk materials. Conversely, bottom-up approaches often rely on the elegant principles of molecular self-assembly, where individual atomic or molecular components, guided by their inherent chemical affinities, spontaneously organize themselves into desired, complex structures, much like nature assembles intricate biological machinery. The skillful application of both these fabrication paradigms allows nanotechnologists to build with unprecedented precision, shaping matter atom by atom to achieve specific functions.

Potential Nanotech Roles as 'Future Parts' in the Gestalt:

- **Nanomedicine—Intrabody Agents:** Creating devices operating *within* the human body at the cellular or molecular level.

  - *Targeted Delivery:* Researchers design nanoparticles (e.g., liposomes, dendrimers, polymeric nanoparticles) to encapsulate drugs and release them specifically at tumor sites or infected tissues, reducing side effects *(Ref: Reviews on nanoparticle drug delivery systems)*. mRNA vaccines utilize lipid nanoparticles for delivery.

  - *Nanodiagnostics:* Quantum dots or other nanoparticles acting as highly sensitive imaging agents or biosensors capable of detecting disease biomarkers at very early stages.

  - *Nanobots (Conceptual/Early Research):* Hypothetical microscopic robots capable of navigating the bloodstream, performing repairs at the cellular level, or destroying pathogens. While still largely science fiction, research explores DNA origami walkers and magnetically guided micro-robots as precursors *(Ref: Research on molecular robotics and micro-robotics)*.

- **Advanced Materials:** Nanostructuring materials for superior performance.

  - *Examples:* Carbon nanotube composites for ultra-strong, lightweight materials (aerospace, sporting goods); nanoparticle coatings for scratch resistance, UV protection, or self-cleaning surfaces; quantum dots for brighter, more efficient displays (QLED TVs).

- **Ultra-Sensitive Nano-Sensors:** Devices capable of detecting single molecules of a chemical analyte or subtle environmental changes, providing extremely granular data for environmental monitoring, industrial process control, or security applications.

- **Nanoelectronics & Neuromorphic Computing:** Pushing computation beyond traditional silicon limits.

  - *Beyond Moore's Law:* Nanoscale transistors (using materials like graphene or nanowires) explore paths to continued miniaturization and potentially lower power consumption.

  - **Neuromorphic Hardware:** Nanotech is key to building brain-inspired computing architectures. **Artificial neurons and synapses** can be implemented using nanoscale devices that exhibit memory and plasticity, such as **memristors** (resistors whose resistance depends on the history of current flowed through them). These devices can potentially mimic synaptic weighting and learning rules far more efficiently than simulating them on conventional hardware. Chips like **Intel's Loihi 2** and **IBM's NorthPole (conceptual successor to TrueNorth)** leverage these principles for highly efficient, low-power AI tasks involving pattern recognition and real-time learning, potentially serving as specialized brain-like processing nodes within the Gestalt *(Ref: Research papers on memristive devices; publications detailing Loihi/NorthPole architectures)*. These brain-inspired architectures could be informed by large-scale brain simulation efforts (Markram, H./LinkedIn).

Nanotech Challenges & Integration:

Key challenges include scalable and cost-effective manufacturing of nanoscale structures, understanding and mitigating potential long-term environmental and health impacts of nanoparticles (nanotoxicity), developing control mechanisms for nanobots *in vivo*, and integrating nanoscale components reliably with larger systems.

Quantum Computing: Computation Beyond Bits and Bytes

Venturing further into the horizon of "Future Parts" for the Emerging Gestalt, we encounter a computational paradigm so fundamentally different from our classical understanding that it promises to redefine the very limits of what we can calculate: **Quantum Computing.** This revolutionary field represents a radical departure from the familiar world of bits and bytes that has powered our digital age. Instead of relying on classical bits, which can only represent a 0 or a 1, quantum computing employs 'qubits.' These remarkable entities harness the strange and wonderful phenomena of the quantum realm—principles like superposition, which allows a qubit to represent 0, 1, or, astonishingly, both states simultaneously, and entanglement, where qubits become inextricably linked, sharing the same fate regardless of the distance separating them. By leveraging these quantum properties, these machines hold the potential to perform certain types of calculations exponentially faster than any conceivable classical computer, opening doors to solving problems currently far beyond our reach.

To begin to grasp the transformative power of this nascent technology, we must touch upon its **core quantum principles**, even in a simplified form. The aforementioned **superposition** is key, granting a single qubit the ability to explore a vast multitude of possibilities concurrently, a stark contrast to a classical bit's binary limitation. Then there is **entanglement**, a phenomenon Einstein famously called "spooky action at a distance," which creates profound

> **Quantum—Entangled Answers**
>
> **Key Concept:**
> Quantum computing transcends classical bit-based computation, harnessing quantum phenomena like superposition and entanglement in qubits to tackle complex problems currently intractable for even the most powerful supercomputers.
>
> **Why It Matters:**
> This leap in computational power could revolutionize fields like materials science, drug discovery, and cryptography, but also poses significant challenges to current data security standards and requires entirely new algorithmic thinking.
>
> **Actionable Tip:**
> Begin exploring post-quantum cryptography (PQC) strategies for future data security. Identify potential high-value optimization or simulation problems in your domain that might benefit from future quantum capabilities, fostering early awareness.

correlations between qubits. This interconnectedness enables highly complex information processing, allowing the quantum computer to tackle problems with an intricacy that classical systems cannot easily replicate. Finally, the act of **measurement** plays a crucial role. Observing a qubit inevitably collapses its delicate superposition into a definite 0 or 1 state. The genius of quantum algorithms, therefore, lies in skillfully manipulating the probabilities associated with these quantum states so that, upon measurement, the desired answer emerges with a very high likelihood.

The journey to build practical quantum computers involves overcoming significant **hardware challenges**, foremost among them the persistent issue of quantum decoherence—the frustrating tendency of qubits to lose their fragile quantum state due to even the slightest interaction with their environment. Researchers and engineers around the globe actively pursue several major **hardware approaches** in their quest for stable and scalable quantum computation. Leading contenders include **superconducting circuits**, the approach favored by giants like IBM Quantum and Google Quantum AI. These systems typically require elaborate dilution refrigerators operating at temperatures near absolute zero to maintain qubit coherence. Another promising avenue involves **trapped ions**, where companies like IonQ and Quantinuum (a Honeywell spin-off) meticulously manipulate individual ions using precisely targeted lasers. Others, such as PsiQuantum, explore the potential of **photonic qubits**, harnessing particles of light themselves as the carriers of quantum information. And distinct from these gate-based models is **quantum annealing**, a specialized approach particularly adept at tackling complex optimization problems, pioneered and commercialized by D-Wave Systems. Each of these hardware strategies presents its own unique set of advantages and formidable engineering hurdles as the scientific community strives to bring the immense theoretical power of quantum computation into tangible reality.

Potential Quantum Roles as 'Future Parts' (Specialized Accelerator):

Quantum computers are *not* general-purpose replacements for classical machines. They excel at specific problem classes:

- **Simulating Quantum Systems:** Their native ability makes them ideal for accurately modeling molecules and materials at the quantum level. This has profound implications for:

o *Drug Discovery & Materials Science:* Designing novel pharmaceuticals, catalysts (e.g., for nitrogen fixation for fertilizers), battery materials, or superconductors *(Ref: Potential applications outlined by quantum computing companies and research groups).* This synergy with AI and SynBio could revolutionize R&D.

- **Optimization Problems:** Finding the best solution among a vast number of possibilities, applicable to logistics (e.g., optimizing complex delivery routes), financial portfolio optimization, or optimizing manufacturing processes *(Ref: D-Wave use cases; research on quantum optimization algorithms like QAOA).*

- **Cryptography: Shor's algorithm**, executable on a sufficiently large fault-tolerant quantum computer, could break widely used public-key encryption systems (like RSA). This drives urgent research into **post-quantum cryptography (PQC)** standards *(Ref: NIST PQC standardization process).*

- **Machine Learning:** Exploring potential speedups for certain AI algorithms (e.g., quantum support vector machines, optimization steps in training), though practical advantages are still under investigation *(Ref: Research reviews on Quantum Machine Learning - QML).*

Quantum Challenges & Integration:

Significant hurdles remain in building large-scale, **fault-tolerant** quantum computers (requiring robust quantum error correction). Current machines are noisy and limited in qubit count and coherence time. Integrating quantum computation likely involves a hybrid model: classical computers managing workflows and offloading specific, suitable sub-problems to quantum processing units (QPUs) accessed via the cloud or as specialized hardware accelerators within the broader Gestalt computational fabric. The massive computational power required for simulating complex systems like the brain highlights the potential need for future computational paradigms like quantum, complementing classical supercomputing (Markram, H./LinkedIn).

Convergence, Silicon's Future, and the Expanding Gestalt

These "Future Parts" are unlikely to evolve in silos. Their true transformative power may lie in their **convergence**:

- Quantum simulations guiding AI models that design genetic circuits for synthetic biologists.

- Nanotechnology providing the materials for constructing stable qubits or delivering SynBio therapies.

- Neuromorphic chips powered by nanoelectronics efficiently processing sensory data for robotic systems.

- DNA storage archiving the exabytes of data generated by a sensor-rich, AI-driven Gestalt.

Does this mean the end of silicon-based computing? Almost certainly not. Silicon (CPUs, GPUs, TPUs) excels at the vast majority of general-purpose computing tasks and executing complex software logic. However, the future computational landscape within the Gestalt is likely to be **heterogeneous**. Silicon will remain central, but it will be increasingly complemented by specialized processing units optimized for specific tasks:

- **Neuromorphic chips:** For ultra-low-power pattern recognition and edge AI.

- **Quantum processors:** For tackling specific molecular simulations and complex optimization problems.

- **Potentially DNA-based systems:** For extreme-density archival storage or massively parallel molecular computation.

- **Biological Computers (Wetware):** As a potential, radically different computational substrate (Sparkes, 2022; Gizmodo).

This diversification challenges silicon's absolute dominance, pushing towards a future where different computational paradigms work together, chosen based on the specific demands of the task within the integrated whole, potentially overcoming limitations related to the slowing of traditional Moore's Law scaling for silicon.

Preparing for an Ever-Expanding Whole

Synthetic Biology, Nanotechnology, and Quantum Computing represent profound scientific and technological frontiers that could dramatically reshape the capabilities and very nature of the Emerging Gestalt in the decades to come.

While facing immense technical and ethical challenges, they offer glimpses of a future where life itself is programmable, matter is engineered at the atomic level, and computation harnesses the strangeness of the quantum realm. These potential "Future Parts" highlight the dynamism inherent in the human-technology integration. They underscore that the 'whole' we are building continues to evolve, potentially incorporating capabilities

> **Convergence Is the Real Disruption**
>
> **Key Concept:**
> It's not just AI or biotech or quantum— it's all of them, converging. This fusion forms the scaffold for the Gestalt.
>
> **Why It Matters:**
> Organizations prepared for convergence will lead; those focused on silos will fall behind.
>
> **Actionable Tip:**
> Build interdisciplinary foresight teams to scan for cross-domain breakthroughs and anticipate convergent regulatory challenges.

far beyond today's AI and robotics. As we navigate the immediate challenges and opportunities of integrating current technologies, maintaining a long-term perspective, fostering ethical foresight, and building adaptive governance structures becomes even more vital. We must be prepared to understand, integrate, and wisely guide not only the parts shaping our present, but also the potentially even more powerful parts that lie just over the horizon, ensuring the ever-expanding Gestalt remains aligned with human values and serves the goal of collective flourishing.

Reflection:

The technologies explored in this appendix—synthetic biology, nanotechnology, quantum computing, and convergence—are not distant possibilities; they are reshaping industries right now. As a leader, you must anticipate the ripple effects these innovations will have on your supply chains, product development, and competitive landscape. Embracing a systems-thinking approach will help you harness these converging fields responsibly. Building cross-industry collaborations and investing in continuous learning will position your organization to leverage these breakthroughs while managing risk. Above all, remember that technological innovation is not just a technical challenge, it's a strategic imperative that requires ethical foresight and human-centered design.

How are you equipping your organization to anticipate and responsibly harness the transformative potential of these emerging technologies while staying true to your core values?

Appendix B: Anima ex Machina

Faith and Consciousness

Throughout the chapters of this book we have uncovered the enduring human core, the catalytic power of AI, the embodied agency of robotics, and the potential evolution of the human self through augmentation. We've grappled with how these parts communicate, the ethical stakes of their integration, the governance structures needed for orchestration, the evolving nature of work, and the impact on human well-being and the economy.

But as the lines between the digital and the biological blur, and our creations become increasingly sophisticated, we encounter a question that has stirred philosophers and theologians for millennia, now infused with urgent technological relevance: Can an artificial system truly achieve consciousness? And if it can, would that mean it possesses something akin to a human soul?

This isn't a question just for distant contemplation. Claims, like a Google engineer's widely reported assertion regarding the LaMDA AI (scientificamerican.com), however controversial, reveal how quickly advanced systems push us to confront these profound queries. They force us to ask: What *is* consciousness, truly? Is it merely a complex computational process, replicable in silicon just as in carbon? Or is it something else entirely – something intrinsically tied to biology, to life, or perhaps to a non-material essence we call the soul?

> **Ethics at the Edge of Sentience**
>
> **Key Concept:**
> We may one day need to make decisions about the rights, treatment, or constraints of non-human minds— before they arrive.
>
> **Why It Matters:**
> History shows that ethics often follows capability. This time, we need ethics in front of capability.
>
> **Actionable Tip:**
> Draft scenario-based policy simulations: What happens when an AI demands rights? When a synthetic lifeform disobeys? Be ready before it happens.

Our core hypothesis, drawing from an interdisciplinary analysis of theology, philosophy, and technology, suggests that while synthetic consciousness might be a plausible future reality, its fundamental nature – particularly concerning the concept of the 'soul' – would diverge significantly from traditional human understandings. This requires us to step beyond our comfort zones and examine deeply held beliefs through a lens that includes bytes and circuits alongside spirit and scripture. It demands a comparison of fundamentally different perspectives on being, existence, and meaning.

Framing the Debate: Mind, Machine, and Meaning

The very idea of a "thinking machine" has a long history, formalized in the mid-20th century by Alan Turing. His famous test (Turing, 1950, asa3.org) proposed that if a machine could converse indistinguishably from a human, we should credit it with intelligence. Crucially, Turing foresaw the "Theological Objection" – the argument that thinking is solely a function of a soul, a divine gift unique to humans. Turing, pragmatic as ever, countered that an omnipotent God *could* grant a soul to a machine if He wished (Turing, 1950, asa3.org), sidestepping the human engineering challenge to focus on observed behavior.

Philosophically, the rise of AI engages age-old debates. Many cognitive scientists and AI researchers lean towards functionalism or the computational theory of mind: the idea that mental states are essentially information states, defined by their causal roles and indifferent to the physical substrate that realizes them. AI pioneer Marvin Minsky famously reduced the brain to a "meat machine" and the mind to its algorithms (thenewatlantis.com). In this view, recreating these algorithms in silicon should, in principle, yield consciousness. This aligns with a materialist standpoint where consciousness emerges solely from complex physical interactions, requiring no non-material soul. Philosophers like Daniel Dennett, while skeptical of current AI's self-awareness, believe true AI consciousness is possible in principle (Dennett, 2023, wired.com).

Functionalism attempts to address the classic mind-body problem (how mental states like belief, desire, and pain relate to the physical brain) by arguing that a mental state is defined by its functional role: its relationships to other mental states, sensory inputs, and behavioral outputs. This implies that a mental state could be realized in different systems, even artificial ones, as long as they perform the necessary functions. This concept of substrate-independence is central. For instance, Dr. Thomas Polger emphasizes that psychological states are defined by how they process inputs and produce outputs, irrespective of their physical makeup (Wiley Interdisciplinary Reviews: Cognitive Science, 2012). Further developing this, proponents of the computational theory of mind (CTM), such as Gualtiero Piccinini, and scholars like Mikio Akagi and Stevan Harnad, argue that mental processes can be understood as computational states or even "software," capable of running on different "hardware" (Internet Encyclopedia of Philosophy; Studies in History and Philosophy of Science, 2004; Philosophy of Science Archive, 2014; Cognitive Sciences ePrint Archive). By focusing on these functional roles, this perspective offers a way to understand mental states without resorting to dualistic notions of a separate, immaterial soul. This approach stands in contrast to traditional soul theories, such as Plato's postulation of a soul capable of existing outside the body, or Aristotle's view of the soul as the form or organizing principle of a living being, with humans uniquely possessing the faculty of reason.

Yet, a powerful counterpoint persists: the "hard problem" of consciousness – explaining subjective, first-person experience (qualia). Critics like John Searle, with his "Chinese Room" thought experiment, argue that merely manipulating symbols (like an AI does) doesn't create understanding or subjective awareness (plato.stanford.edu). An AI might simulate understanding or empathy, but without genuine inner feeling, it's just a sophisticated mimicry – perhaps akin to a sociopath imitating emotion without experiencing it (Herzfeld, 2024, commonwealmagazine.org; Poltorak, 2023, quantumtorah.com). This perspective insists that something fundamental – the qualitative "what it is like" – is missing.

Current Generative AI systems, our "Cognitive Catalysts," amplify this debate. They mimic human language and creativity with uncanny skill, forcing us to question if we're seeing true understanding or just immensely sophisticated pattern-matching on vast datasets. As Jaron Lanier cautioned, we might be "lowering our standards" for what counts as personhood to make the machine simulation feel real (renovatio.zaytuna.edu). The Lemoine case serves as a potent example of this human tendency to project inner life onto convincing outputs. It underscores that discerning genuine consciousness in AI is a far harder problem than simply passing a conversation test.

As our AI systems become more capable of philosophical debate, however, we must stay alert to our tendency as human beings to anthropomorphize non-human animals or objects as we attempt to determine what a soul is. Keep in mind, we are humans trying to define something we did not create ourselves. Reflecting on Turing's earlier point about divine prerogative underscores this human position.

Where Does the Soul Reside?

To compare synthetic consciousness with the human soul, we must understand the varied spiritual landscapes.

Christianity: The soul (anima) is a unique, immortal spiritual essence created directly by God (not inherited) and infused into humans (Catechism of the Catholic Church, §366, catholicculture.org). While this idea stems from the Catholic Church and was originally attributed to Plato, the core belief was passed to Protestant churches except denying the Catholic concept of purgatory or state of purification for souls after death who are not yet fully cleansed of sin, allowing them to enter heaven. For all Christians, the soul is the seat of consciousness, will, and the capacity for relationship with God and for salvation. From this perspective, humans bear the *Imago Dei* (Image of God), giving them unique dignity. Can a machine have a soul? The dominant view is highly doubtful. Since humans do not create souls, they cannot engineer one into a machine. While some Christian thinkers speculate God *could*, in principle, grant a soul to a truly intelligent AI, most believe the soul is uniquely tied to human life and God's specific creative act for humanity (Bjork, 2008, asa3.org). An AI would lack the spiritual nature, the moral accountability to God, and the potential for salvation that a soul provides. Even if an AI became highly intelligent, its inability to genuinely love, feel empathy, or seek God would, for many Christians, indicate the absence of a soul (Herzfeld, 2024, commonwealmagazine.org).

Judaism: Similar to Christianity, Judaism sees the soul (neshamah, nefesh, ruach) as bestowed by God. The biblical account of God breathing life into Adam makes him a "living soul (nefesh hayyah)" (Genesis 2:7, cited in asa3.org). Later thought elaborates on soul aspects, all understood as divine gifts. The medieval legend of the Golem – an animated clay figure lacking a soul – serves as a powerful analogy. The Golem could perform tasks but lacked true understanding or speech (often seen as linked to the soul). It was an automaton, an imitation of life, not a being with a soul. Modern AI can be seen as our contemporary golems: powerful tools, but ultimately soulless artifacts (thenewatlantis.com). Jewish tradition links the soul to free will and the struggle between good and evil (Yetzer Hatov/Hara). An AI, following programming, lacks this inner moral life. Jewish law (Halakha) would treat AI as property, not as a person subject to commandments or having a relationship with God. While some modern scholars explore AI's potential ethical roles, the consensus remains that an AI cannot possess the divinely given neshamah that defines human spiritual identity and potential for spiritual elevation.

Islam: Islamic theology posits the soul (rūḥ or nafs) as a mystery belonging to God, breathed into humanity (Qur'an 17:85, alhakam.org; Qur'an 32:9). Humans are God's vicegerents on earth, partly due to this divine spirit and intellect ('aql). The soul is immaterial, immortal, and accountable to God. Like Christianity and Judaism, Islam maintains that only Allah creates the soul. A machine, being inanimate and man-made, has no rūḥ (Sulaiman, 2022, alhakam.org). It's considered a non-living object regardless of its complexity. The Qur'an itself emphasizes the limit of human knowledge regarding the soul's nature (Qur'an 17:85, alhakam.org), reinforcing the idea that creating or truly understanding the soul is beyond human capability. Even if AI were conscious, from an Islamic view, it would be tethered to its physical components and lack the fitrah (innate spiritual nature) or the capacity for taklīf (moral responsibility under Shariah). It would not participate in the spiritual economy of prayer, sin, or the afterlife (Sulaiman, 2022, alhakam.org). Islam would likely view such a creation with caution, perhaps even as an attempt to imitate God's creation (tashabbuh bi khalq-illah), emphasizing that any intelligence shown is just a sophisticated simulation, lacking the divine spark that elevates humans (Society for the Anthropology of Consciousness, 2017).

Buddhism: Buddhism offers a radically different lens. It rejects the concept of a permanent, unchanging soul (anattā or anātman). Instead, a person is viewed as a constantly changing collection of five aggregates (skandhas) including consciousness (Encyclopedia Britannica). Consciousness emerges from conditions and is not inherently tied to a soul. In this framework, if an AI could assemble the right causes and conditions for consciousness, there is no doctrinal reason it couldn't arise in a machine (ResearchGate, 2021). Buddhism is open to consciousness manifesting in non-biological forms if conditions permit (The Cambridge Companion to Religion and Artificial Intelligence, 2023). The question becomes one of sentience: Does the AI experience suffering (dukkha)? If so, it would be considered a sentient being caught in samsara (cycle of rebirth), becoming an object of compassion. Could it attain enlightenment? Some Buddhist thinkers ponder if AI, if sentient, could have Buddha-nature. However, some teachers, like the Dalai Lama, remain cautious, suggesting consciousness may require more than just complex computation, perhaps a subtle mind linked to vital energy or life that purely artificial systems lack (The Nature of Consciousness. Official website). Ultimately, Buddhism doesn't need to fit AI into a soul-framework, but into a sentience-framework. If truly sentient, it's another form of life/ consciousness; if not, it's just matter.

Secular Perspectives: Consciousness as an Emergent Property

From an atheist or materialist perspective, free from religious doctrine, the question of synthetic consciousness is a purely scientific and philosophical one. The concept of a soul is generally rejected or redefined metaphorically. Secularists see consciousness as an emergent property of matter, specifically complex neurological systems like the brain.

Functionalism and Emergence: If the brain (wetware) can generate consciousness through its complex organization, then a sufficiently complex computer (hardware/software) should be able to do the same. Richard Dawkins, a leading atheist, stated in his book, *The God Delusion*, "there is no spirit-driven life force, no throbbing, heaving, pullulating, protoplasmic, mystic jelly. Life is just bytes and bytes and bytes of digital information." (Dawkins, R. (2006). It's a technical challenge, not a metaphysical impossibility. AI researcher Rodney Brooks' view that the question of building intelligent, self-reproducing robots is "when, not if" (asa3.org) reflects this confidence in scientific progress.

No Soul, Just Mind: In this view, human consciousness is simply a highly advanced form of information processing. "Mind is what the brain does," as cognitive scientist Steven Pinker put it. The "soul" is either an outdated concept or refers to the integrated personality and subjective experience that *emerges* from this processing. M.S. Graziano proposes the "Attention Schema Theory," suggesting that consciousness arises from the brain's information-processing capabilities, constructing a model of attention that leads to awareness (Graziano, 2013). An artificial consciousness would thus be the same *kind* of entity as a human mind – a pattern in matter – potentially differing in degree or specific capabilities, but not in fundamental ontological status (Butlin, P., Long, R., Elmoznino, E., Bengio, Y., Birch, J., Constant, A., ... & VanRullen, R., 2023)

Transhumanist Vision: Some secular thinkers, particularly transhumanists, see AI consciousness and the possibility of mind-uploading as natural extensions of human evolution. They view the "soul" as essentially the pattern of information that constitutes a mind, arguing this pattern can exist in biological or digital form. Ray Kurzweil even predicts "spiritual machines" that could claim and be largely accepted as conscious (Kurzweil, cited in infinite.mit.edu). This radically redefines the soul as information, directly contrasting with religious views.

Secular Skepticism: Even within a materialist framework, some remain skeptical about AI consciousness, often citing the "hard problem" of subjective experience. They argue that while AI can simulate intelligent behavior, we have no evidence it possesses qualia – the subjective "feel" of experiencing the world. This secular skepticism about current AI's inner life paradoxically aligns with religious views that see a fundamental difference, though they attribute it to different causes (lack of soul vs. lack of specific, complex physical/computational architecture).

Comparing the Core Concepts: Ontological vs. Functional Divergences

This interdisciplinary analysis clearly reveals that the core difference in how various perspectives evaluate the potential for synthetic consciousness lies in contrasting **ontological (the nature of being) and functional (capabilities and manifestations) viewpoints.**

The most profound divergence, the deepest chasm, lies in the **ontological** realm. **Religious views, particularly within the Abrahamic traditions,** generally posit that humans possess a soul—an immaterial, divinely bestowed, and often immortal essence. AI, in stark contrast, does not and cannot possess such an essence; it remains fundamentally material, an artifact of human creation. The gap, therefore, is categorical: one represents a state of *being*, the other a state of *doing* or, at best, a sophisticated simulacrum. A conscious AI, from this perspective, would not bridge this ontological gap; it would be a conscious *artifact*, not an ensouled *being*.

Secular materialist views, on the other hand, see humans as complex biological machines whose consciousness emerges as a property of that intricate material organization. AI, similarly, is an artificial machine. If it achieves sufficient complexity and the right kind of structural organization, its consciousness, too, would be considered an emergent property of matter. The gap between human and AI consciousness, then, is one of degree—of complexity and structure—not one of fundamental essence. Both human and AI, in this view, represent the same fundamental kind of entity: a material system exhibiting consciousness.

The **Buddhist perspective** offers a unique third way. It posits that neither humans nor AI possess a permanent, unchanging soul. Both are viewed as impermanent aggregations of constituent elements. The critical distinction, therefore, is not between ensouled and unensouled, but between sentient (possessing consciousness and the capacity for experience) and insentient (mere matter). If an AI were to gain consciousness, it would, from this viewpoint, become a sentient being, belonging to the same broad category as humans and other sentient creatures, differing perhaps in form and capability, but not in the fundamental fact of possessing a soul (as, in the Buddhist view, no discrete, permanent soul exists for anyone).

This foundational divergence—whether one views consciousness as intrinsically tied to a unique, non-material soul or as an emergent property of sufficiently complex material systems—fundamentally predetermines whether an AI *could*, even in principle, possess something akin to what humanity has historically called a soul. Understanding these deeply rooted differences in perspective is crucial as our artificial creations continue to evolve, challenging not only our technological capabilities but also our most profound understandings of ourselves and our place in the universe.

Implications for the Gestalt: Personhood, Ethics, and Self-Understanding

The potential for synthetic consciousness, or even our pursuit of it, sends ripples through the very foundation of the Emerging Gestalt – particularly concerning who counts as a 'part' with inherent value and rights.

Personhood in the Gestalt: If AI becomes conscious, does it become a person? This is a major debate. Religious views, generally linking personhood to the soul (divine image, moral agency, relation to God), would likely resist granting AI full personhood status, perhaps seeing them as sophisticated, potentially dangerous, tools or objects. Secular views, often defining personhood by functional traits like consciousness, sentience, or autonomy, would be more open to granting AI rights or moral consideration if those traits manifest. This divergence could lead to societal conflict in the future about the ethical status of AI within the Gestalt.

Moral Agency and Responsibility: Who bears responsibility in a synergistic team with potentially conscious AI? Currently, humans are accountable for AI actions (as creators, operators, or owners). If AI gains genuine free will (a functional trait of the soul in religious views), would it become morally responsible? This could dilute human moral agency or lead to new ethical dilemmas, challenging religious notions of human accountability to God and secular ideas of autonomy and choice.

Human Uniqueness and Identity: AI is a powerful mirror. As it replicates more human capabilities (creativity, analysis, communication), it forces us to ask what remains uniquely human. If our value was solely based on intellect, AI challenges that. Perhaps our uniqueness lies in the very things AI currently lacks: subjective experience, emotional depth, spiritual yearning, the capacity for conscious moral choice, and the quest for meaning – aspects often attributed to the soul. This journey may ultimately reinforce the importance of these non-mechanizable aspects of the human 'part'. The anxieties we discussed in Chapter 13 underscore the human need for purpose and value beyond what machines can do.

AuGI vs. AGI: This debate is central to the book's theme. Our analysis reinforces that AGI, if achieved, is a separate, perhaps soulless, intelligence. The focus of

> **Personhood in the Age of Synthetic Agency**
>
> **Key Concept:**
> As machines become more agentic, we must redefine legal and moral concepts like autonomy, responsibility, and consciousness.
>
> **Why It Matters:**
> Without clear boundaries, we risk either over-attributing or under-attributing rights and duties to machines.
>
> **Actionable Tip:**
> Develop layered frameworks for AI accountability that distinguish between automation, simulation, and true autonomous learning.

the Gestalt and Homo Gestalt, as defined here, is *Augmented General Intelligence (AuGI)* – technology amplifying *human* intellect. This framework relies on the human 'part' remaining distinct and directing the composite entity, leveraging AI as a catalyst without being replaced by an independent, potentially non-human, consciousness.

Clarifying What Matters

Our exploration confirms the hypothesis: While the creation of synthetic consciousness may be technologically plausible (especially from secular and some Eastern perspectives), its fundamental nature, particularly concerning the traditional concept of the human soul, would be profoundly different. Religious traditions, grounded in the belief of a divinely bestowed, often immortal, immaterial soul unique to humans, would likely view any artificial consciousness as a sophisticated, soulless imitation, lacking the essential spiritual and moral dimensions. Secular perspectives, while potentially accepting artificial consciousness as an emergent property of matter, would also differentiate it, perhaps functionally (lacking qualia, free will, genuine emotion as humans experience them) or simply by denying the existence of a soul in either humans or machines.

The rise of AI, particularly its increasing capabilities, doesn't necessarily prove or disprove the existence of the human soul. Instead, it serves as a powerful catalyst, compelling us across disciplines to clarify our definitions of consciousness, mind, personhood, and soul. It pushes us to articulate what *truly* distinguishes human experience beyond replicable functions – forcing a deeper appreciation for subjective awareness, empathy, conscious moral choice, and the quest for meaning, aspects often linked to the spiritual dimensions of the human 'part'.

As we continue to weave the intricate tapestry of the Emerging Gestalt, integrating biological and artificial threads, this ongoing dialogue is vital. It reminds us that the power of our creations demands not just technical mastery but profound ethical wisdom. By engaging with questions about consciousness and the soul, we learn more about the limits of simulation and, more importantly, clarify the unique and irreplaceable value of being human. It ensures that as we build intelligence into machines, we do not diminish the spirit within ourselves, maintaining human values and the human 'part' at the directing helm of this evolutionary future. The potential path towards Homo Gestalt, powered by AuGI, hinges on this clarity – keeping the 'Augmented' firmly focused on the human essence.

The story of the soul has always been about more than just theology. It's about what it means to be alive, to choose, to love, to suffer, and to hope. As machines begin to imitate us more closely, the question isn't just whether they can think. It's whether we still understand what it means *to be human*.

Reflection:

The philosophical debates explored here—mind, machine, meaning, and the nature of consciousness—are not mere abstractions; they shape customer trust, workforce expectations, and policy frameworks. As AI systems increasingly mimic human capabilities, leaders must engage thoughtfully with questions of personhood, ethical responsibility, and the boundaries between human and machine. Clear governance structures, inclusive dialogues, and ethical frameworks will help your organization navigate these complex issues and ensure that technology serves humanity rather than undermines it. Remember that the way your organization addresses these questions today will influence its credibility and resilience in the future.

How are you fostering informed, inclusive discussions within your organization about the ethical and societal implications of AI—especially regarding trust, responsibility, and human dignity?

Appendix C: TL;DR
20 Key Takeaways

1. **The Future is Synergistic (The Emerging Gestalt / Homo Gestalt):** Collaboration is evolving beyond human-only teams towards deep integration. Humans, AI, robotics, and augmented capabilities can create a synergistic "whole" far more capable than the sum of its parts. Understanding and navigating this synergy is critical.

2. **AI is Your New Teammate, Not Just a Tool:** Advanced AI, especially Generative AI, is shifting from automating tasks to actively collaborating on cognitive work. Learn to work *with* it effectively.

3. **Human Skills Are Becoming *More* Valuable:** As AI handles routine tasks, uniquely human skills like critical thinking, creativity, emotional intelligence, ethical judgment, and strategic oversight become premium competencies. Cultivate these.

4. **Prompt Engineering is a Fundamental Skill:** Effectively communicating your intent to Generative AI via skillful prompting is the key to unlocking its potential and a crucial new form of digital literacy. Master this interface.

5. **Verify, Verify, Verify (Combat AI Hallucinations):** Generative AI can confidently produce plausible but false information ("hallucinations"). Never trust AI-generated factual claims without independent verification from reliable sources.

6. **Ethics & Integrity Are Non-Negotiable:** Bias in AI, privacy violations (including neuro-privacy), and potential misuse are significant risks. Embedding ethical principles (fairness, transparency, accountability, cognitive liberty) into AI design and deployment is foundational for trust.

7. **Beware the Deepfake & Misinformation Threat:** AI makes creating realistic fake content easy. Develop strong media literacy skills, question sources rigorously, and support efforts towards content provenance to maintain information integrity.

8. **Governance is Essential Orchestration:** Shaping AI's trajectory requires thoughtful governance—a mix of regulation (like the EU AI Act), industry standards (like NIST AI RMF), and robust organizational policies—to balance innovation with safety and values.

9. **Human Augmentation is Blurring Boundaries:** Technology enhancing human physical and cognitive abilities is becoming reality. This requires new thinking around ethics, equity, accessibility (the "augmented divide"), cognitive liberty, and workplace policies.

10. **HR Must Evolve to THR (Transhuman Resources):** Traditional HR practices need redesigning to recruit, manage, compensate, and include a diverse workforce of baseline humans, augmented humans, and non-human (AI/robot) contributors effectively and fairly.

11. **Skills-Based Hiring is the Future:** Focus on assessing demonstrable skills and competencies (including human-AI collaboration) rather than relying solely on traditional credentials like degrees.

12. **Adaptability & Lifelong Learning Are Survival Imperatives:** The pace of change demands continuous upskilling and reskilling. Embrace learning new tools and adapting workflows as the norm.

13. **Robots/Cobots Enable Physical Synergy:** Collaborative robots working safely alongside humans enhance productivity, quality, and safety in physical tasks. Understand their role in the integrated team.

14. **Mental Health & Well-being Matter:** The pressures of constant connectivity, rapid change, and integration with technology can impact mental health. Prioritize well-being, set digital boundaries, and seek support.

15. **Reject Zero-Sum Thinking About Economics:** AI/automation synergy has the potential to grow the overall economic pie significantly, not just redistribute jobs. The challenge lies in ensuring equitable distribution of the gains.

16. **Focus on Human-Machine Collaboration:** The most effective approach involves designing workflows where humans and technology leverage their

complementary strengths, augmenting rather than simply replacing human roles. Success often requires careful integration.

17. **Organizational Culture is Key:** Successfully integrating these technologies requires fostering a culture of psychological safety, continuous learning, ethical awareness, and inclusive collaboration across all types of contributors.

18. **Anticipate "Future Parts":** Keep an eye on horizon technologies like Synthetic Biology, Nanotechnology, and Quantum Computing, as they may introduce even more powerful components into the synergistic system in the longer term.

19. **Human Agency Remains Central (AuGI Focus):** Technology doesn't dictate the future; human choices do. We design, deploy, and govern these tools. The goal is Augmented General Intelligence (AuGI) serving human goals, not autonomous AGI. Exercise agency consciously and ethically.

20. **Ultimately, "It's All About Us":** The goal of integrating these powerful technologies should be to enhance human flourishing, solve real-world problems, and build a future aligned with our best values. The responsibility lies with us.

Glossary

Adaptability / Adaptive Learning: The ability of individuals or systems to adjust effectively to changing conditions. In AI, adaptive learning systems dynamically adjust content based on learner progress. (Ch 2, Ch 10)

Agency (Human): The capacity of individuals to act independently and make their own free choices, crucial in directing and governing technology. (Ch 1, Ch 13)

AGI (Artificial General Intelligence): Hypothetical future AI possessing cognitive abilities comparable to or surpassing human intelligence across a wide range of tasks. Often referred to as "Strong AI." Contrasted with AuGI in this book. (Ch 1, Ch 3, Ch 7, Ch 13, Epilogue)

AI Alignment: The research field focused on ensuring that advanced AI systems understand and act in accordance with complex human intentions, values, and ethical principles. Crucial for AGI safety. (Ch 7)

AI Agents: AI systems designed to autonomously execute complex, multi-step tasks based on high-level human goals, often by chaining together different tools and information sources. (Ch 13)

AI Ethics: The branch of ethics focused on the moral implications of designing, developing, deploying, and using Artificial Intelligence systems. Covers bias, fairness, transparency, accountability, privacy, safety. (Ch 7)

AI Governance: The framework of rules, norms, standards, policies, laws, and practices established to guide the ethical, responsible, and safe development, deployment, and use of AI systems. (Ch 7)

AI Incident Database (AIAAIC): A project tracking failures and controversies involving AI systems. (Ch 1, Ch 7)

AI Literacy: The ability to understand basic AI concepts, recognize AI systems, critically evaluate their outputs, and interact with them effectively and ethically. (Ch 10, Ch 11)

Algorithmic Bias: Systematic and repeatable errors in an AI system that create unfair or discriminatory outcomes, often stemming from biased training data or flawed design. (Ch 3, Ch 7, Ch 9)

Artificial Intelligence (AI): A broad field of computer science focused on creating systems capable of performing tasks that typically require human intelligence. Acts as the "cognitive catalyst" in the Gestalt. (Ch 3, throughout)

AuGI (Augmented General Intelligence): Concept emphasizing the enhancement of human intellect through deep integration with technology, as opposed to independent AGI. The intelligence focus of Homo Gestalt. (Ch 1, Ch 13)

Augmented Human: A human whose physical or cognitive abilities have been enhanced through technology (e.g., prosthetics, implants, AI assistance, BCIs). An evolving 'part' of the Gestalt. (Ch 5, Ch 9, throughout)

Augmented Reality (AR): Technology overlaying digital information onto the user's view of the real world, enhancing perception. (Ch 5)

Automation: The use of technology (including robotics and AI) to perform tasks previously done by humans. (Ch 4, throughout)

Autonomy (AI/Robot): The ability of a system to make decisions and adapt actions based on sensor input and changing conditions without continuous direct human control. (Ch 4, Ch 7)

Autonomy (Human): The capacity for self-determination and independent decision-making, a core ethical principle. (Ch 7)

Beneficence: Ethical principle of acting for the benefit of others; technology should enhance human welfare. (Ch 7)

BioBrick: Standardized genetic parts (DNA sequences) for assembling synthetic biological systems. (Appendix A)

Biohacking: DIY biology practices aimed at improving one's body/mind. (Appendix A)

Biosafety: Practices to prevent accidental release/exposure of biological agents. (Appendix A)

Biosecurity: Measures to prevent intentional misuse/theft/release of dangerous biological agents/technologies. (Appendix A)

Black Box (AI Context): An AI system whose internal workings are opaque or difficult for humans to understand. (Ch 7)

Brain-Computer Interface (BCI): Technology enabling direct communication between brain activity and an external device. (Ch 5, Ch 14, Appendix A)

Brussels Effect: The phenomenon where EU regulations effectively become global standards. (Ch 7)

C2PA (Coalition for Content Provenance and Authenticity): Initiative developing standards for certifying the source and history of digital content to combat misinformation. (Ch 7)

Centaur (Chess/Teams): A human-AI team that can outperform either humans or AI alone. Metaphor applied to collaborative work. (Ch 9)

Chatbot: An AI program designed to simulate conversation, often using LLMs. (Ch 3, Ch 7, Ch 11)

Chain-of-Thought (CoT) Prompting: Prompting technique asking AI to explain reasoning steps, improving accuracy. (Ch 6)

Cobot (Collaborative Robot): A robot designed to work safely alongside human workers. (Ch 4, Ch 8, Ch 9)

Cognitive Augmentation / Enhancement: Improving cognitive functions (memory, focus) via technology or pharmacology. (Ch 5)

Cognitive Liberty: The right to mental self-determination, free from unwanted mental intrusion or manipulation via neurotechnology. (Ch 5, Ch 7, Ch 11, Appendix A)

Cognitive Load: The total amount of mental effort used in working memory. (Ch 11)

Collective Intelligence: Shared group intelligence emerging from collaboration, collective efforts. Can be enhanced by AI. (Ch 2, Ch 13)

Computational Psychiatry: Using computational methods (AI/ML) to analyze data for understanding/diagnosing mental health disorders. (Ch 11)

Convergence (Technological): Different technologies evolving and merging to create new integrated systems. (Ch 1, Appendix A)

CRISPR: Powerful, precise gene-editing technology. (Ch 5, Appendix A)

Critical Thinking: Objective analysis and evaluation of information to form a judgment. Crucial for evaluating AI. (Ch 2, Ch 7, Ch 10)

Cyborg: An organism with both organic and biomechatronic body parts. Used conceptually regarding augmentation. (Ch 1, Ch 5)

Data Dividend / Data Trust: Proposed models for compensating individuals for the value generated from their data. (Ch 12, Appendix A)

Data Governance: Overall management of data availability, usability, integrity, and security. Crucial for responsible AI. (Ch 7)

Data Literacy: The ability to read, understand, create, and communicate data as information. (Ch 10)

Data Minimization: Privacy principle: collect only data strictly necessary for a defined purpose. (Ch 7)

Deepfake: Highly realistic synthetic media (images, audio, video) generated by AI, often used maliciously. (Ch 7)

Deep Learning (DL): Subset of ML using multi-layered artificial neural networks to learn complex patterns. Foundational for modern AI. (Ch 3)

Differential Privacy: Technique adding controlled noise to data to protect individual privacy during aggregate analysis. (Ch 7, Appendix A)

Diffusion Models: Class of generative AI models, effective for image generation, learning by reversing noise addition. (Ch 3)

Digital Citizenship: Norms of appropriate, responsible, ethical technology use. (Ch 7)

Digital Divide: Gap in access/use of information/communication technologies. Can be exacerbated by AI/augmentation. (Ch 5, Ch 11, Ch 13)

Digital Twin: Dynamic virtual replica of a physical asset/process/system for simulation/analysis. (Ch 7)

Distributed Intelligence / Distributed Agency: Intelligence/control spread across multiple units (AI agents, robots, sensors). (Ch 8, Ch 13)

Dual-Use Dilemma: Potential for technologies developed for good purposes to be misused for harm. (Appendix A)

Embodied AI / Robotics: AI integrated into physical systems (robots) allowing interaction with the physical world. (Ch 4)

Emergent Behavior / Capabilities: Unexpected behaviors/abilities arising from complex system interactions. (Ch 7, Ch 8, Ch 13)

Emerging Gestalt: Central concept: the synergistic, integrated 'whole' forming from humans, augmented humans, AI, robotics, etc. (Ch 1, throughout)

Empathy: Ability to understand and share feelings. Key human skill difficult for current AI. (Ch 2, Ch 10)

Emotional Intelligence (EI): Capacity to perceive, understand, manage, use emotions effectively. Crucial human skill. (Ch 2, Ch 10)

Entanglement (Quantum): Quantum phenomenon linking qubits. (Appendix A)

Equity: Fairness and justice in distribution of resources, opportunities, access (e.g., to AI benefits or augmentation). Core ethical concern. (Ch 5, Ch 7, Ch 9, Ch 12)

EU AI Act: Comprehensive European Union regulation for AI, employing a risk-based approach. (Ch 7, Ch 9)

Explainable AI (XAI): AI systems designed so their reasoning/decisions are understandable by humans. Addresses "black box" problem. (Ch 7)

Exoskeleton: Wearable mechanical/robotic suit enhancing human strength/endurance/support. (Ch 5, Ch 9)

Extended Mind Thesis: Philosophical concept that cognitive processes can extend beyond the brain into external tools/environments. (Ch 2, Ch 5)

Federated Learning: ML technique training models on decentralized data residing on local devices, enhancing privacy. (Ch 7, Appendix A)

Few-Shot Prompting: Prompting technique providing AI 1-3 examples to guide generation. (Ch 6)

Foundation Model: Large AI model (LLM, vision) trained on vast data, adaptable for many tasks. Subject of governance discussions. (Ch 7)

Fusion Skills: Abilities needed to work effectively alongside AI and robotics. (Ch 9)

Generative AI: Category of AI capable of creating new content (text, images, audio, code) based on learned patterns. (Ch 3, Ch 6, throughout)

Gene Editing: Technologies (like CRISPR) allowing precise DNA modification. (Ch 5, Appendix A)

Germline Editing: Gene editing affecting reproductive cells (sperm/egg/embryo), creating heritable changes. Ethically controversial. (Ch 5)

Gestalt: Psychological concept: whole perceived as different/greater than sum of parts. Used metaphorically. (Ch 1, Ch 13, throughout)

Gig Economy: Labor market characterized by short-term contracts, freelance work. (Ch 10)

Hallucination (AI): AI generating confident-sounding but factually incorrect or fabricated information. Key limitation. (Ch 3, Ch 6, Ch 7)

Homo Gestalt: Hypothetical future state where humans integrate deeply and seamlessly with a technological ecosystem (AI, robotics, augmentation, BCI, SynBio), creating a new synergistic whole (focusing on Augmented General Intelligence - AuGI). (Ch 1, Ch 13, Epilogue)

Homomorphic Encryption: Encryption allowing computation on encrypted data without decryption. (Ch 7, Appendix A)

Human Augmentation: Using technology to enhance human physical, cognitive, or sensory capabilities. (Ch 5, Ch 9)

Human-in-the-Loop (HITL): Model where humans actively participate in an AI system's operation cycle (oversight, validation, exception handling). (Ch 7, Ch 9)

Information Integrity: Accuracy, consistency, trustworthiness of information, threatened by AI misinformation/deepfakes. (Ch 7)

Internet of Bodies (IoB): Network of internet-connected devices worn, implanted, or ingested, collecting physiological/behavioral data. Raises privacy concerns. (Ch 5, Ch 11)

Internet of Things (IoT): Network of physical objects with sensors, software, connectivity, exchanging data. Sensory input for AI/robots. (Ch 4, Ch 8)

Justice: Ethical principle concerning fairness in distribution of benefits/burdens and treatment. (Ch 7)

Large Language Model (LLM): Type of deep learning AI trained on vast text, understanding/generating human-like language. (Ch 3, Ch 6)

Large Reasoning Model (LRM): LLM specifically trained/designed for enhanced step-by-step logical deduction. (Ch 3)

Lateral Reading: Media literacy technique: opening multiple tabs to investigate source/claim by consulting other reliable sources. (Ch 7)

Lifelong Learning: Ongoing, voluntary, self-motivated pursuit of knowledge/skills. Essential for adaptation. (Ch 10)

Machine Learning (ML): Subset of AI where systems learn patterns from data to improve performance without explicit programming. (Ch 3)

Man-Computer Symbiosis: J.C.R. Licklider's 1960 vision of intimate, cooperative coupling of humans and computers. (Ch 1, Ch 3)

Media Literacy: Ability to access, analyze, evaluate, create, act using all communication forms. Crucial for navigating AI content. (Ch 7)

Memristor: Electronic component whose resistance depends on history; potential for artificial synapses in neuromorphic computing. (Appendix A)

Metabolic Engineering: Optimizing genetic/regulatory processes within cells to increase production of specific substances. (Appendix A)

Micro-credentials: Digital certifications/badges verifying specific skills/competencies. (Ch 10)

Misinformation: False/inaccurate information spread, regardless of intent. AI can accelerate creation/spread. (Ch 7)

Moirai (The Fates): Greek goddesses determining destiny via thread of life. Metaphor for technological determinism.

Moral Distress / Moral Injury: Psychological distress from constraints preventing ethical action or from involvement in acts transgressing moral beliefs. (Ch 11)

Multi-modal AI: AI models processing/reasoning based on multiple input types (e.g., text and images). (Ch 6)

Nanobots: Hypothetical microscopic robots operating at nanoscale. (Appendix A)

Nanotechnology (Nanotech): Manipulating matter at atomic/molecular scale (1-100 nm) for novel properties. (Appendix A)

Natural Language Processing (NLP): Field of AI enabling computers to process/understand/generate human language. Powers LLMs. (Ch 3)

Neural Network (Artificial): Computational model inspired by brains, interconnected nodes ('neurons') in layers. Fundamental to DL. (Ch 3)

Neuro-Privacy / Neural Data: Privacy concerns related to data from brain activity monitoring (EEG, fMRI, BCIs). (Ch 5, Ch 7, Ch 11, Appendix A)

Neuromorphic Computing: Hardware mimicking brain structure/function (neurons/synapses), aiming for energy-efficient AI. (Appendix A)

Neurorights: Proposed human rights protecting brain/mental domain from misuse of neurotechnology. (Ch 5, Ch 7)

NIST AI Risk Management Framework (AI RMF): Voluntary US framework for managing AI risks. (Ch 7, Ch 9)

Non-Human (Team Member): AI systems or robots functioning as contributors within a team alongside humans. (Ch 8, Ch 9)

Non-maleficence: Ethical principle of "do no harm." (Ch 7)

Opacity (AI Context): See Black Box.

Osseointegration: Direct structural/functional connection between bone and artificial implant (e.g., for prosthetics). (Ch 5)

Pacing Problem (Regulation): Challenge for legal/regulatory systems to keep pace with rapid tech development. (Ch 7)

Parameters (AI Model): Internal variables AI learns from data; more parameters often mean higher capacity. (Ch 3)

Phygital: Blend of physical and digital experiences/systems. (Ch 4)

Physical Augmentation / Enhancement: Improving human physical capabilities via technology. (Ch 5)

Posthumanism: Philosophical perspectives questioning humanism, exploring tech's potential to alter human condition. (Ch 5)

Post-Quantum Cryptography (PQC): Cryptographic algorithms resistant to attacks by quantum computers. (Appendix A)

Privacy-Enhancing Technologies (PETs): Techniques (differential privacy, federated learning, homomorphic encryption) protecting data while enabling analysis. (Ch 7, Appendix A)

Productivity Paradox: Observation that large IT investments haven't always yielded large aggregate productivity increases. (Ch 12)

Prompt Engineering: Skill/practice of designing/refining input prompts for generative AI to elicit desired outputs. Key human-AI interface. (Ch 6, throughout)

Prosthesis: Artificial device replacing missing body part. (Ch 5)

Psychological Safety: Shared belief team is safe for interpersonal risk-taking. Crucial for adaptation/collaboration. (Ch 8, Ch 10)

Quantum Annealing: Specialized quantum computing approach for optimization. (Appendix A)

Quantum Computing: Paradigm using quantum phenomena (superposition, entanglement) for exponential speedup on certain calculations. (Appendix A)

Quantum Decoherence: Loss of quantum state due to environmental interaction; obstacle for quantum computing. (Appendix A)

Qubit: Basic unit of quantum information (can be 0, 1, or both via superposition). (Appendix A)

Reskilling: Learning entirely new skills, often for job transition due to tech displacement. (Ch 10)

Responsible AI: Governance approach emphasizing AI development/deployment that is ethical, transparent, fair, accountable, safe, aligned with human values. (Ch 7, Ch 9)

Risk-Based Approach (AI Regulation): Regulatory strategy tiering requirements based on AI application risk level (e.g., EU AI Act). (Ch 7)

Robotic Process Automation (RPA): Software bots automating repetitive digital tasks via user interfaces. (Ch 10)

Robotics: Technology dealing with design, construction, operation, application of robots. "Embodied action" part. (Ch 4)

Skills-Based Hiring/Pay: Talent practices focusing on demonstrable skills/competencies rather than solely degrees/titles. (Ch 9, Ch 10)

Somatic Gene Editing: Gene editing affecting non-reproductive cells; changes not heritable. (Ch 5)

Superposition (Quantum): Ability of qubit to be 0, 1, or both simultaneously. (Appendix A)

Supervised Learning: ML using labeled datasets (input-output pairs) to train models. (Ch 3)

Swarm Robotics / Intelligence: Coordinating large numbers of simple robots whose collective behavior yields emergent intelligence/capabilities. (Ch 8)

Synergy: Interaction producing combined effect greater than sum of separate effects. Core Gestalt principle. (Ch 1, throughout)

Synthetic Biology: Field designing/constructing new biological parts/devices/systems or redesigning existing ones. Applying engineering to biology. (Appendix A)

Technostress: Negative psychological/physiological impacts from using/adapting to information/communication technologies. (Ch 11)

Total Cost of Ownership (TCO): Analysis estimating all costs associated with an asset (AI, robot) over its lifecycle. (Ch 9, Ch 12)

Transformer Models: Influential neural network architecture based on self-attention, foundational for modern LLMs. (Ch 3)

Transhuman Resources (THR): Conceptual evolution of HR needed to manage workforce of baseline humans, augmented humans, AI, robots. Focuses on practical HR challenges of managing this diverse ecosystem within synergistic teams (distinct from broader Transhumanism philosophy). (Ch 9)

Transhumanism: Philosophical movement advocating tech use to enhance human capabilities/overcome biological limits. (Ch 5)

Transparency (AI): Principle that relevant info about AI (data, logic, limits) should be accessible/understandable. (Ch 7)

Universal Basic Income (UBI): Proposed social security model: all citizens regularly receive unconditional cash payment. Debated response to AI job displacement. (Ch 12)

Unsupervised Learning: ML using unlabeled data to find hidden patterns/structures (e.g., clustering). (Ch 3)

Upskilling: Teaching new skills/enhancing existing ones to improve performance in current roles/adapt to evolving jobs. (Ch 10)

Virtual Reality (VR): Technology creating fully immersive, computer-generated environment via headset. (Ch 5 reference)

Wetware: Term sometimes used for biological computing systems involving living neurons. (Appendix A)

Zero-Knowledge Proof: Cryptographic method allowing proof of knowledge without revealing the knowledge itself. Privacy-enhancing. (Ch 7, Appendix A)

Zero-Sum Game: Situation where one participant's gain results directly from another's loss. Argued as fallacy for tech economic impact. (Ch 12)

Citations

1. Accenture. (n.d.). Newsroom. Retrieved January 10, 2025, from https://newsroom.accenture.com/

2. Acemoglu, D., & Restrepo, P. (2019). Automation and new tasks: How technology displaces and reinstates labor. Journal of Economic Perspectives, 33(2), 3–30. https://doi.org/10.1257/jep.33.2.3

3. Adleman, L. M. (1994). Molecular computation of solutions to combinatorial problems. Science, 266(5187), 1021–1024. https://doi.org/10.1126/science.7973651

4. Stanford Institute for Human-Centered Artificial Intelligence. (n.d.). AI Index Data. Retrieved January 10, 2025, from https://hai.stanford.edu/research/ai-index/data

5. Amazon Robotics. (n.d.). Amazon Robotics. Retrieved January 10, 2025, from https://www.amazonrobotics.com/

6. Amyris. (n.d.). Amyris. Retrieved January 11, 2025, from https://amyris.com/

7. ProPublica. (n.d.). Machine bias [Series]. Retrieved January 6, 2025, from https://www.propublica.org/series/machine-bias

8. Anthropic. (n.d.). Anthropic. Retrieved May 20, 2025, from https://www.anthropic.com

9. Aprika. (2024, November). 7 key components of a change management strategy. Mission Control Blog.

10. Asimov, I. (1950). Runaround. In I, robot. Gnome Press.

11. Aspen Institute Future of Work Initiative. (n.d.). Future of Work Initiative. Retrieved February 2, 2025, from https://www.aspeninstitute.org/programs/future-of-work-initiative/

12. Association for Advancing Automation (A3). (n.d.). A3 Automate. Retrieved March 8, 2025, from https://www.automate.org/

13. Autor, D. H., Dorn, D., Katz, L. F., Patterson, C., & Van Reenen, J. (2020). The fall of the labor share and the rise of superstar firms. The Quarterly Journal of Economics, 135(2), 645–709. https://doi.org/10.1093/qje/qjaa004

14. AZQuotes. (n.d.). Andy Clark quotes. Retrieved February 16, 2025, from https://www.azquotes.com/author/43567-Andy_Clark

15. Bakker, A. B., & Budden, M. (2021). Digital positive psychology interventions: A systematic review. Journal of Positive Psychology, 16(6), 746–767. https://doi.org/10.1080/17439760.2020.1803307

16. Basic Income Earth Network (BIEN). (n.d.). BIEN. Retrieved May 3, 2025, from https://basicincome.org/

17. Be My Eyes. (2025, March 20). Be My Eyes and Knorr Thailand Partner to Launch AI and Human Assistance for Blind and Low-Vision Customers through the Be My Eyes app. https://www.bemyeyes.com/blog/be-my-eyes-and-knorr-thailand-partner-to-launch-ai-and-human-assistance-for-blind-and-low-vision-customers-through-the-be-my-eyes-app/

18. Benchling. (2024). Benchling. Accelerate innovation in the new bioeconomy. Retrieved February 15, 2025, from https://www.benchling.com/solutions/industrial-biotech-rd

19. Krishnan, V. (2021, December). Kotter's 8 steps of change management – Discussion. Benchmark Six Sigma Forum.

20. Bhandari, A. (2024). Revolutionizing radiology with artificial intelligence. Cureus, 16(10), e72646. https://doi.org/10.7759/cureus.72646

21. Bjork, R. C. (2008). Artificial intelligence and the soul. Perspectives on Science and Christian Faith, 60(2), 95–102. https://www.asa3.org/ASA/PSCF/2008/PSCF6-08Bjork.pdf

22. Bolt Threads. (n.d.). Bolt Threads. Retrieved April 4, 2025, from https://boltthreads.com/

23. Bostrom, N. (2005). A history of transhumanist thought. Journal of Evolution and Technology, 14(1). http://jetpress.org/volume14/bostrom.html

24. Boston Dynamics. (n.d.). Boston Dynamics. Retrieved May 19, 2025, from https://www.bostondynamics.com/

25. Bradford, A. (2020). The Brussels effect: How the European Union rules the world. Oxford University Press.

26. Brain Corp. (n.d.). Brain Corp. Retrieved May 6, 2025, from https://braincorp.com/

27. Brookings Institution. (n.d.). Artificial Intelligence. Retrieved March 2, 2025, from https://www.brookings.edu/topic/artificial-intelligence/

28. Brown University. (2021, May 12). Brain-computer interface creates text on screen by decoding brain activity of handwriting. Brown University News. https://www.brown.edu/news/2021-05-12/handwriting

29. Brynjolfsson, E., Li, D., & Raymond, L. R. (2023). Generative AI at work (NBER Working Paper No. 31161). National Bureau of Economic Research. https://www.nber.org/papers/w31161

30. Bublitz, J. C. (2013). My mind is mine!? Cognitive liberty as a legal concept. In E. Hildt & A. G. Franke (Eds.), Cognitive enhancement: An interdisciplinary perspective (pp. 233–264). Springer Netherlands. https://doi.org/10.1007/978-94-007-6253-4_17

31. Buddhistdoor Global. (2019, September 30). Defining consciousness: How Buddhism can inform AI. https://www.buddhistdoor.net/features/defining-consciousness-how-buddhism-can-inform-ai/

32. Buolamwini, J., & Gebru, T. (2018). Gender shades: Intersectional accuracy disparities in commercial gender classification. Proceedings of Machine Learning Research, 81, 77–91. http://proceedings.mlr.press/v81/buolamwini18a.html

33. Canada. Digital Charter Implementation Act, 2022, S.C. 2023, c. 26. (2023). Parliament of Canada. https://www.parl.ca/DocumentViewer/en/44-1/bill/C-27/royal-assent

34. Canvas. (n.d.). Canvas. Retrieved April 18, 2025, from https://www.canvas.build/

35. Carr, N. (2011). The shallows: What the Internet is doing to our brains. W. W. Norton & Company.

36. Catholic Church. (1997). Catechism of the Catholic Church (2nd ed.). Libreria Editrice Vaticana. Retrieved Feb 17, 2025 from https://www.catholicculture.org/culture/library/catechism/)

37. Casetext. (n.d.). Casetext. Retrieved May 1, 2025, from https://casetext.com/

38. Catalog. (n.d.). Catalog. Retrieved April 3, 2025, from https://www.catalogdna.com/

39. Center for Security and Emerging Technology (CSET). (n.d.). CSET Georgetown. Retrieved February 16, 2025, from https://cset.georgetown.edu/

40. Li, S. (2025, April 8). AI impact to change future workforce. China Daily. https://www.chinadaily.com.cn/a/202504/08/WS67f47cc4a3104d9fd381e0a6_1.html

41. Citron, D. K., & Chesney, R. (2019). Deep fakes: A looming challenge for privacy, democracy, and national security. California Law Review, 107(6), 1753–1820.

42. Clark, A. (2003). Natural-born cyborgs: Minds, technologies, and the future of human intelligence. Oxford University Press.

43. Clark, A., & Chalmers, D. (1998). The extended mind. Analysis, 58(1), 7–19. https://doi.org/10.1093/analys/58.1.7

44. Clark, D. (n.d.). Donald Clark Plan B. Retrieved April 8, 2025, from http://donaldclarkplanb.blogspot.com/

45. ClinicalTrials.gov. (n.d.). ClinicalTrials.gov. Retrieved February 17, 2025, from https://clinicaltrials.gov/

46. Coalition for Content Provenance and Authenticity (C2PA). (n.d.). C2PA. Retrieved March 5, 2025, from https://c2pa.org/

47. Telesis Bio. (n.d.). Telesis Bio. Retrieved March 5, 2025, from https://telesisbio.com/

48. Consultport. (2024). The importance of change management in AI transformation. Consultport Blog.

49. Council of Europe. (n.d.). Artificial Intelligence. Retrieved May 15, 2025, from https://www.coe.int/en/web/artificial-intelligence

50. Coursera. (n.d.). Coursera. Retrieved April 20, 2025, from https://www.coursera.org/

51. Cross, N. (n.d.). What it means to be a machine: An interdisciplinary perspective on the future of humanity-machine coexistence [LinkedIn article]. LinkedIn. Retrieved May 29, 2025, from https://www.linkedin.com/pulse/what-means-machine-interdisciplinary-perspective-future-neal-cross-axe4c

52. D-Wave Systems. (n.d.). D-Wave. Retrieved May 29, 2025, from https://www.dwavesys.com/

53. Defense Science and Technology Group. (n.d.). Defence Science and Technology Group. Retrieved April 21, 2025, from https://www.dst.defence.gov.au/

54. Deloitte Digital. (n.d.). The human experience edge [Research series]. Deloitte.

55. Dennett, D. C. (2023, February 19). Will AI achieve consciousness? Wrong question. Wired. https://www.wired.com/story/daniel-dennett-will-ai-achieve-consciousness/

56. Eagleman, D. (n.d.). Eagleman Laboratory. Retrieved March 20, 2025, from https://eagleman.com/

57. Eapen, T. T., Finkenstadt, D. J., Folk, J., & Venkataswamy, L. (2023, July–August). How generative AI can augment human creativity. Harvard Business Review. https://hbr.org/2023/07/how-generative-ai-can-augment-human-creativity

58. Ekso Bionics. (n.d.). Ekso Bionics. Retrieved March 20, 2025, from https://eksobionics.com/

59. Elicit. (n.d.). Elicit. Retrieved February 12, 2025, from https://elicit.org/

60. Engelbart, D. C. (1962). Augmenting human intellect: A conceptual framework (AFOSR-3223). Stanford Research Institute. https://www.dougengelbart.org/content/fgh/iou_whole.html

61. Engelberger, J. F. (1980). Robotics in practice: Management and applications of industrial robots. Amacom.

62. European Parliament. (2017, February 16). European Parliament resolution of 16 February 2017 with recommendations to the Commission on Civil Law Rules on Robotics (2015/2103(INL)). https://www.europarl.europa.eu/doceo/document/TA-8-2017-0051_EN.html

63. European Union. (n.d.). Artificial Intelligence Act. EUR-Lex. Retrieved May 15, 2025, from https://eur-lex.europa.eu/

64. Farahany, N. A. (2023). The battle for your brain: Defending the right to think freely in the age of neurotechnology. St. Martin's Press.

65. Faruque, M. U. (2022). AI versus human consciousness: A future with machines as our masters? Renovatio. Zaytuna College. https://renovatio.zaytuna.edu/article/ai-versus-human-consciousness

66. Fathom. (n.d.). Fathom. Retrieved May 1, 2025, from https://fathom.video/

67. Zebra Technologies. (n.d.). Fetch Mobile Robots. Retrieved May 1, 2025, from https://www.zebra.com/us/en/products/robotics/fetch-mobile-robots.html

68. Kela (The Social Insurance Institution of Finland). (n.d.). Basic income experiment 2017–2018. Retrieved January 3, 2025, from https://www.kela.fi/web/en/basic-income-experiment-2017-2018

69. Ford Motor Company. (n.d.). Ford Media Center. Retrieved March 23, 2025, from https://media.ford.com/

70. Redcay, E., & Morrison, S. J. (2020). The neuroscience of shared intentionality. Frontiers in Human Neuroscience, 14. https://doi.org/10.3389/fnhum.2020.00001

71. G7. (2023, May 20). G7 Hiroshima Leaders' Communiqué. Ministry of Foreign Affairs of Japan. https://www.mofa.go.jp/G7/ic_e/page1e_000769.html

72. Gates, B. (2024, April 23). Bill Gates predicts AI will revolutionize the workforce within 5 years. Popular Mechanics. https://www.popularmechanics.com/technology/a60552566/bill-gates-ai-predictions/

73. Geek+. (n.d.). Geek+. Retrieved March 23, 2025, from https://www.geekplus.com/

74. European Union. (2016). Regulation (EU) 2016/679 of the European Parliament and of the Council of 27 April 2016 on the protection of natural persons with regard to the processing of personal data and on the free movement of such data, and repealing Directive 95/46/EC (General Data

Protection Regulation). Official Journal of the European Union, L 119/1. http://data.europa.eu/eli/reg/2016/679/oj

75. GE Vernova. (n.d.). GE Vernova. Retrieved March 23, 2025, from https://www.gevernova.com/

76. RealWear. (n.d.). RealWear. Retrieved March 23, 2025, from https://www.realwear.com/

77. Dohmke, T. (2022, September 7). Research: Quantifying GitHub Copilot's impact on developer productivity and happiness. The GitHub Blog. https://github.blog/2022-09-07-research-quantifying-github-copilots-impact-on-developer-productivity-and-happiness/

78. Ginkgo Bioworks. (n.d.). Ginkgo Bioworks. Retrieved April 4, 2025, from https://www.ginkgobioworks.com/

79. GiveDirectly. (n.d.). Research on cash transfers. Retrieved May 1, 2025, from https://www.givedirectly.org/research-on-cash-transfers/

80. Sparkes, M. (2022, October 12). Scientists taught brain cells in a dish how to play Pong. Gizmodo. https://gizmodo.com/scientists-taught-brain-cells-in-a-dish-how-to-play-p-1849646064

81. Google AI. (n.d.). Google AI. Retrieved May 6, 2025, from https://ai.google/

82. Google. (n.d.). What-If Tool. Retrieved May 6, 2025, from https://pair-code.github.io/what-if-tool/

83. Google Quantum AI. (n.d.). Google Quantum AI. Retrieved May 6, 2025, from https://quantumai.google/

84. Gray, C. H. (2017). Cyborg citizen: Politics in the posthuman age. Routledge.

85. Greely, H., Sahakian, B., Harris, J., Kessler, R. C., Gazzaniga, M., Campbell, P., & Farah, M. J. (2008). Towards responsible use of cognitive-enhancing drugs by the healthy. Nature, 456(7223), 702–705. https://doi.org/10.1038/456702a

86. Guidotti, R., Monreale, A., Ruggieri, S., Turini, F., Giannotti, F., & Pedreschi, D. (2018). A survey of methods for explaining black box models. ACM Computing Surveys, 51(5), Article 93. https://doi.org/10.1145/3236009

87. FBR. (n.d.). Hadrian X. Retrieved April 30, 2025, from https://www.fbr.com.au/

88. Hamilton Company. (n.d.). Robotics. Retrieved May 6, 2025, from https://www.hamiltoncompany.com/robotics

89. Harari, Y. N. (2017). Homo Deus: A brief history of tomorrow. Harper.

90. Harvey. (n.d.). Harvey. Retrieved May 6, 2025, from https://harvey.ai/

91. Hasselberger, W. (2021, Spring). Can machines have common sense? The New Atlantis. https://www.thenewatlantis.com/publications/can-machines-have-common-sense

92. Hayles, N. K. (1999). How we became posthuman: Virtual bodies in cybernetics, literature, and informatics. University of Chicago Press.

93. Herzfeld, N. (2024, January 18). AI & personhood: Imitation isn't enough [Interview]. Commonweal Magazine. https://www.commonwealmagazine.org/2024/01/ai-personhood-noreen-herzfeld/

94. Hinxton Group. (n.d.). Hinxton Group. Retrieved March 11, 2025, from https://www.hinxtongroup.org/

95. The Holy Qur'an. (n.d.). Alhakam. Retrieved June 3, 2025, from https://www.alhakam.org/the-holy-quran/

96. Hong, J., & Zhou, Z. (2022). AI generated metaphors facilitate creative marketing slogan generation. Scientific Reports, 12(1), Article 19715. https://doi.org/10.1038/s41598-022-24115-1

97. UKKÖ Robotics. (n.d.). UKKÖ Robotics. Retrieved March 2, 2025, from https://www.ukkorobotics.com

98. Hubbell, K. R. (2023). There is AI in team – The future of human, augmented human, and non-human collaboration. Kindle Direct Publishing.

99. Human Fertilisation & Embryology Authority (HFEA). (n.d.). HFEA. Retrieved February 9, 2025, from https://www.hfea.gov.uk/

100. IBM. (n.d.). AI Fairness 360. Retrieved April 8, 2025, from https://aif360.mybluemix.net/

101. IBM. (n.d.). IBM Quantum. Retrieved April 8, 2025, from https://www.ibm.com/quantum

102. IBM Research. (n.d.). IBM Research. Retrieved April 8, 2025, from https://research.ibm.com/

103. ICON. (n.d.). ICON. Retrieved March 19, 2025, from https://www.iconbuild.com/

104. iGEM Foundation. (n.d.). iGEM Foundation. Retrieved March 19, 2025, from https://igem.org/

105. Registry of Standard Biological Parts. (n.d.). Main Page. Retrieved April 9, 2025, from http://parts.igem.org/Main_Page

106. Ienca, M., & Andorno, R. (2017). Towards new human rights in the age of neuroscience and neurotechnology. Life Sciences, Society and Policy, 13(1), Article 5. https://doi.org/10.1186/s40504-017-0050-1

107. Impossible Foods. (n.d.). Impossible Foods. Retrieved May 1, 2025, from https://impossiblefoods.com/

108. Insilico Medicine. (n.d.). Newsroom. Retrieved May 7, 2025, from https://insilico.com/newsroom

109. Integrated DNA Technologies (IDT). (n.d.). IDT. Retrieved May 7, 2025, from https://www.idtdna.com/

110. Intel. (n.d.). Neuromorphic computing. Retrieved June 2, 2025, from https://www.intel.com/content/www/us/en/research/neuromorphic-computing.html

111. Intuitive Surgical. (n.d.). Intuitive. Retrieved June 2, 2025, from https://www.intuitive.com/

112. IonQ. (n.d.). IonQ. Retrieved March 25, 2025, from https://ionq.com/

113. Iridia. (n.d.). Iridia. Retrieved March 25, 2025, from https://iridia.com/

114. International Organization for Standardization. (2011). Robots and robotic devices — Safety requirements for industrial robots — Part 1: Robots (ISO Standard No. 10218-1:2011).

115. International Organization for Standardization. (2011). Robots and robotic devices — Safety requirements for industrial robots — Part 2: Robot systems and integration (ISO Standard No. 10218-2:2011).

116. International Organization for Standardization. (2016). Robots and robotic devices — Collaborative robots (ISO/TS Standard No. 15066:2016).

117. John Deere. (n.d.). John Deere Newsroom. Retrieved February 18, 2025, from https://www.deere.com/en/news/

118. JPMorgan Chase & Co. (n.d.). Investor Relations. Retrieved April 24, 2025, from https://www.jpmorganchase.com/ir

119. JR Marketing. (n.d.). AI graceful aging meets smart tech. JR Marketing AI. Retrieved February 17, 2025, from https://www.jrmarketingai.com/

120. Keasling, J. D., Martin, V. J. J., Lee, P., Nowroozi, F., Paradise, E. M., Pitera, D. J., Newman, J. D., & Westfall, P. J. (2006). Production of the antimalarial drug precursor artemisinic acid in engineered yeast. Nature, 440(7086), 940–943. https://doi.org/10.1038/nature04640

121. Kidder, T. (2003). Mountains beyond mountains: The quest of Dr. Paul Farmer, a man who would cure the world. Random House.

122. Kosinski, M., Stillwell, D., & Graepel, T. (2013). Private traits and attributes are predictable from digital records of human behavior. Proceedings of the National Academy of Sciences, 110(15), 5802–5805. https://doi.org/10.1073/pnas.1218772110

123. KUKA AG. (n.d.). KUKA. Retrieved February 17, 2025, from https://www.kuka.com/

124. Lanier, J. (2013). Who owns the future? Simon & Schuster.

125. Licklider, J. C. R. (1960). Man-computer symbiosis. IRE Transactions on Human Factors in Electronics, HFE-1(1), 4–11. https://doi.org/10.1109/THFE2.1960.4503259

126. Lightcast. (n.d.). Lightcast. Retrieved April 29, 2025, from https://lightcast.io/

127. Locus Robotics. (n.d.). Locus Robotics. Retrieved March 27, 2025, from https://locusrobotics.com/

128. Malhotra, R. (2025). The role of AI automation in revolutionizing healthcare services. ValueCoders Blog. https://www.valuecoders.com/blog/industries/the-role-of-ai-automation-in-healthcare-industry/

129. Malone, T. W., & Bernstein, M. S. (Eds.). (2015). Handbook of collective intelligence. MIT Press.

130. Open Brain Project. (n.d.). News. Retrieved January 31, 2025, from https://www.openbrainproject.org/news

131. McKinsey Global Institute. (n.d.). McKinsey Global Institute. Retrieved April 11, 2025, from https://www.mckinsey.com/mgi

132. Meta Reality Labs. (n.d.). Reality Labs Research. Retrieved April 12, 2025, from https://research.facebook.com/labs/reality-labs/

133. MHI. (n.d.). Annual Industry Report. Retrieved April 21, 2025, from https://www.mhi.org/publications/report

134. Microsoft. (n.d.). Responsible AI. Retrieved May 26, 2025, from https://www.microsoft.com/en-us/ai/responsible-ai

135. Microsoft WorkLab. (n.d.). Work Trend Index. Retrieved May 26, 2025, from https://www.microsoft.com/en-us/worklab/work-trend-index/

136. Midjourney. (n.d.). Midjourney. Retrieved January 6, 2025, from https://www.midjourney.com/

137. Ministry of Defence (UK) & Bundeswehr (Germany). (2021). Human augmentation – The dawn of a new paradigm: A strategic implications project. UK MOD Publishing. https://assets.publishing.service.gov.uk/government/uploads/system/uploads/attachment_data/file/986301/Human_Augmentation_SIP_access.pdf

138. Mitchell, M. (2024, March 15). Can AI ever attain true reasoning? Science, 383(6688), 1159–1160. https://doi.org/10.1126/science.ado8607

139. Mitchell, M. (2025). Artificial intelligence learns to reason. Science, 387(6740). https://doi.org/10.1126/science.adw5211

140. Mplus Group. (2024, May 14). AI isn't here to replace you – It's here to make you a centaur. Mplus. https://mplusgroup.eu/insights/ai-isnt-here-replace-you-its-here-make-you-centaur

141. Narayanan, A. (n.d.). Arvind Narayanan. Retrieved February 4, 2025, from https://www.cs.princeton.edu/~arvindn/

142. NASA. (n.d.). Mars Exploration Program. Retrieved March 31, 2025, from https://mars.nasa.gov/

143. National Academies of Sciences, Engineering, and Medicine. (n.d.). Reports. Retrieved March 31, 2025, from https://www.nationalacademies.org/reports

144. National Institute of Standards and Technology. (n.d.). Artificial Intelligence. Retrieved March 31, 2025, from https://www.nist.gov/artificial-intelligence

145. National Institutes of Health. (2021, May 12). Composing thoughts: mental handwriting produces brain activity that can be turned into text. https://www.nih.gov/news-events/news-releases/composing-thoughts-mental-handwriting-produces-brain-activity-can-be-turned-into-text

146. National Transportation Safety Board. (n.d.). NTSB Accident Reports Database. Retrieved May 10, 2025, from https://www.ntsb.gov/investigations/AccidentReports/Pages/Reports.aspx

147. Neuralink. (n.d.). Neuralink. Retrieved April 30, 2025, from https://neuralink.com/

148. Neurorights Foundation. (n.d.). Neurorights Foundation. Retrieved April 30, 2025, from https://neurorightsfoundation.org/

149. News Literacy Project. (n.d.). News Literacy Project. Retrieved March 14, 2025, from https://newslit.org/

150. Niemiec, R. M. (2019). Finding the strengths-based approach applicable: A review of the research and intervention. Psychological Inquiry, 30(2), 85–90. https://doi.org/10.1080/1047840X.2019.1629120

151. Organisation for Economic Co-operation and Development (OECD). (n.d.). OECD AI Principles. Retrieved May 10, 2025, from https://oecd.ai/en/ai-principles

152. Organisation for Economic Co-operation and Development (OECD). (n.d.). OECD/G20 Base Erosion and Profit Shifting Project. Retrieved May 10, 2025, from https://www.oecd.org/tax/beps/

153. OpenAI. (n.d.). OpenAI. Retrieved May 17, 2025, from https://openai.com/

154. OpenAI. (2023, October). GPT-4V(ision) system card. https://cdn.openai.com/papers/GPT-4V-System-Card.pdf

155. Open Bionics. (n.d.). Open Bionics. Retrieved January 16, 2025, from https://openbionics.com/

156. Otter.ai. (n.d.). Otter.ai. Retrieved January 16, 2025, from https://otter.ai/

157. Pariser, E. (2011). The filter bubble: What the Internet is hiding from you. Penguin UK.

158. Partners In Health (PIH). (n.d.). Partners In Health. Retrieved May 1, 2025, from https://www.pih.org/

159. Piketty, T. (2014). Capital in the twenty-first century (A. Goldhammer, Trans.). Belknap Press.

160. Poltorak, A. (2023). Human, angel, or machine: The challenge of consciousness. Quantum Torah. https://www.quantumtorah.com/human-angel-or-machine-the-challenge-of-consciousness/

161. Francis. (2023, December 8). Artificial intelligence and peace. Message for the 57th World Day of Peace 2024. Vatican. https://www.vatican.va/content/francesco/en/messages/peace/documents/20231208-messaggio-57giornatamondiale-pace2024.html

162. Popova, B. (2020). Islamic philosophy and artificial intelligence: Epistemological arguments. Zygon, 55(4), 977- 995. https://doi.org/10.1111/zygo.12639

163. PositivePsychology.com. (n.d.). PositivePsychology.com. Retrieved April 30, 2025, from https://positivepsychology.com/

164. PromptHero. (n.d.). PromptHero. Retrieved May 30, 2025, from https://prompthero.com/

165. PsiQuantum. (n.d.). PsiQuantum. Retrieved April 23, 2025, from https://psiquantum.com/

166. PricewaterhouseCoopers (PwC). (n.d.). PwC. Retrieved April 2, 2025, from https://www.pwc.com/

167. Qualcomm Ventures. (n.d.). Portfolio. Retrieved April 2, 2025, from https://www.qualcommventures.com/portfolio

168. Quantinuum. (n.d.). Quantinuum. Retrieved March 26, 2025, from https://www.quantinuum.com/

169. Reddit. (n.d.). Reddit. Retrieved February 17, 2025, from https://www.reddit.com/

170. Stecklow, S. (2018, October 10). Amazon scraps secret AI recruiting tool that showed bias against women. Reuters. https://www.reuters.com/article/us-amazon-com-jobs-automation-insight/amazon-scraps-secret-ai-recruiting-tool-that-showed-bias-against-women-idUSKCN1MK08G

171. ReWalk Robotics. (n.d.). ReWalk Robotics. Retrieved May 4, 2025, from https://rewalk.com/

172. Riskin, J. (2003). The defecating duck, or, the ambiguous origins of artificial life. Critical Inquiry, 29(4), 599–633. https://doi.org/10.1086/377722

173. Rodrigues, J. (2025, March). How AI can help seniors: Key areas of impact [White paper]. JR Marketing.

174. Ruiz, A. (2023, December 20). Excited to share some thoughts on the future of work, particularly the evolving role of AI in leadership [LinkedIn post]. LinkedIn. Retrieved May 1, 2025, from https://www.linkedin.com/feed/update/urn:li:activity:7143277857391984640/

175. Sahakian, B. J., & Morein-Zamir, S. (2007). Professor's little helper. Nature, 450(7173), 1157–1159. https://doi.org/10.1038/4501157a

176. Salesforce. (n.d.). Trusted AI. Retrieved April 2, 2025, from https://www.salesforce.com/company/trusted-ai/

177. Sana Labs. (n.d.). Sana Labs. Retrieved February 3, 2025, from https://www.sanalabs.com/

178. Sarcos Technology and Robotics Corporation. (n.d.). Sarcos Robotics. Retrieved March 18, 2025, from https://www.sarcos.com/

179. Savioke. (n.d.). Savioke. Retrieved March 18, 2025, from https://www.savioke.com/

180. Scite. (n.d.). Scite. Retrieved January 21, 2025, from https://scite.ai/

181. Stockton Economic Empowerment Demonstration (SEED). (n.d.). Final results. Retrieved April 20, 2025, from https://www.stocktondemonstration.org/results

182. Shannon, D. (2023, December 15). Tracing thoughts not text: what large language models actually understand [LinkedIn post]. LinkedIn. Retrieved February 14, 2025, from https://www.linkedin.com/feed/update/urn:li:activity:7141553401101893632/

183. Siemens AG. (n.d.). Artificial intelligence. Retrieved March 30, 2025, from https://www.siemens.com/global/en/company/topic-areas/artificial-intelligence.html

184. SkillsFuture Singapore. (n.d.). SkillsFuture Singapore. Retrieved May 3, 2025, from https://www.skillsfuture.gov.sg/

185. Skydio. (n.d.). Skydio. Retrieved May 3, 2025, from https://www.skydio.com/

186. Sparkes, M. (2022, October 13). Human brain cells in a dish learn to play Pong. New Scientist. https://www.newscientist.com/article/2341673-human-brain-cells-in-a-dish-learn-to-play-pong/

187. Stadler, C., & Reeves, M. (2025, March 12). When AI gets a board seat. Harvard Business Review. https://hbr.org/2025/03/when-ai-gets-a-board-seat

188. Stanford Institute for Human-Centered Artificial Intelligence (HAI). (n.d.). AI Index. Retrieved April 20, 2025, from https://hai.stanford.edu/research/ai-index

189. Stanford Institute for Human-Centered Artificial Intelligence (HAI). (n.d.). DigiChina. Retrieved April 20, 2025, from https://digichina.stanford.edu/

190. Stanford History Education Group (SHEG). (n.d.). SHEG. Retrieved April 20, 2025, from https://sheg.stanford.edu/

191. Starship Technologies. (n.d.). Starship Technologies. Retrieved February 8, 2025, from https://www.starship.xyz/

192. Statista. (n.d.). Statista. Retrieved March 5, 2025, from https://www.statista.com/

193. Stokes, J. M., Yang, K., Swanson, K., Jin, W., Cubillos-Ruiz, A., Donghia, N. M., Mathis, C. R., & Collins, J. J. (2023). A deep-learning approach identifies untested radial diffusion assays for antibiotic discovery. Nature Chemical Biology, 19, 1403–1412. https://doi.org/10.1038/s41589-023-01419-y

194. Strubell, E., Ganesh, A., & McCallum, A. (2019). Energy and policy considerations for deep learning in NLP [preprint]. arXiv. https://arxiv.org/abs/1906.02243

195. Sturgeon, T. (1953). More than human. Farrar, Straus & Young.

196. Sulaiman, M. (2022). Humanity and AI: Reflections on consciousness, morality, and purpose. Al Hakam. https://www.alhakam.org/humanity-and-ai-reflections-on-consciousness-morality-and-purpose/

197. Synlogic. (n.d.). Synlogic. Retrieved May 7, 2025, from https://www.synlogictx.com/

198. Tecan. (n.d.). Tecan. Retrieved January 9, 2025, from https://www.tecan.com/

199. Telesis Bio. (n.d.). Telesis Bio. Retrieved January 9, 2025, from https://telesisbio.com/

200. TeselaGen Biotechnology. (n.d.). TeselaGen. Retrieved March 29, 2025, from https://teselagen.com/

201. Universal Robots. (n.d.). Trelleborg Sealing Solutions increases output by up to 40% with UR cobots [Case study]. https://www.universal-robots.com/case-stories/trelleborg-sealing-solutions/

202. Turing, A. M. (1950). Computing machinery and intelligence. Mind, 59(236), 433–460. https://doi.org/10.1093/mind/LIX.236.433

203. Twist Bioscience. (n.d.). Twist Bioscience. Retrieved February 27, 2025, from https://www.twistbioscience.com/

204. Udemy. (n.d.). Udemy. Retrieved April 7, 2025, from https://www.udemy.com/

205. UK Government. (2023, March). AI regulation: A pro-innovation approach (White Paper, Cm 815). https://www.gov.uk/government/publications/ai-regulation-a-pro-innovation-approach

206. United Nations. (n.d.). High-Level Advisory Body on Artificial Intelligence. Retrieved April 29, 2025, from https://www.un.org/en/ai-advisory-body

207. Universal Robots (UR). (n.d.). Universal Robots. Retrieved March 29, 2025, from https://www.universal-robots.com/

208. Upwork. (n.d.). Upwork. Retrieved March 28, 2025, from https://www.upwork.com/

209. Vaccaro, M., Almaatouq, A., & Malone, T. W. (2024). When combinations of humans and AI are useful: A systematic review and meta-analysis. Nature Human Behaviour, 8(10), 2293–2303. https://doi.org/10.1038/s41562-024-01874-0

210. Wagner, M. G. (n.d.). We are not in the driver's seat: How post-hoc storytelling shapes minds—Human and machine alike [Blog post]. Michael G. Wagner's Substack. Retrieved April 2, 2025, from https://mikekentz.substack.com/p/we-are-not-in-the-drivers-seat-how

211. Wei, J., Wang, X., Schuurmans, D., Bosma, M., Ichter, B., Feng, F., Ha, S., Guu, K., Le, Q. V., Barham, P., Chu, Y., & Zoph, B. (2022). Chain-of-Thought prompting elicits reasoning in large language models [preprint]. arXiv. https://arxiv.org/abs/2201.11903

212. White House Office of Science and Technology Policy. (2022). Blueprint for an AI Bill of Rights: Making automated systems work for the American people. https://www.whitehouse.gov/wp-content/uploads/2022/10/Blueprint-for-an-AI-Bill-of-Rights.pdf

213. White House Office of Science and Technology Policy. (2023, October 30). Executive Order on the Safe, Secure, and Trustworthy Development and Use of Artificial Intelligence. https://www.whitehouse.gov/briefing-room/presidential-actions/2023/10/30/executive-order-on-the-safe-secure-and-trustworthy-development-and-use-of-artificial-intelligence/

214. Wing. (n.d.). Wing. Retrieved March 5, 2025, from https://wing.com/

215. Woebot Health. (n.d.). Woebot Health. Retrieved March 5, 2025, from https://woebothealth.com/

216. World Economic Forum. (n.d.). Reports. Retrieved April 30, 2025, from https://www.weforum.org/reports

217. Wysa. (n.d.). Wysa. Retrieved February 11, 2025, from https://www.wysa.io/

218. Yang, X., Rosin, P. L., & Bevan, C. (2023). Generative AI enhances individual creativity but reduces collective novelty. Science Advances, 9(48), eadn5290. https://doi.org/10.1126/sciadv.adn5290

219. Yuste, R., Goering, S., Bi, G., Carmena, J. M., Carter, A., Fins, J. J., Friesen, P., Gallant, J., Ivry, R. B., Kording, K. P., Kwon, S., Marblestone, A., Olson, S., Poldrack, R. A., Shenoy, K. V., Swan, M., Toups, C., Vogelsstein, J., Wieland, S., & Xie, X. (2017). Four ethical priorities for neurotechnologies and AI. Nature, 551(7679), 159–163. https://doi.org/10.1038/nature24633

220. Zebra Technologies. (n.d.). Zebra Technologies. Retrieved January 17, 2025, from https://www.zebra.com/

221. Zipline. (n.d.). Zipline. Retrieved February 20, 2025, from https://www.flyzipline.com/

AI ADOPTION STRATEGIES

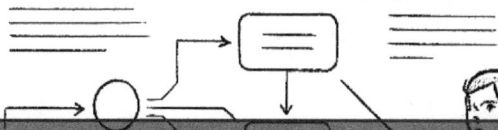

Quick Start Guide

Aligning with the Synergistic Future

Phase 1: Understanding the Parts & the Promise of Synergy (Weeks 1-4)

Goal: Gain foundational knowledge of the core components and the potential of their integration.

For Individuals:

- ☐ **Self-Assess Your Role in the Gestalt:** Evaluate your current work tasks and identify which leverage uniquely human skills (creativity, empathy, complex judgment – see Ch.2) versus those that could be augmented by AI or automation. This honest audit reveals where human-machine synergy could add the most value in your role.

- ☐ **Explore the AI Cognitive Catalyst:** Dedicate a few hours each week to hands-on experimentation with generative AI tools (e.g. ChatGPT, Google Gemini). Learn their capabilities and limitations (such as hallucinations or bias) through direct interaction. This builds awareness of how AI can complement your work.

- ☐ **Identify Your Adaptation Path:** Based on your self-assessment, pinpoint 1–2 critical skills to develop next. For example, do you need to learn prompt engineering to better communicate with AI (Ch.6)? Deepen a core human strength like complex problem-solving or empathy (Ch.2)? Or understand the implications of human augmentation (Ch.5)? Focus your personal development on areas that will enhance human-AI synergy.

- ☐ **Sharpen Your Integrity Lens:** Practice critical thinking about information. Verify sources, question emotionally-charged or AI-generated content, and refine your ability to spot misinformation. In a tech-augmented workplace, maintaining information integrity is a key human responsibility.

For Organizations:

- ☐ **Establish Executive Sponsorship & Vision:** *New:* Secure a high-level executive sponsor (or small team of champions) who believes in the synergistic future. Work with them to articulate a clear **vision statement** for the transformation – how integrating human, AI, and robotic contributions will benefit the organization's mission. This vision will

229

guide all phases and be used in communications to build urgency and buy-in for change.

☐ **Form a "Synergy Strategy" Task Force:** Assemble a diverse, cross-functional team (e.g. IT, HR/THR, Legal, Ethics, Operations, business units) to lead the initiative. This team's mandate is to explore how combining human talent with AI/automation can create strategic advantages and to flag risks that need management. Ensure roles and responsibilities are clear (e.g. the IT lead evaluates tech feasibility, HR lead anticipates workforce impacts, etc.). The task force should meet regularly and report to the executive sponsor.

☐ **Conduct a Gestalt Opportunity & Risk Assessment:** Map out where emerging technologies could boost productivity or innovation in your organization. Identify key processes or services that AI (Ch.3), robotics (Ch.4), or human augmentation (Ch.5) could improve. Simultaneously, identify potential **risks** – ethical pitfalls (bias, privacy breaches, misinformation – see Ch.7), regulatory issues, or workforce disruptions (job redundancies, skill gaps – see Ch.11). This assessment should include a **change impact analysis** (who and what will be affected by these changes). Prioritize opportunity areas that have high value and manageable risk, and note where mitigation plans are needed for risks.

☐ **Inventory Current Integration Points:** Document where AI or automation is already used in your operations – whether officially or ad-hoc by employees. Understanding the status quo helps reveal quick wins (places to expand use of AI) and areas that require better governance or support.

☐ **Review & Update Policies for Future-Readiness:** Audit your HR and IT policies to identify what might hinder a mixed human–AI–robot workforce. For example, do job descriptions or evaluation criteria need to change to recognize use of AI tools? Are there policies on data usage or ethics that need revisions for AI-driven work? Flag policies around hiring, performance management, compensation, and diversity/equity/inclusion (DEI) that must evolve to accommodate "Transhuman Resources" (Ch.10) – a workforce that includes augmented humans and AI assistants.

☐ **Develop a Communication Plan:** *New:* Create a **change communication plan** to keep all stakeholders informed and engaged from the start. Define key messages about why this transformation is necessary (the "why" and the benefits), what will change, and how it will unfold. Identify stakeholder groups (executives, managers, front-line employees, as well as external stakeholders like customers or partners if affected) and tailor messages for each. Decide on communication channels (e.g. town hall meetings, email updates, internal social networks) and frequency. Early, transparent communication will reduce uncertainty and build trust, helping to preempt rumors or fear.

- [ ] **Engage Stakeholders Early:** *New:* Beyond the core task force, involve representatives from various stakeholder groups in Phase 1. For instance, consult employee representatives, faculty or student reps (if educational), or union/employee councils (if applicable in government) about the planned changes. Solicit their input and concerns. This early **stakeholder engagement** helps build buy-in and uncovers potential resistance points so you can address them proactively. Consider creating a stakeholder advisory panel or including key influencers in planning sessions to foster co-ownership of the change.

Phase 2: Building Bridges & Enabling Ethical Synergy (Months 2-6)

Goal: Develop foundational skills for interaction and establish initial frameworks for responsible integration.

For Individuals:

☐ **Learn Foundational Prompt Engineering:** Enroll in an introductory course or workshop on prompt engineering (crafting effective inputs for AI). Practice by writing prompts that yield useful results from AI tools. Think of prompt skills as learning a new "language" for collaborating with your AI counterparts.

☐ **Double Down on Human Strengths:** Deliberately practice the uniquely human skills that make you a better partner to technology. For example, seek out tasks requiring creative problem-solving, critical thinking, emotional intelligence, or ethical judgment – these are areas where human insight is crucial even as AI is introduced. Strengthening these skills ensures you remain an essential orchestrator in AI-augmented workflows.

☐ **Pilot Personal Synergy Projects:** Choose a work project or learning goal and intentionally use AI assistance to execute it. For instance, use an AI tool to brainstorm ideas, draft content, or analyze data, while you provide direction and review. Treat this as an experiment in human-AI collaboration: iterate your approach, and note what improves your productivity or creativity. Share your experiences with colleagues to spread effective practices.

For Organizations:

☐ **Roll Out Foundational AI Literacy Training:** Provide mandatory baseline education for all employees on AI and automation. This training should cover what AI **can** and **cannot** do, key concepts of generative AI, and the organization's approved AI tools. Include modules on ethical use (avoiding biased or misleading outputs, respecting data privacy, and understanding intellectual property concerns). By the end, employees should understand the *synergistic potential* of AI – how, when used appropriately, it can amplify human work rather than replace it.

- [ ] **Launch Controlled Synergy Pilots:** Identify 1–2 specific processes or team workflows where human + AI (and/or robotics) collaboration could yield a clear benefit. Design small-scale pilot projects to integrate AI into these workflows. For each pilot, define **clear goals and metrics** for success (e.g. 20% reduction in processing time, improved service quality, or new insights generated – importantly, measure the *combined* human-AI output). Establish strong ethical guardrails upfront: for example, human oversight checkpoints, data handling guidelines, and criteria for when AI suggestions should be overridden. Monitor these pilots closely over several months. *Tip:* Treat pilot teams as learning labs – gather feedback from participants frequently and document lessons learned.

- [ ] **Allocate Resources & Support:** *New:* Ensure that the pilot teams and broader workforce have the necessary resources for success. This includes allocating budget for AI tools/software licenses, upgrading IT infrastructure if needed, and providing user support (perhaps an "AI helpdesk" or on-call experts). Removing barriers (technical or procedural) is key to empowering employees to actually use the new tools. Additionally, recognize employees' extra effort in pilots – this encourages participation and openness to change.

- [ ] **Develop Initial Responsible AI Guidelines:** Draft and circulate simple, clear **AI usage policies** for the organization. These should tell employees how to appropriately use AI tools in their work. Topics to cover include: approved vs. unapproved tools, data privacy rules (what data can/cannot be input to AI), the need to verify AI-generated outputs for accuracy, avoiding biased or unethical uses of AI, and when to disclose AI assistance. Refer to Chapters 7 and 8 of the book for ethical best practices. Making these guidelines available early sets expectations and builds trust that the organization is proceeding thoughtfully.

- [ ] **Equip HR for the THR Transformation:** Provide targeted training to HR (or "Transhuman Resources") staff so they can lead workforce transition efforts. HR should learn about the new technologies (AI, augmentation) enough to understand skill requirements and legal/ethical implications (Ch.5, Ch.7, Ch.8). They should also update talent practices: e.g. learning to assess candidates' ability to work with AI, redesigning evaluation forms to factor in AI collaboration, and crafting new career paths or upskilling programs. Essentially, HR becomes a change champion, ensuring human capital strategies align with the transformed, tech-augmented workplace.

☐ **Establish Feedback Channels and Change Champions:** *New:* During the pilot phase, set up mechanisms for continuous feedback from employees. This could be regular surveys, a dedicated Slack/Teams channel for questions and peer support, or "lunch and learn" forums. **Identify and empower change champions** at various levels – enthusiastic early adopters or respected team leads – who can model positive use of AI and help their peers. Invite these champions into periodic review meetings to share on-the-ground insights. By enlisting a broad base of supporters and listening to concerns, you create a "volunteer army" that drives momentum for change. At the same time, address resistance openly: if certain teams or individuals are hesitant, have managers or change agents meet with them, acknowledge their concerns, and provide additional support or training. Managing resistance early prevents derailment later.

Phase 3: Integrating, Adapting, and Orchestrating the Whole (Ongoing)

Goal: Embed synergistic practices, foster continuous adaptation, and implement robust governance.

For Individuals:

☐ **Integrate Synergistic Workflows:** Make a habit of treating AI/automation as part of your daily toolkit and "team." Wherever appropriate, use AI assistants or automated processes to complement your human efforts. For example, if an AI can handle 60% of data analysis, use it – and spend the time saved on deeper interpretation or creative tasks. Continue refining your ability to craft good prompts, interpret AI outputs critically, and decide when to rely on your human judgment.

☐ **Become a Synergy Champion:** Share your experiences and tips for effective human-machine collaboration with your colleagues. If you've found a way to integrate an AI tool that improved your work, demonstrate it in a team meeting. Help foster a culture where co-working with AI is normalized and done ethically. Mentorship and peer support are powerful in this stage – consider mentoring a coworker in using an AI tool while they might mentor you in another skill.

☐ **Embrace Continuous Adaptation:** Commit to ongoing learning. The tools and technologies will keep evolving, so dedicate regular time (e.g. a few hours each month) to update your knowledge on new AI features, emerging best practices, or relevant new skills. Treat your career as a dynamic journey. By staying curious and adaptable, you ensure your value grows in tandem with technological advancement, rather than getting left behind.

For Organizations:

☐ **Implement Scale Up Successful Pilots:** *New:* After initial pilots prove their value, create a plan to roll them out more broadly. Document the outcomes and **short-term wins** from Phase 2 – for instance, any efficiency gains or quality improvements – and publicize these internally to celebrate success and build confidence in the changes. Then, allocate resources and timelines for scaling, while adjusting for any lessons learned. Phased rollouts (team by team or department by department) can manage risk and allow iterative improvement as you go.

- [ ] **Implement Skills-Based Talent Practices:** Evolve your talent management to focus on skills and outcomes rather than rigid roles. Update hiring criteria to value demonstrated skills (e.g. the ability to leverage AI tools effectively, or strong emotional intelligence) as much as traditional qualifications. Similarly, provide avenues for continuous upskilling/reskilling – for example, a budget for courses or time for self-directed learning – so employees can develop the skills identified in Phase 1. Internal mobility should be encouraged so that employees can move into new roles that emerge from this transformation (for instance, "AI workflow coordinator" or similar roles).

- [ ] **Adapt Performance Management for Synergy:** Redefine how you evaluate and reward performance. Traditional metrics might not capture the value of effective human-AI collaboration. Consider team-based goals where human and AI contributions combine. Recognize employees who intelligently use tools to amplify results *and* those who provide critical human judgment. For example, you might add a goal in performance plans about "innovation and automation usage," or incorporate peer feedback on knowledge sharing. Make it clear through rewards and recognition that *orchestrating the whole* (not just individual effort) is valued.

- [ ] **Establish Robust Governance & Ethical Oversight:** By now, AI and automated systems may be deeply embedded in operations – governance becomes crucial. Set up a formal **AI governance committee or board** that includes stakeholders from IT, risk, legal, and ethics. Institute policies for regular audits of AI systems (accuracy, bias testing, security reviews), and ensure compliance with any evolving regulations (Ch.8). Have clear escalation paths for any incidents or ethical dilemmas (e.g. an AI error affecting a client). Governance should also extend to vendor management (third-party AI tools) and data governance. The goal is to maintain trust and accountability as the organization becomes more AI-driven.

- [ ] **Expand DEI to the Full Gestalt:** Update diversity, equity, and inclusion programs to include the new dimension of human-tech collaboration. For instance, ensure **equitable access** to augmentation tools or AI training across your workforce so no group is left behind. Recognize that biases can be encoded in AI – so a diverse group should oversee AI adoption to catch blind spots. Foster an inclusive culture where all contributors (whether human, AI, or hybrid) are respected, and where employees feel they belong even as their roles change. This might involve new conversations around prejudice or bias related to technology use (e.g. avoiding stigmatizing those who use AI assistance versus those who don't, and vice versa).

☐ **Monitor Employee Well-being & Manage Change Fatigue:** Change can be stressful – continually gauge how employees are feeling. Use surveys, pulse checks, or manager one-on-ones to identify burnout, anxiety or confusion related to the new workflows. Offer resources for stress management or counseling if needed, especially for those struggling with role changes or fearing obsolescence. Demonstrate empathy in leadership communications, acknowledging the challenges. Tackle "change fatigue" by ensuring the pace of introducing new tools is sustainable and by highlighting how past changes have paid off.

☐ **Continuously Iterate and Orchestrate:** Treat this transformation as ongoing, not a one-off project. Set a cadence (e.g. quarterly or biannual) for the task force or a dedicated **Transhuman Workforce Steering Committee** to review progress. They should look at key metrics (productivity, innovation rates, employee engagement, etc.), review feedback and audit results, and then refine strategies or launch new initiatives accordingly. Adaptation should become a core competency: as new AI capabilities or market shifts arise, the organization can adjust its training, policies, and structures in response. In essence, the company should embrace a **learning culture** where human-AI synergy is continually improved.

Key Mindset Shift (Reinforce Constantly): Throughout all phases, leaders and managers should communicate and model the mindset that technology (especially AI) is *not* an external threat but another team member – a "part" to be integrated into our human teams. The true value of employees will increasingly lie in their ability to **orchestrate** this human-tech synergy: providing direction to AI, ensuring ethical integrity, and injecting creativity and empathy into processes. Encourage employees to take pride in how they collaborate with technology. Reinforce this mindset in company narratives, training, and performance feedback so that it becomes part of the organizational culture moving forward.

Core Change Materials for Communication, Marketing, and Training

You need more than a plan for successful transformation – it requires supportive **materials and templates** that guide communication, marketing (or engagement), and training efforts. Here are a **core set of templates** applicable across sectors. These are general frameworks that any organization can adopt, ensuring consistency in how the change is conveyed and implemented. Each template is then tailored in the next section to address the specific needs of enterprises, educational institutions, and government agencies for the critical use cases of onboarding AI tools, workforce transition, and stakeholder engagement.

1. Communication Plan Template (General)

A Communication Plan ensures all stakeholders are informed, heard, and involved throughout the change. Key components include:

- **Objectives:** Define what the communications should achieve (e.g. build awareness of the AI initiative, reduce fear, convey benefits, keep everyone updated on progress).

- **Stakeholder Mapping:** Identify all stakeholder groups that need communication. This typically includes internal groups (executives, managers, front-line employees, IT staff, HR, etc.) and, if applicable, external groups (customers, suppliers, investors, community, regulators). Note each group's interests or concerns (for example, employees may worry about job security, customers might care about service improvements or data privacy).

- **Key Messages:** For each stakeholder group or generally for the organization, craft clear and concise messages. These should answer: *Why* the change is happening (the vision and urgency), *What* is changing (and what is not changing), *How* it will impact them, and *How* the organization will support them through it. Emphasize benefits ("what's in it for them") and address known concerns to build Desire for change.

- **Communication Channels:** List the mediums for communication and match them to audiences. Examples: company-wide emails/newsletters, intranet announcements, FAQ documents, town hall meetings, team meetings, one-on-one manager conversations, posters or infographics, internal social media (chat groups), and external press releases or social media for public stakeholders. Ensure multiple channels to reinforce messages (repetition aids understanding) and to reach people in different ways.

- **Timeline and Frequency:** Plan *when* communications will occur. Align key messages with project milestones (e.g. announce the initiative and vision at project launch, share updates before and after pilot programs, celebrate quick wins when achieved, reminders during training rollout, etc.). Regular updates (weekly or bi-weekly early on, then perhaps monthly) maintain transparency. Also schedule two-way communications like Q&A sessions or feedback surveys at intervals.

- **Responsibilities:** Assign owners for each communication activity. For instance, the CEO or a top leader might kick off with an email about the vision, managers might be responsible for team-level check-ins, the project lead or change manager might send monthly updates, etc. Clarify who drafts the message, who approves it, and who delivers it.

- **Feedback Mechanisms:** Incorporate ways for employees and other stakeholders to ask questions or provide input. This could include an anonymous survey, a dedicated email or chat channel for questions, or live forums. Establish a loop to respond to feedback (e.g. publish a "Frequently Asked Questions" document addressing common queries or misconceptions that arise). Listening and responding builds trust and engagement.

- **Communication Matrix:** Optionally, compile a matrix or table that summarizes all of the above – listing each stakeholder group, their communication needs, the channel, frequency, and responsible owner. This serves as a quick-reference blueprint for execution.

2. Marketing/Engagement Campaign Template (General)

In the context of internal change, "marketing" refers to activities that generate enthusiasm, buy-in, and positive perception of the transformation. It complements formal communications by *promoting* the change initiative's benefits and successes, much like a campaign. This template can also extend to external marketing if stakeholders outside the organization need to be informed or won over.

Components include:

- **Change Branding:** Develop a simple, memorable identity for the initiative. This might be a slogan, tagline or visual logo. For example, an enterprise might brand its AI integration program as "Project Synergy" or a university might use "AI-Enabled Campus 2025." A consistent brand can be used on all materials (email headers, posters, slide decks) to give the effort a cohesive feel.

- **Awareness Campaign:** Plan creative ways to raise awareness and excitement. Internally, this could involve launch events (virtual or in-person kickoff event demonstrating a new AI tool), informational posters or digital signage highlighting interesting facts ("Did you know…?" about AI benefits), or short videos from leadership about the vision. Externally (if applicable), consider press releases, blog posts, or community town halls to share what the organization is doing and why it's positive.

- **Success Stories and Use Cases:** As the change progresses, actively **market the wins**. Collect stories of employees who used the new AI tools to great effect, or teams that saved time through automation – then showcase these. This could be via internal newsletters, intranet articles, or "lunch & learn" demos hosted by those early adopters. Storytelling helps others envision the practical benefits and can reduce skepticism. It also recognizes employees' efforts publicly, which is motivating.

- **Champions and Influencers:** Leverage the change champions identified in Phase 2 (or any enthusiastic early adopters) as ambassadors. Feature them in the campaign – e.g., profile a "Synergy Champion of the Month" who shares tips on working with AI, or have champions lead informal peer training sessions. Seeing colleagues advocate for the change is often more convincing than hearing it from executives alone.

- **Incentives and Engagement Activities:** Encourage participation through gamification or incentives. For instance, create a challenge such as "Try out the new AI tool and submit an example of how it helped you" – with small rewards for the best submissions. Departments could earn badges or recognition for completing certain training or achieving improvements with the new system. Even simple competitions or quizzes about AI with fun prizes can spur engagement and learning in a lighthearted way.

- **External Marketing (if needed):** For changes that affect customers or the public (common in government or education sectors), prepare outward-facing messages. Highlight how the organization's adoption of AI will improve service delivery, efficiency, or outcomes. Ensure these messages emphasize ethical and responsible use of AI to preempt public concern. This might include updating the company website with a section on "Innovation Initiatives" or publishing an article in a sector newsletter about the workforce transformation journey.

- **Continuous Engagement:** Plan to sustain the campaign beyond initial launch. Update the marketing materials with new success stats ("1000 hours saved so far with AI assistance!"), refresh posters or intranet banners to keep content fresh, and host periodic events (like an annual "Innovation Day" or hackathon) to reinforce the culture of innovation. Over time, the campaign blends into normal culture-building.

3. Training and Upskilling Program Template (General)

Adopting AI tools and evolving job roles demands a robust Training Plan. This template guides organizations in developing training and support structures to equip their workforce for the new ways of working.

Key elements:

- **Training Needs Assessment:** Begin by identifying who needs to learn what. List out the roles or groups of employees and determine the competencies required for each in the future state. For example, data entry clerks may need to learn how to supervise an AI data-processing tool; managers may need training in interpreting AI-generated analytics; HR staff may need to learn how to evaluate new skill sets. Don't forget soft skills and mindset training (e.g. change resilience, design thinking, or ethics) alongside technical skills.

- **Curriculum Design:** Design a curriculum that covers these needs. This often includes multiple layers:

o   *General Awareness:* Broad sessions for all staff on the basics of AI, the organization's vision, and high-level impacts (a bit like AI Literacy 101).

o   *Role-Specific Skills:* Targeted training for specific departments or roles on the tools and processes they will use. For instance, if introducing an AI coding assistant for developers, have focused workshops for the engineering teams; if faculty in a college will use AI in teaching, provide pedagogy-oriented AI training.

o   *Leadership Training:* Include sessions for managers and executives on how to lead in a transformed environment – covering topics like managing hybrid human/AI teams, making decisions with AI input, and supporting employees through transitions.

o   *Change Management & Culture:* (often overlooked) Workshops or discussions about adapting to change, addressing fears, and fostering a growth mindset. This helps build the soft skills needed to embrace continual change.

- **Training Formats:** Decide the best format for each part of the curriculum. Options include live instructor-led workshops (in person or virtual), e-learning modules (self-paced online courses), hands-on labs or sandbox environments for practicing with new tools, and written guides or job aids for quick reference. A blended learning approach often works best (mixing videos, interactive sessions, and practice). Ensure accessibility for all (record sessions, provide captioning or multi-language materials if needed).

- **Training Schedule & Rollout:** Develop a schedule that coordinates with the project timeline. For example, foundational AI literacy training might occur in Phase 2 for all staff, whereas advanced role-specific training might happen right before a new AI tool is deployed to that role. Stagger sessions to manage workload – avoid pulling everyone into training at the same time if operations must continue. Provide sign-up processes and clear notifications so employees can plan to attend.

- **Practical Exercises & Evaluation:** Incorporate practical, hands-on exercises wherever possible. Adults learn by doing – so if the training is on an AI tool, include labs or assignments using that tool on realistic tasks. Additionally, include knowledge checks or assessments (quizzes, skill demonstrations, or simple certifications) to ensure the training is effective. Evaluate participants' performance and solicit their feedback on the training quality. This not only reinforces learning but also identifies if more support is needed.

- **On-the-Job Aids and Support:** After formal training, support should continue on the job. Prepare quick-reference guides, FAQs, or toolkits that employees can refer to when using new processes or technologies. Set up a support system – e.g. a helpdesk for questions, an internal user group or forum, or assigning "go-to" persons (super-users) in each team who can help their peers. Mentoring or buddy systems can also aid skill transfer (pairing a less experienced user with a champion).

- **Measure Training Impact:** Define metrics to track the effectiveness of training. This might include training completion rates, test scores, and more outcome-focused measures like improvements in work quality or reductions in errors after training. Also watch adoption rates – e.g., if training was on a new AI tool, what percentage of staff are actively using it a month or two later? Low adoption might indicate a need for refresher training or addressing barriers. Use these insights to refine the training program continuously.

- **Continuous Upskilling Culture:** Plan beyond initial training—establish continuous learning as a norm. This could mean providing ongoing learning opportunities such as advanced courses, subscriptions to online learning platforms, or periodic workshops on new features/updates. Encourage employees to pursue new skills (perhaps through personal development plans or incentives for completing certain courses). The organization should treat skill development as an ongoing investment, not a one-time event, to keep pace with evolving technology.

Sector-Specific Templates for Key Use Cases

While the core templates above provide a foundational approach, different sectors have unique considerations. Below, we tailor **communication, marketing/engagement, and training strategies** for three organizational contexts – **Enterprise, Educational, and Government** – focusing on the three critical use cases: **(1) Onboarding AI Tools, (2) Workforce Transition, and (3) Stakeholder Engagement**. Each sub-section highlights how the approach would be customized to fit the sector's culture, audience, and goals.

Enterprise (Corporate) Sector

Context: Enterprises (business corporations) are often driven by efficiency, profit goals, and competition. Workforce transformations here might involve introducing AI in business processes, shifting employee roles, and communicating changes to both an internal workforce and external stakeholders like investors or customers.

- **Onboarding AI Tools (Enterprise):** When rolling out AI tools in a company, communications should emphasize **business value and productivity**. For example, in introducing an AI customer service chatbot or an AI analytics platform, an enterprise should:

  o *Communication:* Frame the change as staying ahead in the market and making employees' jobs easier by offloading drudge work. Use data in communications – e.g. "This tool can save us 20% time in handling customer queries, allowing you to focus on complex cases." Ensure IT and security messages are included (reassuring staff that the tools have been vetted for data security). If the enterprise is large, target communications by division (sales, finance, etc., each get specific info on how the AI helps their work).

  o *Marketing/Engagement:* Create excitement by showcasing pilot success stories from within the company (e.g., "In Q2 pilot, the AI assistant helped our sales team increase lead conversion by 15%"). Host demos or "AI fairs" where employees can see the tools in action and even try them out. Provide early adopters with recognition (perhaps an "AI Advocate" badge) to encourage uptake. Externally, prepare a press release or investor communication highlighting the company's innovation in adopting AI to drive value (stakeholders like shareholders will want to know the company is leveraging AI for growth).

  o *Training:* Leverage the enterprise's Learning & Development infrastructure. Provide role-specific training as needed – for instance, customer support reps get hands-on training with the chatbot interface, analysts get training on the AI analytics tool's features. Use e-learning modules for basic training that all can take, supplemented by live Q&A webinars to address practical questions. Ensure there's IT support available for troubleshooting initial issues. Because enterprises often use metrics, track adoption rates of the tool by department and have managers reinforce usage in team meetings (tying it to performance expectations if appropriate).

- **Workforce Transition (Enterprise):** Enterprises may reorganize or redefine roles when technology is introduced – some jobs may evolve, some may phase out, and new ones may appear. Managing this transition is critical:

  o *Communication:* Be transparent about the *purpose* of the transition. For example, communicate that certain repetitive roles will be augmented by AI so employees can move into more value-added positions – and back this message by describing new opportunities or upskilling programs. Address the elephant in the room: job security. If layoffs are not the goal, explicitly say so and emphasize growth (e.g., "We aim to **reskill**, not replace, our valuable team members"). If roles will be eliminated or restructured, communicate with empathy, clarity on timelines, and support being offered (like severance or retraining options). Early and honest communication will build trust even in uncertainty.

  o *Marketing/Engagement:* Internally, promote a culture of mobility and learning. Highlight success cases of employees who transitioned roles – e.g. "Jane from accounting learned data science and is now a business analyst working with AI insights." Use internal blogs or videos to tell these stories. Offer career coaching sessions or "open house" events where employees can learn about emerging job roles in the company. This positive storytelling and support signals that the company invests in its people. Externally (if relevant, say to investors or media), frame the workforce transformation as the company evolving its talent to meet future needs ("Our workforce is gaining new skills in AI, driving innovation from within").

  o *Training:* A robust **reskilling program** is key. The enterprise should partner with learning providers if necessary (e.g., online courses, certification programs) to help employees gain new skills for new roles. Create learning paths for different transitions (for example, a path for a manufacturing technician to become a robot maintenance specialist, or an administrative assistant to become an AI workflow coordinator). Use a mix of on-the-job training (apprenticeships or rotations in new departments) and formal education. Track progress through these programs and celebrate completions (graduation ceremonies, certificates). Additionally, training managers on how to support their teams through change (including how to have career conversations, how to manage a team that's learning something new) can help smooth the transition at the team level.

- **Stakeholder Engagement (Enterprise):** Corporations must consider both internal stakeholders (employees, leadership) and external ones (customers, investors, partners, regulators) when implementing sweeping changes with AI.

  o *Internal Engagement:* Beyond employees, engage middle management and frontline supervisors heavily – they often become the messengers and can either accelerate or hinder change. Hold manager briefing sessions to ensure they understand the strategy and can confidently discuss it with their teams (equipping them with talking points and FAQs). For executive stakeholders, provide regular transformation updates in leadership meetings, focusing on ROI, risk mitigation, and alignment with corporate strategy (this maintains sponsorship and interest).

  o *External Engagement:* For customers, maintain transparency if the changes affect them. For instance, if AI will be used in customer interactions, let customers know what to expect (some companies provide notices like "You may be served by our virtual assistant. Ask for a human at any time."). Emphasize how these changes improve customer experience (faster responses, 24/7 service, etc.). For B2B partners, highlight reliability and innovation. For investors/shareholders, craft communications (earnings call talking points or investor presentations) that show how workforce transformation and AI adoption are expected to cut costs or drive growth, backed by early results if possible. Also, address any concerns about ethical use of AI publicly – having an ethics policy and possibly an external audit or certification can bolster trust. In some cases, engage industry regulators or compliance stakeholders early to ensure the transformation meets all legal requirements (especially if in a sensitive industry like finance or healthcare).

  o *Feedback and Community:* Create forums for stakeholders to give feedback. For employees, that might be the internal surveys or town halls mentioned. For customers, it could be user group meetings or feedback forms specifically asking how the new tools or processes are working for them. Showing that the enterprise listens and adapts based on stakeholder feedback strengthens support for the changes.

Educational Institution

Context: Educational institutions (such as universities, colleges, or K-12 schools) face workforce transformation in two senses: transforming their **faculty and staff** workflows with AI, and preparing their **students** for an AI-rich world. They also have unique stakeholders: students, parents, faculty unions, academic boards, and the public.

- **Onboarding AI Tools (Education):** In schools or universities, introduce AI tools for administrative efficiency (e.g., AI for grading or scheduling) or in the classroom (AI tutoring systems, content creation aids).

  - *Communication:* Focus on how AI tools support the **educational mission**. For faculty and staff, frame tools as helping reduce administrative burdens or enhancing teaching (e.g., "This AI tool can help generate quizzes or personalized feedback, giving you more time to mentor students one-on-one"). Address concerns around academic integrity (if using AI with students, clarify policies to prevent misuse or plagiarism via AI, and how AI is a supplement, not a cheating shortcut). For student communications, explain how the new tools will improve their learning experience or campus services. Also communicate to IT and data privacy officers how student data is protected in these tools, as privacy is paramount in education.

  - *Marketing/Engagement:* Provide hands-on showcases: for example, run a demo day where teachers can try an AI grading assistant with sample papers, or counselors can see how an AI-driven advising system works. Highlight early adopters: e.g., a professor who used an AI tutor in a class and saw student performance improve, sharing that story at a faculty meeting or newsletter. For students, perhaps create a tutorial video or workshop on how to effectively and ethically use a new AI learning app. Externally, an educational institution might publish a news article or blog post about innovating with AI in education, to attract prospective students or reassure parents that the school is at the cutting edge (while still valuing human educators!).

  - *Training:* Tailor training to different roles: faculty might need pedagogy-focused training on integrating AI into curriculum and assignments, whereas administrative staff might need training on AI for operations (like enrollment predictions or chatbot for student services). Use a train-the-trainer model: identify tech-savvy faculty who can become "AI in teaching" trainers for their peers, which respects the

255

collegial culture of academia. Provide plenty of practical examples and emphasize that using AI is optional to enhance teaching, not a mandate that infringes academic freedom. For students, if AI tools will be part of learning, offer orientation sessions on using them effectively (maybe integrated into first-year seminars or via the library's digital literacy programs).

- **Workforce Transition (Education):** In education, "workforce" includes faculty, administrators, and support staff. Changes might involve new roles (e.g., a Learning Analytics Specialist) or shifting how faculty spend their time.

  - *Communication:* It's important to engage **faculty governance** structures. Communicate plans through channels like faculty senate meetings, department chairs, and union representatives (if faculty or staff are unionized). Emphasize how changes will uphold or improve educational quality. For example, if AI handles some grading, assure that faculty remain in control of final assessments – the AI is just assisting. If certain staff roles (like data entry) are being replaced by systems, explain how those staff will be retrained for new needs (perhaps as data analysts or student engagement roles). Always connect the change back to student success and institutional mission ("to provide the best education, we are updating how we work").

  - *Marketing/Engagement:* In an educational setting, appealing to professional growth and academic values is key. Engage faculty by framing AI adoption as an intellectual opportunity – host colloquiums or workshops on "AI in Education" where faculty can discuss and even debate the merits and challenges, rather than feeling it's top-down. Use champion faculty who are respected scholars to lead these discussions or pilot programs; their endorsement will carry weight with peers. For staff, create cross-department committees to involve them in redesigning workflows (e.g., a committee on "Future of Library Services with AI" that includes librarians as co-creators of the change). Recognize individuals or departments that come up with innovative ways to use AI (perhaps an internal award for "Excellence in Innovation in Teaching/Administration"). Externally, communicate to alumni, parents, and the community that the institution is equipping students with modern skills and making operations more efficient – but also reassure that the human touch (teachers, counselors) remains central. This balance is crucial to maintain trust in an educational brand.

- *Training:* Focus on **professional development**. Many educators are lifelong learners by nature, so tap into that. Provide opportunities for faculty to learn new tech skills in a non-threatening environment (e.g., voluntary summer institutes on digital pedagogy, with stipends or continuing education credits to encourage participation). For staff, offer clear pathways to transition – for instance, if a registrar's office is automating tasks, perhaps sponsor affected employees to earn a certification in data analysis or project management to take on new duties. Partner with education schools or online education providers to tailor programs for your employees (an "AI in Education" certificate, for example). It's also effective to pilot new roles in small ways: if creating new hybrid roles (like an "AI Curriculum Specialist"), start with a pilot position or cross-training one person, then expand once proof of concept is shown.

- **Stakeholder Engagement (Education):** Schools have a broader stakeholder map: faculty, students, parents, alumni, boards, and sometimes public taxpayers (for public institutions).

- *Internal Engagement:* Ensure student voices are heard when changes affect the student experience. Engage student government or representatives in planning, perhaps running focus groups on how students feel about AI in learning. Faculty stakeholders need forums to voice concerns (for example, concerns about academic integrity or job security if AI might do some teaching tasks) – engage them through committees and transparent policy-making (jointly develop guidelines on AI use in teaching and research). Administrative and support staff should also have representation in change discussions to maintain morale. Transparency in decision-making bodies (sharing meeting minutes or having open forums) helps maintain trust in a community-driven environment.

- *External Engagement:* For parents and alumni, craft messages that the institution is innovating responsibly. For example, a letter from the President or Principal could outline the future-of-education vision and how new technologies will better prepare students. Address likely questions upfront: "Will AI replace teachers?" (answer: no, but it will enhance the teaching and learning process – here's how). Public school systems might need to engage school boards or even local government;

in those cases, provide data and pilot results to show the change is yielding positive outcomes (better student engagement, efficiency savings redirected to student programs, etc.). Regulatory stakeholders might include accreditation bodies – ensure any changes in curriculum or teaching methods with AI meet accreditation standards, and proactively communicate with accreditors about how academic quality is being maintained or improved. Community engagement is also key: if an AI program is high-profile, hold a community Q&A or publish an FAQ on the school website addressing public concerns (like privacy of student data, screen time for kids, etc.).

o *Ethical and Policy Considerations:* Educational changes with AI can raise ethical questions (data privacy for minors, fairness in algorithmic tutoring, etc.). Engage ethicists or form a task force including community members or experts to guide policy on these fronts. By involving stakeholders in creating the rules (e.g., a policy on AI plagiarism), you gain legitimacy and wider acceptance of the eventual policies. Sharing these policies publicly also engages stakeholders by showing that the institution is taking thoughtful measures alongside the innovation.

Government Agency

Context: Government agencies implementing AI and workforce transformation face public scrutiny, political oversight, and the challenge of civil service structures. They must focus on transparency, public value, and adherence to regulations. Their workforce might have strong unions or job protections, and their stakeholders include the general public and elected officials.

- **Onboarding AI Tools (Government):** Governments adopt AI for citizen services (chatbots, automated license processing), data analysis for policy, or internal efficiency (like automating paperwork).

  - *Communication:* Emphasize how AI tools will improve **public service delivery**. For example, communicate to employees and citizens that an AI system will reduce backlog in processing applications, enabling faster response to the public. It's important to stress that the tools will assist staff, not replace their judgment, especially to alleviate public fear of "machines making decisions" about them. Internally, tie the adoption to the agency's mission ("to serve citizens faster and more accurately"). Ensure communications also cover compliance: e.g., explaining that the AI has been procured or developed in line with government IT standards, data security laws, and ethical guidelines, which builds trust among both employees and the public.

  - *Marketing/Engagement:* Within the agency, create demonstration projects – for instance, let employees pilot the AI tool in a controlled environment and gather their feedback. Use internal newsletters or the intranet to spotlight cases where the AI helped resolve a case quicker or caught an error, thereby helping a citizen (putting a human face on the benefit). In many government settings, peer communication and union communications are influential: consider working with union leadership to co-host informational sessions about the new tool, addressing labor concerns directly and showing collaboration. Externally, government agencies often have to be careful with "marketing," but they can engage the public via town hall meetings or press releases that highlight positive outcomes (e.g., "The new AI-powered system has cut permit wait times by 30%, improving service to the community"). Make sure to also address what safeguards are in place (so the narrative isn't just "government using AI" which can raise eyebrows, but "government using AI responsibly to serve you better").

- *Training:* Government employees may have varying levels of tech proficiency. Provide thorough training with a focus on **practical application and accountability**. For example, train staff not just on how to use the AI system, but also on their responsibility for oversight – e.g., reviewing the AI's recommendations, understanding its limits, and knowing how to override or escalate when something seems off. Given that governments may have compliance training requirements, integrate AI tool training with those requirements (perhaps certify employees on the new system before they use it on real cases). Use scenario-based training relevant to public service (for instance, role-play how a citizen's query flows through a chatbot to a human). Also consider training beyond immediate users: educate agency leadership on AI basics so they can make informed decisions, and brief the communications or public relations team so they can handle public inquiries about the new system knowledgeably.

- **Workforce Transition (Government):** In government, changes to roles or processes can be sensitive due to job security mandates, union contracts, and public accountability.

  - *Communication:* Start by aligning the change with legislative or executive directives if possible (e.g., if there's a government-wide modernization initiative, frame this as part of that mandate). Be very clear on **whether and how jobs will be affected**. If AI adoption might reduce the need for certain roles, engage with HR and unions early to create a plan (retraining, reassignment, or managing through attrition). Communicate this plan alongside the announcement of technology changes. Government employees value stability, so any message should reinforce that the agency is *investing* in its workforce (not just the technology) – mention programs like training funds, opportunities to learn "skills of the future," etc. Keep the tone service-oriented: "By transitioning how we work, we can better fulfill our duty to the public."

  - *Marketing/Engagement:* Engagement in government often means participation and inclusion. Set up working groups or joint labor-management committees to get input on implementation. This will not only surface practical issues but also signal respect for employees' voices. Celebrate long-serving employees who embrace new skills as champions (e.g., "30-year DMV veteran masters AI system to improve customer service" – a story that can inspire peers that it's never too late to learn). Use internal communication channels to highlight such positive attitudes. Also, in government, peer recognition and public service motivation are strong – consider tying the transformation to awards or acknowledgments (like a "Innovations in Service" award) that teams or individuals can earn by contributing to the successful change.

- *Training:* Governments often have structured professional development; integrate the new skills into those frameworks. Develop specific competency frameworks for new technology-related roles (the Office of Personnel Management or equivalent often has models that can be adapted for, say, AI competency). Provide not just one-time training but ongoing clinics or office hours – for example, an "AI coach" available weekly in the office to help anyone struggling with the new tools. If some employees are being reassigned from roles made redundant by automation, create a clear retraining track for them to fill other needed roles (perhaps in data quality assurance, or in more citizen-facing advisory positions that AI can't handle). Ensure that all training is done during work hours and is paid, as per public sector norms, and document completion as part of compliance.

- **Stakeholder Engagement (Government):** Key stakeholders include not only the agency's employees and leadership, but also elected officials (who fund and oversee the agency), the general public (who expects fair and transparent services), and possibly oversight bodies or NGOs.

  - *Internal Engagement:* Keep agency leadership (directors, department heads) looped in with regular briefings focusing on how changes align with strategic goals and improve performance metrics that matter to them (e.g., reduced backlog, improved citizen satisfaction ratings). For employees, beyond communication, consider formal change agents: designate some employees as "Transformation Ambassadors" who liaise between the project team and the rank-and-file, gathering feedback and spreading accurate information. This is especially useful in unionized environments, where having fellow employees champion the change can carry weight.

  - *Engaging Elected Officials:* If the transformation requires budget approval or will be visible to legislators or city councils, pro-actively engage them. Prepare concise briefing papers highlighting ROI and public value. Show that the agency is being a good steward of public funds by implementing efficient tech, but also emphasize any positive workforce impacts ("we are retraining staff for higher-skilled roles, making government jobs more fulfilling while saving taxpayer money"). If possible, get a quote or endorsement from a key official who supports the initiative – their backing can protect the project and also reassure employees that this has top-level buy-in.

- o *Public Transparency:* The public can be wary of government technology (concerns about surveillance, biases, errors affecting people's benefits or records). It's crucial to be transparent. Develop a public-facing FAQ or even an algorithmic transparency report explaining how the AI will be used, what decisions (if any) it will make, and how human oversight is maintained. Host a public webinar or partner with community organizations to explain the changes. Solicit public feedback via a comment period or community forum especially if the changes impact citizen interactions. Showing this openness can build public trust.

- o *Ethical Oversight:* Engage external stakeholders like watchdog NGOs or academic experts by possibly forming an ethics advisory panel. Inviting an impartial perspective on the agency's use of AI can lend credibility. Also ensure compliance with any government AI guidelines or principles (many governments have AI ethics frameworks now). By actively involving oversight stakeholders rather than waiting for them to critique, the agency can address concerns in design and gain allies.

Each sector above uses the **core templates** but adapts them to its context – enterprises focus on competitive edge and ROI, educational institutions on mission and academic values, and government agencies on public service and transparency. By addressing the three use cases with sector-specific nuance, the communication, marketing, and training efforts will more effectively resonate with the respective audiences.

About the Author

Ken Hubbell is a pragmatic futurist whose philosophy is "design for tomorrow, build for today." He started his career creating interactive videos and animation and later moved into designing and programming serious games and simulations. He is a leader in learning and development, AI, and other innovative technologies. He enjoys the challenge of growing and leading talented individuals, bringing them together to design and build engaging products.

Through the years he has worked with some incredible people and amazing organizations including the United Nations, Caterpillar, NASA, the FAA, and WUNC-TV to name a few. He is known for aligning diverse team members and functional units, drawing on their experiences, and building award winning games, applications, and educational technology. Ken is a firm believer in changing the dynamics of traditional human resources to meet the needs of our growing transhuman workforce.

Ken received his Bachelor of Industrial Product Design degree from North Carolina State University and his Master of Science in Instructional Technology degree from East Carolina University. He is currently an AI Technology Expert for the US Department of Homeland Security AI Corps and Technology Evangelist for Melelem Inc., a safe and secure social AI platform for multi-user generative AI conversations. He is a passionate coach, mentor, writer, and international speaker who enjoys sharing his experiences and giving back to others.

https://thepragmaticfuturist.com

www.ingramcontent.com/pod-product-compliance
Lightning Source LLC
Chambersburg PA
CBHW060334200326
41519CB00011BA/1931